PRAISE FOR

WHERE THE LIGHT FELL

"[Raw], honest, beautifully written, and at times searing . . . We live in a world that is always clouded by ungrace, by strife and anger and division, according to Yancey, and Christians should be on the other side. . . . The pain of [Yancey's] early life gives his words and his witness an authority and authenticity that he would otherwise not have. He has become, over time, a person to whom the wounded and the brokenhearted are drawn, compelled by his message of grace."   —*The Atlantic*

"*Where the Light Fell* is in many ways a classic spiritual autobiography tracing one man's conversion from cynic to believer. But it's more. It's a searing family story as revelatory as gothic Southern fiction. It's an exposé. It's a social critique. It's a tragedy. It's a tale of redemption. . . . The memoir itself is an answer to the question that looms throughout: What do we do with the burdens, sins, and pain of our past?"   —*Christianity Today*

"Searing . . . heartrending . . . This stunning tale reminds us that the only way to keep living is to ask God for the impossible: love, forgiveness, and hope."
—KATE BOWLER, *New York Times* bestselling author of
Everything Happens for a Reason

"An illuminating autobiography that could very well have been titled *The Philip Yancey Philip Never Knew*. Delicate, tender, humorous, and brutally honest, *Where the Light Fell* accomplishes quite significantly not only as the author's biography, but also as a biography of our nation grappling with her faith. At once pain-filled and healing, through this book we come to know a 'trickster' who falls into the 'mysterious power of words,' revealing the cracks and fragments of our culture at large, but reminding us afresh how grace can ultimately prevail over us."
—MAKOTO FUJIMURA, founder of the International Arts Movement,
artist, and author of *Silence and Beauty: Hidden Faith Born of Suffering*
and *Art and Faith: A Theology of Making*

"[A] graceful, illuminating memoir, a gift to [Yancey's] readers."
—*Booklist*

"[A] gripping memoir . . . Yancey's eloquent descriptions of coming to faith and his exacting self-examination make this a standout. Exploring the corrosive role of fear in faith, Yancey's piercing and painful account invites comparison to *Hillbilly Elegy*."
—*Publishers Weekly* (starred review)

"*Where the Light Fell* could be a Faulkner novel, with racist preachers, off-kilter parenting, tormented siblings, and religious hypocrisy right and left. It's not an overstatement to say that this stunning memoir might be the miracle we've all waited for. I believed every word."
—Carolyn S. Briggs, author of *Higher Ground*

"A forthright recounting of a rocky journey to self-knowledge."
—*Kirkus Reviews*

"We've known for years Philip Yancey carries a well of sorrow. . . . Now we know where the well is, and how deep. . . . In *Where the Light Fell*, Yancey opens the door wide into his heart and soul. . . . Trauma casts a long shadow, a very long shadow. The reader will look for where the light finally falls, perhaps not realizing it's all around and always just a step away."
—*Baptist Standard*

"What raises it above [a misery memoir], however, is Yancey's lucid writing, and his preparedness to look clear-eyed into the paranoia of the funda-mentalist Christianity that forms the background to much recent political activity among the Evangelical right in the States. And, ultimately, it is still a story of grace."
—*Church Times*

"It's a story of how one man's painful upbringing birthed a passionate cu-riosity and fueled a writing career behind some of the most celebrated Christian books of the last 40 years."
—*Religion Unplugged*

WHERE
THE LIGHT FELL

WHERE
THE LIGHT FELL

A Memoir

PHILIP YANCEY

CONVERGENT
New York

2023 Convergent Books Trade Paperback Edition

Copyright © 2021 by Philip Yancey and SCCT

All rights reserved.

Published in the United States by Convergent Books,
an imprint of Random House, a division of
Penguin Random House LLC, New York.

CONVERGENT BOOKS is a registered trademark and its C colophon
is a trademark of Penguin Random House LLC.

Originally published in hardcover in the United States by
Convergent Books, an imprint of Random House, a division of
Penguin Random House LLC, in 2021.

LIBRARY OF CONGRESS CATALOGING-IN-PUBLICATION DATA
Names: Yancey, Philip, author.
Title: Where the light fell / Philip Yancey.
Description: First edition | New York: Convergent, [2021]
Identifiers: LCCN 2021012926 (print) | LCCN 2021012927 (ebook) |
ISBN 9780593238523 (trade paperback) | ISBN 9780593238516 (ebook)
Subjects: LCSH: Yancey, Philip. | Yancey, Philip—Family. |
Christian biography—United States. | Authors, American—20th century—
Biography. | Authors, American—21st century—Biography.
Classification: LCC BR1720.Y36 A3 2021 (print) |
LCC BR1720.Y36 (ebook) | DDC 270.092 [B]—dc23
LC record available at https://lccn.loc.gov/2021012926
LC ebook record available at https://lccn.loc.gov/2021012927

Printed in the United States of America on acid-free paper

crownpublishing.com

2 4 6 8 9 7 5 3

Title page illustration: iStock.com/Anuwat Meereewee
Book design by Alexis Capitini

For Janet, naturally

It was by following the sun's rays that I reached the sun.

—Leo Tolstoy, in *Tolstoy Remembered* by Tatyana Tolstoy

CONTENTS

PART ONE
THE FAMILY PLOT

PART ONE

THE FAMILY PLOT

There is no agony like bearing an untold story inside you.

—Zora Neale Hurston, *Dust Tracks on a Road*

CHAPTER 1

THE SECRET

Not until college do I discover the secret of my father's death.

My girlfriend, who will later become my wife, is making her first visit to my home city of Atlanta, in early 1968. The two of us stop by my grandparents' house with my mother, have a snack, and retire to the living room. My grandparents sit in matching recliners across from the upholstered couch where Janet and I are seated. A television plays softly in the background, tuned to the ever-boring *Lawrence Welk Show*.

Normally my eighty-year-old grandfather snores through the program, waking just in time to pronounce, "Swellest show I ever saw!" Tonight, though, everyone is wide-awake, fixing their attention on Janet. *Philip's never brought a girl over—this must be serious.*

Conversation proceeds awkwardly until Janet says, "Tell me something about the Yancey family. I'm so sorry I'll never get to meet Philip's father." Thrilled by her interest, my grandmother rummages in a closet to fetch some photo albums and family scrapbook   A pages turn, Janet tries to keep straight all the names and faces flashing before her. This ancestor fought for the Confederacy in the Civil War. That distant cousin died of a black widow spider bite. Her father succumbed to the Spanish flu.

Suddenly a folded clipping from *The Atlanta Constitution* flutters from the album to the floor, newsprint yellowed with age. When I lean forward to retrieve it, a photo that I've never seen catches my eye.

A man lies on his back in a hospital bed, his body pitifully withered, his head propped up on pillows. Beside him, a smiling woman bends over to feed him with a spoon. Right away I recognize her as a slimmer, youthful version of my mother: the same prominent nose, the same mass of dark, curly hair, an early trace of the worry lines that now crease her forehead.

The photo caption stops me cold: "Polio Victim and Wife Spurn 'Iron Lung.'" I hold the paper closer and block out the buzz of family chitchat. The printed words seem to enlarge as I read.

> A 23-year-old Baptist minister, who was stricken with polio two months ago, has left the "iron lung" in which he was placed at Grady Hospital because, as he put it, "I believe the Lord wanted me to."
>
> The Rev. Marshall Yancey, of 436 Poole Creek Rd., Hapeville, said about 5,000 people from Georgia to California were praying for his recovery and he was confident he would be well "before too long."
>
> He signed his own release from Grady against medical advice.

Those three words, *against medical advice,* send a chill through my body, as though someone has poured ice water down my spine. Sensing the change, Janet looks at me quizzically, her left eyebrow arched so high that it touches her bangs. I slide the clipping over so that she, too, can read it.

The newspaper reporter quotes a Grady Memorial Hospital doctor, who warns that removal from the respirator "might do serious harm," followed by a chiropractor who claims the patient is "defi-

nitely improving" and may begin walking in six weeks if he continues their course of treatment.

Then the article turns to my mother:

> Mrs. Yancey, the minister's young, blue-eyed wife, explained why
> her husband left Grady:
>   "We felt like he should be out of that iron lung. Lots of people
> who believe in faith healing are praying for him. We believe in
> doctors, but we believe God will answer our prayers and he will
> get well."

I glance at the newspaper's date: December 6, 1950. Nine days
before my father's death. I flush red.

Janet has finished reading. *Why didn't you tell me about this?* she asks
with her eyes. I mime surprise: *Because I didn't know!*

Dozens, scores of times I have heard the saga of my father's
death, how a cruel disease struck down a talented young preacher in
his prime, leaving a penniless widow with the noble task of wresting
some meaning from the tragedy. My growing-up years were dominated, even straitjacketed, by a vow she made—that my brother and
I would redeem that tragedy by taking on the mantle of our father's
life.

Never, though, have I heard the backstory of what led to his
death. When I replace the clipping in the scrapbook, I find on the
facing page a similar account from my mother's hometown newspaper *The Philadelphia Bulletin*. Quite by accident I am discovering that
this man whom I never knew, a saintly giant looming over me all
these years, was a sort of holy fool. He convinced himself that God
would heal him, and then gambled everything—his career, his wife,
his two sons, his life—and lost.

I feel like one of Noah's sons confronting his father's nakedness.
The faith that exalted my father and gained him thousands of supporters, I now grasp, also killed him.

As I lie in bed that night, memories and anecdotes from childhood flash before me, now appearing in a different light. A young

widow lying on her husband's grave, sobbing as she offers her two sons to God. That same widow, my mother, pausing to pray, "Lord, go ahead and take them unless . . ." before seeking help as her sons thrash convulsively on the floor. Her rage that erupts when my brother and I seem to stray from our appointed destiny.

An awful new realization hits me. My brother and I are the atonement to compensate for a fatal error in belief. No wonder our mother has such strange notions of parenting, and such fierce resistance to letting us go. We alone can justify our father's death.

AFTER CHANCING UPON the newspaper article, I have many conversations with Mother. "That was no life for him—paralyzed, in that machine," she says. "Imagine a grown man who can't even swat a fly off his nose. He desperately wanted out of Grady Hospital. He begged me not to let anyone take him back there." Her reasoning is sound, though unsatisfying.

"I get that," I protest, "but why was I never told about the faith healing? The most important fact of my father's death I learned by chance, from a scrapbook. You invited a reporter into the room, and a photographer. You told *them* the truth, but not my brother and me!"

Once exposed, the mystery of my father's death acquires a new, compulsive power. When I start asking around, a family friend confides in me, "So many of us were dismayed at their decision, moving your father from a well-equipped hospital to a chiropractic center."

I feel as if someone has twisted the kaleidoscope of our family myth, scattering the shards to form a wholly new design. I share the news with my renegade brother, who has incurred Mother's wrath by joining Atlanta's hippie counterculture. He immediately jumps to the conclusion that she deprived us of a father by "pulling the plug" on her own husband. A chasm opens in our little family that likely will never be bridged.

I don't know what to think. I know only that I have been misled. The secret is now out, and I determine to investigate and write it down someday, as truthfully as I can.

Love in action is a harsh and dreadful thing
compared with love in dreams.

—Fyodor Dostoevsky, *The Brothers Karamazov*

CHAPTER 2
THE GAMBLE

You would need to have lived in the middle of the twentieth century to appreciate the fear that polio once stirred up—the same degree of fear that pandemics such as HIV/AIDS and COVID-19 would later arouse. No one knew how polio spread. By air or water? Contaminated food? Paper money? Across the country, swimming pools closed as a precaution. When a rumor surfaced that cats might be carriers, New Yorkers killed seventy-two thousand of them.

To add to the terror, polio targeted mostly children. Parents used it as the ultimate threat—to keep their kids from playing too hard, using a public phone, getting dirty, or hanging out with the wrong crowd: "Do you want to spend the rest of your life in an iron lung?!" Newspapers ran daily tallies of the dead, along with photos of breathing machines lined up in rows, like giant sausage rolls with little heads poking out one end.

Not all victims were children. The world's most famous polio patient, President Franklin Delano Roosevelt, contracted the disease at age thirty-nine.

My father fell ill earlier, at twenty-three. His symptoms mimicked the flu at first: a sore throat, headache, mild nausea, general weakness in his muscles. But on October 7, 1950, he awoke to find his legs paralyzed. Unable to move, even to get out of bed, he feared the worst.

When the ambulance came, Mother asked a neighbor to keep three-year-old Marshall Jr. away from the window, but my brother cried so hard that the neighbor gave in to his tears and let him watch. For weeks he had recurring nightmares of his father being carried out of the house, helpless and unmoving.

The ambulance sped to Georgia Baptist Hospital. Doctors gave the patient a quick exam, then abruptly sent him outside in a wheelchair, wearing only a hospital gown. "It's polio," they told my mother. "Get him over to Grady. They're the only hospital around here equipped to treat polios."

Sometime that week, Mother wrote an urgent letter to her home church in Philadelphia and the other congregations that had agreed to support them as missionaries. Her message was simple and direct: "Please pray!"

A SPRAWLING LANDMARK in downtown Atlanta, Grady Memorial was a charity hospital that accepted anybody. In 1950 locals referred to it as "the Gradies" because, like most hospitals in the South, Grady segregated the races, with a tunnel beneath the street joining the separate facilities for whites and "Coloreds." Patients joked that Grady gave equal treatment to all races—equally bad treatment. No matter your race, you could sit for hours in the lobby waiting for your number to be called. Not if you had polio, though: orderlies immediately whisked my father down the hallways to an isolation ward.

We were living in Blair Village at the time, a government housing project built for veterans of World War II. Four or five concrete-block apartments, resembling army barracks, formed a horseshoe shape around a cul-de-sac. When my father got sick, a public health nurse posted a quarantine sign on our door, temporarily barring any visitors.

For the next two months my mother followed the same daily routine: Feed the kids breakfast, pack up their diapers and toys, and bundle them off to whichever neighbor had agreed to babysit that day. Then, because she had not yet learned to drive, she rode the public bus, with its dozens of stops, into the city. Often she was the only white passenger on a bus full of workers, sitting alone in the front section reserved for whites. At Grady she stayed by her husband's side until dark, when she caught a bus home.

The nurses told her that only one in seventy-five adults with polio experienced paralysis. My father was the unlucky one. And because his paralysis included the diaphragm, Grady consigned him to the dreaded iron lung.

A large metal cylinder painted mustard yellow, the apparatus engulfed my father's body except for his head, which rested on a cushioned table. A tight rubber collar around his neck prevented air from escaping. By pumping in air and then sucking it out to form a vacuum, the machine forced his lungs to expand and contract, something they could not do on their own. My father complained that the noise kept him from sleeping: the bellows made rhythmic whooshing sounds and metallic squeaks, like worn wiper blades scraping across a car windshield.

Few hospitals had TV sets then, and my father could not turn the pages of a book. All day and all night he lay still on his back. He stared at the ceiling, passing time by studying the pattern of holes in the acoustic tiles. By shifting his eyes, he could look in a mirror angled toward the doorway and see faces moving past a small window in the door.

From his vantage, anyone who approached him towered like a giant. A masked orderly would shove a spoonful of food in his direction and he would flinch. Access ports lined the side of the machine, and hospital staff reached through the portholes with gloved hands to insert a needle or replace a bedpan. They addressed his head, the only body part outside the machine, as if it led a separate existence from the parts inside.

He lost control over basic functions: going to the bathroom, sleeping, feeding himself. He couldn't even choose when to take a breath; the artificial lung did that for him. The world shrank. Five years before, he had been sailing home on a warship, with all of life awaiting him. Now the iron lung defined his range. It became a kind of exoskeleton, like a cramped shell around a stuck crab.

Grady had strict rules about visitors. When my aunt Doris, a nurse at another hospital, showed up in uniform for a visit, the charge nurse at Grady decided she lacked the proper training for polio. "Honey, you don't want to see how bad he is anyhow," she said.

A few times his mother, my grandmother Yancey, appeared at the window with a mask on and waved. Only once did his father show up, with my brother and me in tow. A blacksmith, this strong man hoisted us onto his shoulders and held us at the window, so that my father could see his own sons, our images reversed in the mirror bolted to the machine.

The only visitor who braved the risk, the only person who touched him other than clinically, was my mother, his emotional lifeline. She read books to him, softly sang hymns, pestered the nurses and orderlies for better treatment, and offered what little encouragement she could—even as her own world collapsed around her.

She kept from him her inner fears, but recorded them in a diary: "Suffering terribly—out of mind most of the time. I asked God to take him home if he had to suffer so."

DURING THE HOUR-LONG bus rides to and from Grady, and the occasions when her husband napped inside the iron lung, Mother had much time to review the whirlwind of the five years she had known him.

She met him in April 1945, when a group of sailors on weekend leave traveled to Philadelphia from their navy base in Norfolk, Virginia, hoping to see the city's sights. He chose to spend Sunday morning at church, where a middle-aged couple responded to the pastor's request to "invite a serviceman home for lunch." There he first encountered Mildred Diem, my mother, who was staying with the couple as she recovered from a medical procedure.

The adventuresome sailor from Atlanta fell madly in love with timid, sheltered Milly, three years his senior. She had never had a boyfriend, and was charmed by his Southern accent and his gentlemanly style. She also marveled at his carefree spirit, exactly the opposite of her own repressed nature.

As they swapped stories about their upbringings, she learned that the young Marshall Yancey had a wild streak. He was something of a gambler, a kid who took risks. With no warning, at age fourteen Marshall ran away from home. His mother worried herself sick until, four days later, he called collect from St. Louis, Missouri. "I heard they had a great zoo, one of the best," he explained. "So I came up to see it."

Proud of his son's brash independence, his father wired him the money to take a train home. "That boy has a mind of his own!" he bragged.

Next, Marshall heard about a Whiz Kids program run by the University of Chicago, which let bright high school students take courses in philosophy. One day, after a family argument, he ran away again. Now sixteen, he hitchhiked to Chicago and talked the university into admitting him into the program. For a few months he flourished, until a bout of strep throat did him in. Rather sheepishly, he called his parents again and asked for help getting home. His father smiled. "My son has guts. He'll try anything."

After sampling the advanced courses in Chicago, Marshall had no desire to enroll again in Atlanta schools. World War II, winding down in Europe, was still raging on the Pacific front; like every American boy of the time, my father wanted to do his part. When he turned seventeen, he got parental permission to enlist as an underage recruit. "Choose the navy," his father advised. "That way you'll always have a bed to sleep in, not like those army foxholes."

Three weeks into basic training at Naval Station Great Lakes, north of Chicago, Marshall made one more call to Atlanta. "I made a mistake, Dad. Please, get me out of this place! It's terrible. I have a sinus infection, I hate the North, and the instructors are tyrants." His father contacted a congressman on his behalf, but to quit the military in wartime is no easy task. For the first time in his life, my father was trapped.

Snow fell early that year, and chunks of ice floated on Lake Michigan. Christmas arrived, his loneliest Christmas ever. One frosty day as he walked along the shoreline, gazing at a fogbank rolling in, it struck him that his entire future was a fog. He lacked even a high school diploma and soon would ship out to war, unsure if he would ever return.

At a friend's suggestion, he caught a ride into downtown Chicago to visit the Pacific Garden Mission, which he knew about from its popular program, *Unshackled*. "The longest running radio drama in history," it mostly told stories of bums and addicts converted to faith at a homeless shelter founded by the evangelist Dwight L. Moody. The stories all had the same plot, and the organ music and sound effects seemed corny—yet there was that promise of "the secret of a new life."

In uniform, Marshall felt reasonably safe walking through Chicago's worst slum, though several times he had to step around men lying on heating grates to keep warm. To his surprise, the volunteer host who greeted him at the mission had read some of his favorite philosophers. "They raise a lot of good questions," the volunteer granted. "But I haven't yet found a philosopher who tells you how to get rid of guilt. Only God can do that. I sense God is after you, Marshall." After a long conversation, having nowhere else to turn, my father prayed to become a Christian that day in late 1944.

Over the next few months, and especially after meeting Milly, he devoted his spare time to studying the Bible, trying to figure out this "new life." Then in June he embarked for war aboard the USS *Chloris*, an aircraft repair ship. On the way to Hawaii, a sensational news report reached them: The United States had dropped two atomic bombs on Japan, which led to an unconditional surrender. The war was over.

• • •

THE REST OF my father's naval career consisted of biding time in Norfolk, waiting for his discharge so he could propose to Milly. Letters flew back and forth, and every free weekend he took his leave in Philadelphia.

One roadblock stood in the way of the romance. Mildred had promised God to serve as a missionary in Africa. That continent of snakes, lions, tropical diseases, and political unrest posed a true test of faith for a Christian of the time, and for that very reason it appealed to my mother's idealism. When she heard others talk about "the dark continent," she had a strong sense that God wanted her there. No prospect of marriage could weaken her resolve.

In the summer, as the couple sat together on a bench by Keswick Lake in New Jersey, Marshall asked nonchalantly, "Would you consider letting me go to Africa with you as your husband?" She made him wait a couple of days before giving an answer, but there was never any doubt. In September, a scant five months after their first meeting, they got married in her home church. Maranatha Tabernacle sponsored many foreign missionaries, and with the church's help the young couple cultivated a mailing list of potential supporters.

My parents spent the next three years in Philadelphia, enrolled in college. My father earned a diploma, but the arrival of Marshall Jr. just after their first anniversary put a halt to my mother's studies. My father decided on further training at a seminary in Indiana. He bought a 1927 Model T Ford for twenty-five dollars. The Ford had only one seat, so he found a cast-off dining-room chair, shortened the legs, and bolted it to the floor. Mildred rode to Indiana in style, holding her eight-month-old baby—my brother—in her lap.

To their dismay, that plan came to nothing. Marshall Jr. developed severe allergies, and a doctor advised them, "If that was my baby, I'd drop everything and move to Arizona." So they headed west, my mother bouncing along in that dining-room chair while nursing a coughing, sputtering infant.

None of my father's hoped-for church jobs materialized, and after a few discouraging months in Arizona, they gave up and made the long road trip to Atlanta. Once again an adventure had soured for my father. He taught for a while at Carver Bible Institute, a "Colored school" located in central Atlanta. The school paid no salary but provided housing, which turned out to be two army cots in an upstairs classroom, with a public bathroom down the hall. My mother insisted that they find better accommodations after I was born, in November 1949.

At last, as a new year began, prospects brightened. My father found work at a home for juvenile delinquents. He drew a modest salary and qualified for veterans' housing in Blair Village. Now the two could plan the next big move—to the mission field. All this while, Mother had been faithfully writing "prayer letters" to people interested in sponsoring young missionaries, a list that had grown into the thousands. Their dream of service in Africa was about to come true.

Instead came polio, two months in an iron lung, a daring leap of faith, and the countdown to death.

In the polio ward at night, sleepless, my father tried to envision life as an invalid. Increasingly he saw himself as an albatross around the neck of his wife, who already had two young children to care for. "I guess you're sorry you married me now," he told her one afternoon. "You got no bargain."

"No!" she protested. "When I vowed 'for better, for worse, in sickness and in health,' I meant it." Alone that night she prayed more fervently, "God, don't take him away from me!"

They had a faint flicker of hope when a doctor told them about some new state-of-the-art treatment techniques at Warm Springs. "It's a therapy center south of Atlanta funded by President Roosevelt, who claimed it helped him," the doctor said. "But it's very hard to get accepted."

To qualify for Warm Springs was like winning the lottery. The Grady nurses favored a handsome young teenager. They did his hair, pampered him, flirted with him. He thought he had won the polio lottery, but died in the ambulance halfway to the destination. One by one, others in the ward passed away.

Early one morning an aide at Grady called my mother at home. "Ma'am, I could get fired for this," she said, "but I know your man's a preacher and I want to hep out. Your husband, why, he died last night. His heart done give out, and they had to bring him back with shots. And when he come back, his first words were 'Why'd you bring me back?'"

Desperate, my mother pleaded with her husband not to give up. "Think of all those people praying for you," she reminded him. Together, they decided to stake everything on a miracle, their only chance. Didn't they believe in a God who had the power to heal? Why not put their faith in his hands? Why would God "take" a man so committed to a lifetime of service?

Newly energized, my father settled on two ambitious goals: to get out of the iron lung and to get out of Grady. Although he trusted God for healing, he wanted to do his part, so he pressed the doctor to allow him a few minutes each day outside the hated apparatus. "How else can I gain strength?" he argued.

The first few days he panted and wheezed as his atrophied lungs struggled to regain function. Mother stood guard, ready to dash for help. Day by day, he breathed a little longer on his own: ten minutes, fifteen minutes, then half an hour. Every moment outside the machine risked catastrophe, for nurses did not always respond to a summons. Without prompt attention he could simply stop breathing, or choke to death.

With the help of a portable respirator, he extended his stays to several hours. He celebrated Thanksgiving by managing eight hours free of the iron lung, still lying flat, unmoving. The miracle was happening, albeit gradually, in stages.

On December 2, Mother recorded a watershed event in her diary: "Moved Marshall to Stanford Chiropractic Center. He begged me to remove him from Grady if I loved him. I believe the Lord gave him that one last desire." It was a giant step of faith, made in the face of disapproving doctors. Grady required them to sign a form stating that the patient was leaving against medical advice.

As the ambulance transported him down Peachtree Street, my father had his first glimpse of sunshine in almost two months and took his first breaths of fresh air. At once he felt weak and anxious, but also free and full of hope.

For the first time since her husband's hospitalization, Mother was allowed to stay through the night. She sat in a chair by his bedside, fearful that he would die that first night. Instead, he slept soundly, away from the noise and bright lights of the polio ward.

He had achieved both goals, escaping at last from the iron lung and from Grady. God the miracle worker was answering their prayers.

Each new morn
New widows howl, new orphans cry, new sorrows
Strike heaven on the face . . .

—Shakespeare, *Macbeth*

CHAPTER 3
DEMISE

As my father planned his move to the chiropractic center, Mother had been working on a better child-care arrangement for Marshall and me. Her sister Violet in Philadelphia offered to travel to Atlanta and stay with us, which seemed the ideal solution—until my grandmother Diem got wind of it. "Not on your life. Mildred's the one who left home and married that Southern preacher. Let her stew in her own juices for a while." My Philadelphia grandmother was a hard woman.

My grandfather Diem, who had lost his own father at age twelve, had more sympathy. "Let me work on it," he said. "We can fly the boys up here, if we can just get permission from the airlines." No unaccompanied child under the age of five could fly without special authorization, so he wrote a letter of appeal and addressed it to "Captain Edward V. Rickenbacker, President, Eastern Air Lines, New York, New York." Somehow the letter reached Rickenbacker, who agreed at once. The permission letter arrived the day my father was moved from Grady to the chiropractic center.

On his first full day at the chiropractic center, after two months of isolation, my father was allowed to see and touch his sons. "Show him what you can do, Philip," Mother said, and for the first time he saw me walk—something he could no longer do. Next, he called Marshall over to his bedside and gave him a pep talk about helping out at home. As we left the room with our Yancey grandparents, Mother kissed us both goodbye.

The next morning, my grandparents brought us to the Atlanta airport, driving out on the tarmac to the steps of the DC-3 airplane. Marshall Jr. carried on board a bag of hard dinner rolls, which he loved to chew. All during the four-hour flight, a stewardess in her smart uniform fussed over us both. She tried to feed us sweet potatoes, but Marshall refused to eat anything except his dinner rolls. A wealthy passenger had offered to look after me. For years afterward, I would brag to schoolmates about my first trip on an airplane, at thirteen months old, when I drooled on a millionaire.

For almost two weeks Marshall and I stayed with our Philadelphia grandparents, doted on by my mother's two younger sisters. On the fateful day of December 15, the entire family gathered around a radio to listen to a national address by President Harry Truman. The United States was being routed on the battlefields of Korea, and that night President Truman declared a state of emergency. In dire terms he described the threat posed by Communists in the Soviet Union and China.

In the midst of Truman's radio address, the phone rang and the operator announced those rare words, "Long-distance call." My grandfather was holding me against his shoulder as he accepted the charges. He listened in silence and mumbled a few phrases as the others stood around awaiting the news. When he hung up the phone, his eyes shone with tears. He looked down at my face and said, "Philip, my boy, you have a rough life ahead of you."

MY FATHER'S MOVE to the chiropractic center had seemed full of promise. No longer bothered by the creaks and groans of the iron lung, the patient slept well. And with her children now in Philadelphia, Mother could give him undivided attention. If he needed suctioning, she buzzed the aides, who proved far more responsive than the staff at Grady. Therapists wrapped his muscles in steamed woolen packs and moved his arms and legs to keep the joints limber.

"We can't guarantee it, but there's a chance you can regain the ability to walk," one doctor told him. Journalists from the Atlanta and Philadelphia papers reported on the young minister's progress and his hopes for healing.

A week later, however, he took an abrupt turn for the worse. His breathing became more labored, and Mother's fears surged back. On December 13 they heard carolers outside the window, and for the only time in her husband's presence, my mother broke down. "What will I do if I have to live without you—with no job, no driver's license, and two babies to look after?" she sobbed.

He tried to comfort her, assuring her that everything would be settled by Christmas. "We must have faith. Remember my motto, Milly. 'God's grace is sufficient.'"

Yet he, too, had premonitions. "What will you do if I die?" he asked—"Take our sons to Philadelphia?" He didn't trust her family, or the North, with his children. She said no. She had left Philadelphia against her parents' wishes and knew she wouldn't be welcomed back.

"Will you move in with the Yanceys?" he pressed. He didn't trust his own family, either, for they didn't share all his religious beliefs. No, she reassured him, she'd find a way to keep us on her own. "Good. That's good," he said, and calmed down.

On Friday, December 15, she got out the razor to give him his morning shave. "Not today," he said. His response surprised her, but she honored his wish. In a few hours his sister, Doris, joined the two of them in the room, and by afternoon his parents arrived. Despite the cold weather outside, he insisted that they open the windows. All four visitors sat around his bed in their winter coats as he lay in cotton pajamas soaked in sweat, fighting to breathe.

Suddenly his body relaxed and the breathing slowed—he had

slipped into a coma. Mother jumped up to hit the emergency button, and a minute later a chiropractic doctor answered the summons. He took one look at his unconscious patient and said, "I'm afraid it's time to call Grady."

The doctor placed an emergency call, asking the hospital to send its portable respirator, the only one in Atlanta. The device worked on the same principle as the iron lung, only it was compact, fitting over the torso like a baseball umpire's chest guard.

My father's eyes remained open even in his comatose state. A tense silence filled the room, a silence that could be felt. Finally, Doris said, "I don't think he can see, but hearing is the last sense to go. Let's keep talking." They all made an effort, though conversation seemed stilted, fake.

When they heard an ambulance siren through the open window, the family felt a rush of hope. It vanished when the Grady attendants entered the room—they had neglected to bring the respirator.

"We can't move him to Grady in his condition," one of the men said. They felt his pulse and checked his temperature, and then for some reason they turned my father over on his stomach, the worst thing you can do to a polio patient. He took one more breath, his last.

A short time later my mother made that long-distance call to Philadelphia.

Her diary has one more entry, dated December 15. "Marshall suddenly went home to be with the Lord. We had a blessed 2 weeks together at this hospital. I was able to spend all my time with him. What precious memories!! . . . May the boys grow to be like him."

The diary ends. She did not record, and could not possibly know, what lay ahead as she fought to pick up the pieces of our lives.

I HAVE NO memory of the airplane trip to Philadelphia or the car trip back to Atlanta for the funeral service. I have no memory of the room in the chiropractic center, or of the yellow machine my grandfather held me up to see at Grady Hospital, or of the frail figure who lay inside it staring at my reversed image in a mirror.

I have only the version of events passed down through relatives, of my father's valiant struggle against a fatal disease that cut short a promising career of Christian service. Seventeen years would pass before I picked up the newspaper article and came upon the story of the miracle that failed. Like every secret, it gained power as it lay hidden.

I have few actual proofs of my father's existence. A handful of black-and-white photos, including a small booklet issued by the navy as a memento of his tour of duty. His Bible with a worn black cover, marked up with notes in his handwriting. Musty copies of *The Complete Works of William Shakespeare* and *The Decline and Fall of the Roman Empire*. Two term papers from college days. A packet of letters he wrote my mother during their courtship.

There is also a tree: a mimosa tree with fernlike leaves and smooth bark that he planted as a sapling in front of his home. On visits to my grandparents, I would climb this tree, which now towered above their house, and sit in the crook of its branches amid the pink blossoms with their sweet scent, wondering about his life—until the ants and yellow jackets found me.

The Yancey relatives, and the house he shared with them, were living reminders of my father. When we arrived there, Marshall and I would dash to the school playground just down the street, where our father attended elementary school. "Your dad used to play on these very swings and monkey bars," Grandpop reminded us, every time.

After his death, my grandparents had assured my mother, "Don't worry. We'll look after you." And they did. Grandpop slipped Mother money on the side and gave Marshall and me a silver dollar at the end of every visit. My grandmother usually served two kinds of meat with each meal, and only later did I realize she did that just for us, knowing how poor we were.

Everything seemed strange and wonderful at my grandparents' house: separate faucets for cold and hot water, the needle arm on the record player that automatically swung out to let the next LP platter drop down with a slapping sound, the private telephone not connected to a party line. Each morning we stepped out on the front porch to collect milk—*chocolate* milk—delivered in glass bottles covered in condensation.

Their house on Virginia Avenue became a refuge. Our horseplay, which might merit a spanking at home, my grandparents thought cute. When I left that house at the end of a visit, I left behind something warm and loving.

As a child, I didn't miss my father. How could I? Barely a year old when he died, I never knew him. Two grainy photos helped me visualize him. One shows a thin, rakish sailor leaning against a rail fence, his navy cap worn at a jaunty angle. A more formal portrait shows him with wire-rim glasses and looking a bit older, even scholarly; he's wearing a double-breasted suit with wide lapels and a wide tie, his curly hair parted on one side and piled in a heap on top.

"That's your daddy," Mother often said as she pointed to the photos, even before I could comprehend the words. She referred to him as "your daddy," but I never called him anything. He died before I could talk.

My brother, three years old when our father died, retains his name (Marshall Watts Yancey Jr.) as well as three actual memories. Once, he ran out to meet our big black Pontiac in the driveway and our father reached over to fetch a Tootsie Pop from the glove compartment. Another time, he recalls, they climbed together what seemed to him an enormous hill of Georgia red clay. Our father pulled Marshall along with one arm while cradling a baby—me—in the other. Marshall returned home boasting, "I climbed a mountain! Philip can't even walk."

The third memory has always haunted him. That same man, now paralyzed and fighting for air, slowly turned his head on a hospital pillow and forced out the words, one or two at a time, between labored breaths. "Son . . . while I'm . . . in here . . . you're the . . . man . . . of the . . . house. It's up . . . to you . . . to take . . . care . . . of your . . . mother . . . and little . . . brother." Marshall nodded and accepted the weight of that burden as solemnly as a three-year-old could do. He informed Mother that he should take charge of my spankings right away.

Years later I came across a photo taken of me when I was a few months old. I look like any baby: fat cheeked, half-bald, with a bright, unfocused look to my eyes. The photo is crumpled and mangled, as if a puppy had gotten hold of it. My mother explained its condition. "When your dad was in the iron lung, he asked for pictures of me and of you and Marshall. I had to jam them in between some metal knobs. That's why it's all crumpled."

I felt a sudden contraction in my chest. For the first time ever, I sensed an emotional tie to my father. It seemed odd to imagine him, a virtual stranger, caring about me. During the last months of his life, my father spent his waking hours staring at those three images of his family, *my* family. There was nothing else in his field of view.

Did he pray for us? Yes, surely. Did he love us? Yes. But there was no way to express that love with his children banned from the room.

I have often thought of that crumpled photo, one of the few links connecting me to the stranger who is my father. Someone I have no memory of, no sensory knowledge of, spent every day thinking of me, devoting himself to me, loving me as well as he could. Then, before he could make much of a mark, he passed from this world.

My relationship with my father ended just when it began. From that point on, Mother was in charge.

> A memory is what is left when something happens
> and does not completely unhappen.
>
> —Edward de Bono, *The Mechanism of Mind*

CHAPTER 4
THE VOW

Growing up, I feel my father's absence more like a presence. He's a ghost figure, summoned like a genie by our mother at key moments. *Your father is watching you. Your father would be so proud.*

At school, not having a father makes me different, and I like that. Sometimes bullies take it easy on me. Other times they act even meaner, for I have no protector to march to their houses and confront their parents.

Some kids don't know better than to ask Marshall or me, "How'd your dad die?" When we tell them polio, our status goes up. In the 1950s rabies or suicide wouldn't have a more dramatic effect. On the walls of every school hang March of Dimes posters of children wearing metal braces on their legs, or lying in a scary-looking contraption. When we add that our father lived in one of those iron lungs, eyes widen like they do when kids don't know what to say next.

Marshall and I get lots of attention at church. "You poor child," women cluck to me as they tamp down a cowlick on my head. "You look just like your daddy, with that same mess of curls," they say. Their husbands take a sudden interest in their fingernails or study their clothes for stray whiskers. I glow in the sympathy that my family's plight coaxes out.

Sometimes church people say words meant to console us: "Your father finished his work on earth and God promoted him to Heaven." Or, worse, "God must have needed him more than you boys did." My brother shyly lowers his head when he hears such comments. Two years older than me, Marshall knows how to look sad, prompting more kind words from those who seek to comfort us.

People also try to comfort our mother, who has gained a following as a Bible teacher. "I declare, I've never met anybody like your husband. What a tragedy. Imagine the missionary couple you two would have made." She nods, and her face shows a respectful, wounded-widow look. "There must be some reason God took him so soon," some say, and that one lodges. *We* are the reason, she has decided—Marshall and me.

Marshall knows what will help settle Mother when she suddenly leaves the dinner table and goes to her bedroom for a spell. Once, he sees her wiping her eyes on the dish towel, and says, "Dad's aliver than we are." Mother retells that story to people at church, or over the telephone, and little Marshall beams at his wisdom.

As for me, the only sure thing is that my father is gone. Although I want to act sad like Marshall, I don't know how. I can see that death makes people cry, and somehow I grasp that what happened to my father is the greatest tragedy of our lives—but inside I feel nothing. My father isn't even a memory, only a scar.

I NOTICE THAT death is a big deal. Mother faithfully reads a small-print page in the newspaper called Obituaries. And whenever we're driving somewhere and a funeral procession passes, we pull over and wait with the other cars, out of respect. Death is the one time when every nobody becomes a somebody.

I tag along with her to several funerals, which in the South usually have an open casket. Dead people look a lot like live people, only they don't move and their eyes stay closed. I want to touch a dead person, to see what they feel like, but being short makes this a challenge. Whenever I try to sneak my arm into the casket, the metal buttons on my coat sleeve scrape along the side. I quickly draw my arm back, hoping no one has heard the noise.

My father lies in an old country graveyard tucked into the woods, and Mother often takes us there right after church. The Georgia sun blazes hot, and Marshall and I loosen our ties, shed our jackets, and step carefully around the mud puddles. We roam among the graves: the fancy monuments, the angel statues and poems carved in granite, the stone lambs and cherubim that mark the dead babies.

Some of the graves hold soldiers killed in the Civil War. One section, for the poor, has no markers, just two planks of wood nailed together in the shape of a cross. A few of the crosses have photos of the buried people tacked onto them. They're covered with clear plastic, and ants crawl underneath it to drink the dew.

While we boys wander around, our mother stands beside the Yancey family plot, set inside a crumbling cement curb. Our father's gravestone, provided by the navy, is one of the plainest, a simple marker level to the ground that records the dates of his birth and death. Mother tries to tell us about the other Yanceys buried there, though we have little interest. We'd rather hunt for snakes.

As we grow older, visiting the cemetery becomes a chore. Mother insists that we clean up the garbage, worn tires, and discarded underwear that rude people have thrown over the fence. If we stop to take a break, she starts repeating the same old stories about relatives we don't even know.

One of those visits, however, is different. I can't remember how old I was—maybe nine or ten—but my memory of that scene stands out as sharp as the present.

We have made our ritual Sunday visit, returned home, and cleaned up. For some reason Mother asks us to sit around the Formica table in the kitchen, where we eat our meals, even though it's not eating time. Marshall and I look at each other, wondering what we've done wrong. Mother holds a white mug of coffee in her left hand, with a spoon handle sticking out of it. She stirs the coffee, though she doesn't drink it. She seems unusually serious, dabbing at her eyes and swallowing a few times before she speaks.

She begins by reminding us of the story of Hannah in the book of 1 Samuel, which we already know from Sunday School. More than anything, Hannah wanted a baby. She would travel to the temple and pray so hard and so long that the priest thought she was drunk.

Mother reads parts of the story to us from her King James Bible. "'Eli said unto her, How long wilt thou be drunken? Put away thy wine from thee. And Hannah answered and said, No, my lord, I am a woman of a sorrowful spirit: I have drunk neither wine nor strong drink, but have poured out my soul before the LORD.'"

Marshall and I sneak a sideways glance. Mother's tone of voice warns us this is no time to giggle about the drinking.

She continues. "Hannah was barren, you see. That means she couldn't have any children. But God heard her prayer: 'For this child I prayed; and the LORD hath given me my petition which I asked of him: Therefore also I have lent him to the LORD; as long as he liveth he shall be lent to the LORD.'"

Mother pauses for a moment, and I silently puzzle over the idea of being lent like that, borrowed by God.

"God answered Hannah's prayer with a child she named Samuel. So as soon as Samuel was weaned, probably around the age of three—your age, Marshall, when your daddy died—she took him to the temple and gave him to God." Marshall's face shows something between surprise and unease. *Where is this going?* Still, we say nothing.

Mother hesitates, as if unsure what to say next. "You boys don't know this, but before I got married I had to have an operation to fix some problems that women have. The doctor told me that probably I would never have children. Well, your dad and I prayed, and almost exactly a year after our wedding, you, Marshall, were born. It was a difficult pregnancy, and I almost died. And then two years later, Philip, you came along."

She stops to wipe her nose with a Kleenex, and then she wipes her eyes. My heart sounds very loud, and I wonder if she can hear it.

"Just a year after that, your daddy died. I didn't know what to do. All my dreams were dashed. I believed God had called me to Africa as a missionary. We had all these people lined up to support us and pray for us over there, and suddenly everything fell apart.

"I had promised your daddy not to move back to Philadelphia, so here I was in a new part of the country, with you two boys to look after. I had no husband and no job. My old church in Pennsylvania agreed to send us fifty dollars a month, but our rent alone was fifty-three dollars. I didn't know if we could make it."

She moves the spoon around in the coffee cup for a while before resuming. "I went to the cemetery, to the grave you just visited, a fresh grave then, still mounded with dirt that hadn't settled. I threw myself facedown on the dirt, prostrate, my arms stretched out across that mound, and sobbed and cried out to God. Like Hannah. This is the story that God gave me. Right then and there, I dedicated you both to God. I asked him to use you boys to fulfill the dream that your dad and I had—to replace us in Africa as missionaries. And for the first time I finally had some peace about his death."

Marshall and I do not move. My stomach is fluttering, and I am afraid even to breathe. We have never seen Mother like this. To cry, usually she goes into another room. She sniffles some, then adds one thing more.

"I made a decision to never remarry. My job was to take care of you two. Both of you had health problems when you were younger. Marshall, in Arizona you caught a desert fever that doctors said was like rheumatic fever. Several times I had to rush you to the hospital with a high temperature, almost convulsing. Philip, you had asthma and pneumonia. You would cough your lungs out. A couple of times I had to drive you, too, to the emergency room. Each time, before putting both of you in the car, I would kneel down and pray, 'Lord, if you don't want them to fill their father's place as missionaries in

Africa, go ahead and take them now. They're yours. I've given them to you.'"

We sit there for a minute that seems to contain an hour, not knowing how to react. I want to say something, but my tongue has swelled up and my mouth has gone dry. I put my hand on her arm as she cries. Marshall hugs her. And that is how we first collide against the awful power of our mother's vow.

I leave the table feeling special, like a chosen one. I have no clue how cruelly that vow will eventually work itself out. Hannah gave her son to God as a thank offering. But Marshall and I have been offered out of something different—guilt, perhaps, or betrayal.

In time, Hannah's story will become my least favorite story in the Bible.

PART TWO
BOYHOOD

> Life, being made up of little separate incidents which
> one lived one by one, became curled and whole like a wave
> which bore one up with it and threw one down with it,
> there, with a dash on the beach.
>
> —Virginia Woolf, *To the Lighthouse*

CHAPTER 5

AWAKENINGS

My earliest memories all involve fear.

When I was three years old, my brother fell from the top bunk of our bed. His startled face, yellow in the glow of a night lamp, passed my own in slow motion just before crashing into the sharp edge of a table. Screams, splashes of blood, a call to the neighbor to look after me as Mother rushed Marshall to the hospital. He returned after midnight with a gauze patch covering the stitches on his forehead.

Another memory begins with a loud knock on the door. Mother moves to answer it. "Must be one of Miz O'Brien's kids. She's about due to have her baby."

Instead, as the door opens, a woman with funny-smelling breath staggers in. "Lock the door!" she says in a blubbery voice as she lurches toward a chair. She is pressing a rag to her right arm, which leaks blood.

Mother steers Marshall and me to our bedroom. We stand just

inside the doorway, straining to hear the muffled words from the living room.

Soon the woman's boyfriend shows up, pounding first on the door and then on the windows. "Don't let him in!" she cries. "He's after me. I tried to get in my mom's house for protection, and that's how I busted my arm—breakin' the damn window." The forbidden word, *damn,* echoes like a gunshot in our home.

After a while the woman leaves, begging our mother not to lock the door behind her. Shouts from the courtyard, doors slamming, police sirens, flashing red lights.

We are living in a housing project full of luckless poor whites. During the day we hear barking dogs and crying babies, squeaky screen doors, mothers yelling, "Git in here—it's time for lunch!" At night we hear thumps from the neighbors who share our bedroom walls. "He's drinking again." The wife shrugs the next morning when Mother eyes her bruises.

I have one more memory from Blair Village, the earliest of all. For no good reason I have bitten Marshall, who immediately runs to the bathroom to tell Mother. "Send him in here at once," she demands, and I creep slowly toward her voice. Marshall has left the bathroom door partly open and there I find my mother sitting in the bathtub with no clothes on, her glasses off, her dark hair loose. I have never seen a woman naked—all that rounded flesh made shiny by the soap. My eyes get very confused because I know I shouldn't look.

"Come over here," she says, stern as a cop. My legs go stiff. Her eyes narrow, her voice tightens. "Now!" My feet move one at a time closer to the sound, closer to the mounds of skin.

"Give me your arm," she says. I hold it out and she bites it, hard, right above the wrist. Too shocked to cry, I look down at the line of tooth marks turning red. "Now you know what it feels like," she says.

I stumble out the bathroom door, staring at my arm, having experienced something new and strange that I have no name for.

• • •

I GROW UP in a world of women. Men are scary, with their rough-ness, their silence, the hint of danger about them. I can't tell what they're thinking. Women usually let you know, one way or another.

In my fourth year a big change takes place. We are in Philadelphia, visiting my mother's family, the Diems, when my fingers get smashed in a car door. "It's your own fault," Mother says when I wail. "You should have moved your hand out of the way." I squeeze a rag around my fingers to stop the blood while she runs back inside the house for a bandage. *How can something be my fault, when I'm the one hurting?*

We drive to church and sit through a service that drags on for a million years. Afterward, as I am sulking in the back seat with my bandaged fingers, the car door opens. I see two saddle oxford shoes and two legs in milky-looking nurses' stockings with seams up the back. Then a strange new person ducks her head inside.

"Marshall, Philip," Mother says, "I want you to meet Aunt Kay. She's going to live with us. She's your new daddy."

Just like that, I forget about my sore fingers. *A new daddy?* The stranger gets into our car. She has gray hair and green eyes and a face that has already started to wrinkle. She's not really our aunt, we just have to call her that.

We head to Atlanta that very afternoon with Aunt Kay riding be-side Mother in the front seat. Everything she owns fits into two cardboardy suitcases, now in our car's trunk. I keep quiet, staring at the back of this woman's head, mulling over the new arrangement. If she's going to live with us, I need to find a way to win her over.

When we stop for the night at a motel in Virginia, I announce, "I want to sleep in Aunt Kay's bed!" It works. She pulls me to her side of the bed and cuddles. No child, no person has ever asked to share her bed. A door to her heart swings open, and from that moment on, I'm her pet.

During the long trip, Mother explains that Aunt Kay is an answer to her prayers. "I promised your dad that I'd keep the two of you, but I just can't handle things by myself anymore. I have my Bible clubs to teach. Aunt Kay will help with that and also with stuff at home."

Kay's own story spills out. Her father walked out when her baby brother was born. From then on, her mother moved the family from place to place, often in the middle of the night whenever the rent came due. Little Kay lost her favorite doll when an angry landlord locked them out of the house and threw away their belongings. They ended up living on a boat, with her mother making a living of sorts as a house cleaner. When Kay graduated from high school, an aunt told her she could either clean houses like her mother or, if she agreed to work hard, the aunt would pay her way through nursing school. Kay jumped at the offer, and after years of nursing, she decided to find some Christian service. That's when the Philadelphia church pointed her to our needy family.

Aunt Kay's arrival in our home changes everything. Worldly-wise, she knows how to use tools, deal with banks, even change the oil in a car, so Mother lets her take charge of such things. She has a gruff manner and a Pennsylvania accent that makes Georgians suspicious, though she usually gets her way. "Men take advantage of widows," she tells Mother. "If you ever think someone's trying to cheat you, let me handle it." I think she has a grudge against men. Not little boys, though.

Aunt Kay lives with us for three years, and she does serve as a kind of new daddy. Since she's a nurse, she always knows what will fix a bloody nose or a bee sting. My life brightens. I learn to play her off against Mother, because Aunt Kay usually takes my side. I prefer for her to bathe me—she has a gentle style with the washcloth, while my mother scrubs till it burns. Aunt Kay never seems in a hurry, even when I want to play with boats and soap bubbles.

Plus, she sometimes talks Mother out of spanking us. I'm guessing she didn't get punished much as a kid.

NEEDING AN EXTRA bedroom, we move from Blair Village to a freestanding house in Ellenwood, a rural town south of Atlanta. We're in farmland now, on a dirt road. Aunt Kay says we've gone from Charles Dickens's world to Tom Sawyer's. I'm not sure what that means, but I love our new place. Instead of quarreling neighbors, we hear birdsong and country quiet, interrupted only by the thrilling sounds from a nearby railroad.

I lie awake the first night, hardly able to sleep for the silence. Then comes the clickety-clack of railcars and the forlorn tones of a fading horn. The next morning my brother and I walk to the train tracks, silver with rain. We jump across puddles that shine like a rainbow from the fine film of oil on top. For most of the morning we stand spellbound as mighty, smoke-belching engines chug past. Squealing at the weight, the rails dip and rise as each long train passes. We count boxcars as they hurtle by . . . 79, 80, 81. When the caboose appears, we wave wildly, trying to get the uniformed man inside to wave back.

Not long after we move in, a few boxcars derail, spilling hundreds of ripe watermelons beside the tracks. Some bounce on the ground and split wide open, and their moist red meat soon attracts a cloud of flies. Marshall and I sort through the sweet-smelling packing hay in search of whole melons small enough for us to tote home. A good watermelon goes for a dollar at the farmer's market, and the next day several country folk set up roadside stands offering large melons for a quarter. We laugh at the dummies driving by who stop and pay money for watermelons they could pick up for free.

Railroads yield all sorts of treasures. Another derailment dumps a load of grand pianos in East Point, on our route to church. Detouring around the scene, we gawk at the jumble of legs, keyboards, and polished black wood scattered on the tracks. A few weeks later, Mother gets stuck at a crossing where emergency crews are cleaning up after a train-auto collision. The delay takes so long that she lets us out to wander, and alongside the tracks I find a pale white hunk of flesh hinged in the middle—surely someone's elbow. I touch it and leave it there, but my reports of this find dazzle my playmates back in Ellenwood.

Mother judges country kids safer than the ones at Blair Village, so she lets us roam outdoors, where a new world beckons. Neighbor kids introduce us to candy cigarettes, which we dangle from the sides of our mouths as we walk. Chewing gum is forbidden in our house, but these kids give us jawbreakers the size of Ping-Pong balls to chomp on. Contraband has a secret pleasure, I learn—as long as I lick my teeth clean before heading home.

Our home has a rule against guns, which puts Marshall and me at a disadvantage among boys who wear cowboy hats and holsters with toy pistols. One kid steals a real bullet from his dad's closet, and we stare at the brass object as if it were an idol. He says you can shoot a bullet without a gun, by hitting the end of it with a hammer. Flush with the danger, we try again and again, but can never get it to fire.

Sometime around age five I awaken to my own body. I can't resist biting my fingernails—until Mother coats them with hot pepper sauce. Even when asleep my body plays tricks on me. I dream of going to the bathroom and wake up to clammy sheets and a wet bed. I dream of jumping off a bridge and awaken to a spastic, jerking leg. Once, I dream of being shot, with blood pouring out of my stomach; it's a gas attack from eating refried beans.

I return from each day's play scabby kneed and covered with Georgia clay, the same color as dried blood. I drink out of the garden hose, waiting until the sun-warmed water turns cool and then letting the water with its strange taste—rubbery from the hose and metally from the well—spill down my mouth onto my clothes. I dribble it over my head, or cover the nozzle with my thumb and aim a jet at an anthill. Hearing a sharp rap on the glass, I look up to see the figure of Mother standing at the kitchen sink, watching.

The world comes alive in summer. Yellow jackets stagger around the fallen apples on the ground, drunk from the fermenting fruit, making easy targets for rocks or rotten apples. I chase fireflies at dusk. As the sky darkens, bats appear, and I toss a ball in the air that they follow jerkily to the ground.

It takes more than dark to drive me back indoors. It takes Mother: "Philip, I mean *now!*"

• • •

AROUND THEN, I discover that words have power. I test this knowledge by repeating lists of rhyming words—*cape, gape, tape, rape*—while watching for that knowing look between the two adults in my life. Usually, though not always, they crack a smile: "Careful, we don't say that word."

I realize I can frustrate, even infuriate Marshall by repeating every word he says. "Stop it." *Stop it.* "I said stop it!" *I said stop it!* "Did you hear me?" *Did you hear me?* "I'm gonna tell." *I'm gonna tell.* "You're in big trouble, Philip." *You're in big trouble, Philip.*

And sometimes I am. I try to leap over a mud puddle, and fall in. I drop coins through the floor heating grate. Summers, the rotating floor fan begs to be tested. Reminding me of a giant mechanical insect, it turns its head back and forth, the blades spinning like a helicopter's. I sing, and the fan chops up each syllable so that I sound like Woody Woodpecker. I shove cardboard in the blades, and stick my fingers as close to them as possible without getting them chopped off.

A whispering voice inside leads me to splash in puddles, to explore the woods until I get lost, to throw berries at passing cars. I am simply following that voice. I don't *mean* to do those things.

"I have eyes in the back of my head," Aunt Kay insists, and for a time I believe her, because she always seems to know when I've done something wrong. One day I walk into a room and Mother and Aunt Kay stop talking. They look at me and Mother says, "Little pitchers have big ears." *Huh? Baseball pitchers?* I leave the room and plant myself just outside the door in case they start talking again.

I learn that the world has two sets of rules, one for adults and one for children. Children must do what big people tell them, whether it makes sense or not, whether they want to or not. Children must apologize when they're wrong; adults never do. Like God, adults make all the rules—and according to my playmates, my God-fearing mother has way too many rules.

Only adults, not children, are allowed to keep secrets. "That's for me to know and you to find out" shuts up my questions if I ask Mother why she whispered on a phone call. Yet if I have a secret, she stoops down to my level, stares right into my eyes, maybe into my brain, and demands to know what I'm concealing. "Tell me the truth. What happened? Don't you lie to me!"

Kids can never make fun of adults, but the other way is fine. "Look at the pouty fish," Mother says when I'm sulking. "Look at that ugly fish pouting with the big lips." The lesson sticks. If you show your feelings, they mock you. If you don't—well, how can you not?

MARSHALL AND I have always assumed that food appears on the table like magic. In Ellenwood we actually see where it comes from. We buy our eggs from a neighbor, and Aunt Kay shows me how she discards the fertilized ones that already have a baby chicken growing inside. I avoid eggs for a while, especially fried eggs that run yellow all over the plate when I poke them. Could that be a liquid baby chicken?

That first summer, Aunt Kay fences in a plot for a vegetable garden, to keep the rabbits out. After a lot of hoeing and planting and weeding, we begin to see the results waving like colorful ornaments in the breeze: tomatoes, rattlesnake beans, bell peppers, okra, stalks of corn. I drink in the hot, moist smell of growing things. Vegetables require a lot of tending, I learn, except for the squashes and cucumbers, which grow like weeds.

Toward the end of the season, I uncover a giant cucumber at the edge of the garden. This monstrosity, hidden by weeds all summer, has grown to the size of a watermelon. It's so fat that I can barely lift it. "We can't eat that one," Mother says. "Why don't you feed it to the mule down the road." With Marshall's help I do just that, only to hear a few days later that the bony mule has died. For weeks I feel guilty about killing the poor mule, despite Mother's assurances that something else must have caused its death.

Marshall and I have different eating styles. He insists on strict separation: Meatloaf cannot touch potatoes, which cannot touch a vegetable, which cannot touch a dinner roll. I carve out elaborate tunnels in the mashed potatoes and carefully pour in brown gravy before covering them up, adding some peas on top for decoration. We have to eat everything on the plate: "Think of all the people starving in China," we're told. I always begin with my least favorite foods and work up to the good stuff.

To me, tomatoes belong in a special class of food—pure slimy poison. According to Mother, my disgust began when Marshall announced, "I hate tomatoes," after trying stewed tomatoes. Hearing that, I associated the glossy, firm fruit that grows in our garden with the maroon-colored goop that comes out of a can and decided to hate all tomatoes.

"I'll never forget the day you threw a fit over tomatoes," Marshall recalls. "I think you were four. Mother tied you to a chair, secured your arms with clothesline, and force-fed you."

I don't remember the clothesline. I do remember Mother saying, "I'll teach you to like tomatoes!" I yelled and writhed and twisted my head back and forth as she forced tomatoes into my mouth—tomatoes with mayonnaise, tomatoes with sugar, tomatoes with salt and pepper. In my memory, red acid juice drips down my chin to mingle with the tears. I cry so hard that the sobs turn into choking, then coughing, until more tomato ends up outside my body than inside.

I still hate tomatoes.

PETS ARE THE highlight of my childhood, my chief source of delight, and for them I have Aunt Kay to thank. When Marshall and I start begging for a pet, any pet, Aunt Kay backs us up. "The boys need one," she tells Mother. "We have an ideal place out here in the country. What about a cat? You don't have to housebreak them, so they aren't nearly as messy as dogs."

Mother, however, detests cats. After their wedding, she and our father lived for a time with her aunt Floss, who kept thirty-two cats in her Philadelphia row house. "They're sneaky, and they get into everything," she says. "They make my skin crawl." If a stray cat meows at our front door, Mother boils water and throws it onto the cat.

Marshall, Aunt Kay, and I keep up the pressure. Finally, after weeks of pleading, we get a six-week-old kitten, solid black except for white "boots" on each of her legs, as if she has stepped in a shallow dish of paint. Naturally, we name her Boots. She lives on the screened-in porch and sleeps on a pillow stuffed with cedar shavings. Aunt Kay insists that Boots must learn to defend herself before going outdoors and fixes a firm date of Easter for the kitten's big test.

At last the day arrives: Easter Sunday, the year I turn five. The Georgia sun, a white hole in the pale blue sky, has coaxed spring into full bloom, and the air itself seems to glow with color. Still wearing our short-pants suits after church, Marshall and I carry Boots outside. She sniffs her first blade of grass that day, bats at her first daffodil waving in the breeze, and stalks her first butterfly, vaulting high in the air and missing. She keeps us gleefully occupied until neighbor kids join us for an Easter egg hunt.

When our next-door playmates arrive, the unimaginable happens. Their Boston terrier, Pugs, who has followed the kids into our yard, catches sight of Boots. He lets out a low growl and charges. I scream, and we all run toward Boots. Already Pugs has the little kitten in its mouth, shaking it like a sock. We kids circle the scene, shrieking and jumping up and down. Helpless, we watch a whirl of flashing teeth and flying tufts of fur. Marshall grabs a stick and tries to hit the snarling dog. Finally Pugs drops the limp kitten on the grass and trots home.

In an instant, my happy world spins away from me. Boots has not yet died. She is mewing softly, and her eyes hold a look of terror. Blood oozes from puncture wounds, and her black coat is spattered with Pugs's saliva. Adults arrive, who quickly shoo us kids away from the scene.

All afternoon I pray for a miracle. *No! It can't be! Tell me it's not true!* Maybe Boots won't die, or perhaps she will die and then come back. Hadn't the Sunday School teacher told us such a story about Jesus? I make vows and promises to God, and a thousand schemes run through my mind, until reality wins out and I accept at last that Boots is dead.

From then on, my childhood Easters are stained by the memory of that day in the grass. To make it worse, sometime later Mother tells us that Pugs didn't really kill Boots. "The kitten was still alive, but she had a broken neck. So Aunt Kay put Boots in a sack and held her underwater in a deep part of the creek until there were no more signs of struggle."

At night I dream about Boots, crazed and desperate, clawing and biting to escape the bag as her tiny lungs fill with water.

I FIND SOLACE in our neighborhood dogs. Sensing no danger from a kid, they emerge stiff-legged from their doghouses and under-porch hollows to greet me. The meaner ones growl until I squat down small and extend my hand, palm up. "Good boy!" I say, and their tails move cautiously back and forth. Like a Pied Piper of dogs, I lead the pack down the road, parceling out head pats to each mutt as they sniff my shoes and check my pockets for treats.

Mother falls for none of the strays I bring back for audition, not even a pitiful three-legged dog who has no home. "That dog's nasty," she says. "Wash your hands—it could have a disease."

I plead for a dog of my own. We'll be eating dinner, talking about Marshall's schoolwork, and I butt in, "Another good thing about dogs . . ."

Miracle of miracles, a kind couple from church gives us a squirmy, squirrel-colored puppy, which they say is a short-haired cocker spaniel. We name him Buster Brown after a line of shoes that has a dog in its ads, and I nickname him Buggy Brown. The first few nights, he sleeps in a box with a towel, a hot-water bottle, and a ticking clock to remind him of his mother's heartbeat. At his first whimper I lift him into bed with me. He starts out under the covers down by my feet and wiggles his way up until he's sleeping directly against my face. In the morning I smell his puppy breath as he yawns, sticking out his long pink tongue and smacking his lips.

We are inseparable. If I sit on the couch, Buggy Brown sits on my lap with his head resting on my arm. I let my arm fall asleep rather than move it, so I won't disturb him. If I go into the bathroom, he sits outside, scratching at the door. Outdoors, he flops down the steps, trips over his own feet, sniffs the vegetables in the garden. Every night I comb him like a monkey, picking burrs from his fur and ticks from his ears. Sometimes the tick comes off with a bit of Buggy's pink flesh caught in its jaw, but my trusting dog never complains.

Buggy Brown's life revolves around me. He sleeps on my socks or discarded clothes, anything that has my scent, and he trots behind me as my constant companion. If I go somewhere without him, he sits by the window motionless until I return, at which point he leaps in the air and makes high-pitched yaps. He treats me like I'm the adult with all the answers, not a kid too young for school.

In turn, I rediscover the world through my dog. I switch on the radio and he jumps backward, startled. I shine a flashlight and Buggy cocks his head, then charges, flinching and licking his nose when it touches the hot glass. Together we explore the woods and creek, and he stops to smell (and eat) mushrooms and bugs I've not even noticed. At night he howls at the moon as if it doesn't belong up there.

Much like humans, puppies have moods. Buggy Brown races around the house with ear-flapping joy, his toenails clicking on the linoleum, then suddenly skids to a halt in front of his bed and hops in for a nap, sighing with contentment. If Mother hits him with a rolled-up newspaper or sticks his nose in a mess he made indoors, he mopes for hours. If I scold him—a rare event—he snuggles up to me, propping his chin on my wrist, pawing me, trying to worm his way back into my good graces.

I check his loyalty one day by taking away a bone he's chewing on. He passes the test, looking at me with a puzzled expression but not growling. "You're the best dog in the world," I say again and again, and his entire body wriggles in gratitude. Buggy Brown is the most dependable goodness in my life.

One fateful day Buggy Brown falls into the open pit in our backyard dug by a septic-tank repairman. After calling for him, I hear a whimper coming from the bottom of what seems like a huge cavern. Poor Buggy Brown—his coat is covered in the grossest sludge I can imagine, and he has never looked so sad. No one knows what to do until a neighbor man steps forward for the bravest deed I have ever seen. He walks carefully down a board angled into that pit, picks up my foul, bedraggled dog, and, holding Buggy to his chest, climbs back out. Normally Buggy Brown hates baths, but on this day he stands stone-still as we spray, lather, and rinse him over and over.

Several months later, Buggy Brown gets sick. Our loyal guardian lies in the shade instead of running out to greet neighbors' dogs or kids on bikes. He coughs constantly. I hold his feverish body, and dab Vaseline on his hardening nose and thickened foot pads. "Distemper," says the veterinarian. "We could have prevented this with a vaccine, you know." No, we didn't know, and we likely wouldn't have spent the money anyway.

In the vet's office, Buggy Brown has some kind of fit. His lips curl back and his teeth chatter like scissors. Liquid the color of curdled milk dribbles out of his mouth, staining my clothes. Mother has to pry him from my arms. The vet agrees to keep him for a few days, and I never see Buggy Brown again. I wonder if the vet really kept him or put him right to sleep—or drowned him in a creek, like Boots.

AFTER A PERIOD of mourning, again I bring up the subject of dogs. I promise I'll do all the feeding, clean up the messes and garbage, and protect the furniture. "Yes," Mother says, "but they break your heart, Philip. You know what it's like around here. A car slams on the brakes, we hear a yelp, and somebody's dog just got run over."

One Sunday afternoon I'm walking along the railroad tracks, and God answers my prayer. I find a bone-thin puppy curled up asleep. Breathless with hope, cupping the puppy in my hands, I hurry home. I pray mightily for him while Aunt Kay feeds him milk from a dropper. Over the next few nights, she sets an alarm clock for feedings, crumbles aspirin into the milk, and somehow nurses the mongrel puppy back to health. He is soot-colored except for a white spot over one eye, so what else can I call him but Blackie?

Blackie has more energy than Buster Brown, and much less desire to behave. He scatters garbage across the yard outside and chews the furniture inside—and, as she often reminds me, Mother ends up doing most of the feeding and yard pickup. Blackie is banished to the outdoors. He runs away for hours at a time. I tie him to the clothesline, which he promptly pulls down. I attach a chain to a tree, and he winds the chain around it until he can hardly move, then howls until I free him.

I try to think like a dog. If I approached things with my mouth, not hands-first, I'd want to chew everything, too. I always find a way to take the dog's side, and Blackie knows that. Whenever he sees me, his tail spins in circles. If I let him off the leash, he dances around as if it's the best day of his life.

My children's books tell stories about animals who can talk and understand words. *Could this be true?* I wonder. In my most soothing tone of voice, I say, "Blackie, you are the stupidest, ugliest dog I have ever seen. You're an idiot, and I can't stand you. You're nothing but trouble." He wags his tail and looks at me with bright, eager eyes. A few minutes later I say as harshly as I can, "Blackie, now you listen to me—you are one great dog and I love you!" His head lowers and he looks up at me with a *What have I done wrong now?* look. It is my very first scientific experiment.

Blackie lets me hold his muzzle in both my hands as I tell him about my day. He may not understand English, but he understands my sorrows and listens to my complaints. I let him lick my sores because everybody knows dog spit helps them heal. I always ask about his day, too. "Were you a good dog? Did you stay in the yard? Did you dig under the garden fence?" He gently takes my hand in his mouth and makes happy whining sounds as if to answer me.

Blackie never does manage to win Mother over. He raids the neighbors' garbage cans as well as our own. He makes piles in the most traveled paths so that Marshall and I have to pry moist dog dirt from the crevices of our shoes. He tears up grass wherever we chain him so that soon our yard looks like an extension of the dirt road. Mother keeps track of all these offenses, and sometimes beats Blackie with a stick.

The final straw comes when a neighbor spies Blackie chasing his chickens and ducks. A man in dungarees and a straw hat shows up at our door. "Ma'am," he says to my mother, "I reckon that's y'all's dog over there, the black one?" She nods yes. "Well, I hate to tell you this, but that dog done killed three of my chickens. Y'all gonna hafta find some way to control that dog." Mother thanks him, and he tips his cap and walks home. I try to deny the crime—*maybe it was a dog who looked just like him*—but Blackie's dead-chicken breath is a sure giveaway.

The next Sunday afternoon we load Blackie in our car and go for a ride. Knowing what is about to happen, my heart is bursting. Blackie suspects nothing. I hold him in my lap as he sticks his nose out the window, speed-reading the air on the way to an adventure. Every so often he turns and licks my face in sheer joy.

"Tell him goodbye," Mother says as the car pulls to a stop on a dirt road in the woods, miles from home. She remains in the car while Blackie and I get out. I hold him close, tell him he'll be OK, and I'm sure somebody else will make a great home for him. He tolerates such talk for a minute or two, and then breaks loose to explore the new territory. He runs down the road to mark a tree and barks at a squirrel rustling in the leaves above.

I return to the car and kneel on the back seat, looking out the rear window. Blackie sits down, panting, his tail moving back and forth behind his body, smoothing the dirt. He stares at the car with a quizzical look. Then he jumps to his feet and lopes in our direction.

Blackie proves no match for a car. My last view of him is a moving dark shadow I can barely make out in a cloud of dust. Finally, even the shadow disappears.

> The writer attempts to bridge the wound of childhood
> with words, knowing all the while that, should the wound heal,
> he would no longer be a writer.
>
> —Richard Selzer, *Down from Troy*

CHAPTER 6

HAZARDS

At the age of five, I encounter the dentist.

I have already lost some of my baby teeth. The first time I felt a tooth beginning to move, I rocked it back and forth with my fingers until it loosened enough that even my tongue could wiggle it. "You'd better tie that thing to a doorknob and slam it shut," Marshall said. "Or else it'll come out at night and you'll choke to death in your sleep."

Not eager to die, I tied one end of a thick string to my tooth and another to the doorknob—and chickened out. It took two or three attempts before I mustered the courage to slam the door. I felt instant relief, like the sensation you get when a piece of food stuck in your throat finally goes down. Over the next few days I wore sores into my tongue, feeling the soft, tender space between the missing tooth's sharp-edged neighbors.

But now two pointy teeth have shown up in the wrong places,

forming a new row in front of my lower teeth. This calls for a visit
to the dentist. "So this is your son Philip," he says to Mother and
shakes my hand as if I'm a grown-up. He's an overweight, grand-
fatherly man with a big nose, whom Mother has chosen because of
his low fees.

The dentist leads me to a padded chair that goes higher as he
pumps a pedal like a bicycle's. "Let's see what you've got here, my
boy," he says. I lean my head back against the crinkly paper on the
headrest and open my mouth. A light strapped to his head makes me
squint, and I listen to his "Uh, huh . . . hmm" grunts as he pokes
around. I can see the hairs in his nose and smell his lunch. At last he
says, "Yep, looks like those two got to come out." My heart skips a
few beats.

"No shots!" I say. "Please. I hate needles."

The dentist looks over at Mother, who shrugs.

"Well, normally we'd use some Novocain," he says. "I dunno. If
that's what you want . . ." He reaches into what looks like a small
refrigerator, though when the door opens, steam comes out. From it
he removes a pair of funny-angled pliers. With his meaty hands he
jiggles the first tooth back and forth a bit, then stands up and braces
himself. I hear a loud *crack,* like when a baseball bat breaks—and
everything goes black.

He has just ripped out an adult canine tooth with its long root. I
shake from the terrific searing pain and lean over the porcelain sink
beside the chair to spit out a gush of warm, salty blood. I can't get
enough air into my lungs.

"Well, I'll be. That's no baby tooth at all." He holds the tooth
closer to examine it. "Still, it was in the wrong place. You're a brave
boy. And as long as you're here, we might as well get the other one."

He gives me a few minutes to recover, and I sip water out of a
paper cone and keep spitting until it comes out mostly clear. He
packs the still-bleeding hole with a wad of cotton, grabs his pliers,
and the nightmare repeats. When he's finished, I notice flecks of my
blood on his white coat.

"See, that wasn't so bad," Mother says, as I'm still gulping mouthfuls of air. She stops for ice cream on the way home, and the shock of cold when it hits my gums blurs my vision.

THE WORLD IS a dangerous place, I am learning, even at home. Twice I fall on the central heat register that warms our house, and for weeks afterward I wear a grid of burn marks on my hands and legs. Black widow and brown recluse spiders hide in corners of the crawl space, and whenever I feel my skin twitch at night, I leap from bed with a start.

Outdoors presents more hazards. We run barefoot across thorns and rusty cans, and scrape our backs ducking through barbed-wire fences. Bees, hornets, wasps, and yellow jackets zoom around looking for young boys to attack. A hornet sting is a badge of honor: I probe with a needle to make sure the stinger is out, then watch the little crater with a blood spot swell and turn red.

Adults like to scare us kids. Cross your eyes and they'll stay stuck that way forever. Swallow a peach pit and you'll choke to death. Masturbate—what's that?—and you'll go blind. Play too hard on a summer day and you may get sunstroke and end up in a hospital or a coffin. Wary of rabies, Mother warns me to avoid dogs that slobber or stagger around in circles. I ignore her and befriend every dog I meet.

My aunt Doris has told me scary stories about people who die from something called "blood poisoning." Whenever I step on a nail or pick up a splinter, I inspect the site every few hours, watching for that red streak that could rise up my leg like mercury in a thermometer and race to my heart.

In this era before vaccinations, I catch the normal childhood diseases: chicken pox, mumps, whooping cough, scarlet fever, strep throat, measles. Aunt Kay, a nurse, takes charge then. Most of these ailments cause a fever, which I almost enjoy. Fever makes everything clear and misty at once, like dreaming while awake. I'm in my own private world. Time stops, and I no longer know what normal feels like. And then one morning, when I wake to a pillow soaked in sweat, Aunt Kay announces happily, "The fever broke!"

The scariest disease, polio, we don't worry about. Dr. Salk and Dr. Sabin have been competing to find a vaccine, and Dr. Salk wins the race with a treatment that requires three shots. His vaccines get off to a bad start, paralyzing several hundred kids and alarming parents all across the country. "Your daddy had it, so you're OK," Mother assures us, and I breathe easier. Then Dr. Sabin produces a vaccine you can take by mouth, on sugar cubes. Marshall makes the most of it. Fond of sugar and convinced he's immune, he looks for hesitant classmates at school and offers to eat their Sabin doses.

Eventually the scientists get the procedure down and polio in the United States almost disappears. It occurs to me that maybe my father just lived too soon.

DESPITE THE DISCOMFORT, being sick has some advantages. I can eat all the ice cream I want, served in Dixie Cups with wooden paddle-spoons. The rule against soft drinks gets suspended, too, and I sip cold, bubbly ginger ale that tickles my throat.

Not only that, sickness brings out the best in Mother. For a while I become the center of her attention. In the daytime she fixes me a makeshift bed on the living-room couch and reads books to me. Every hour or so she asks how I'm feeling, and I hear her giving reports on the phone to her friends. "He's doing better today. A little trouper, doesn't complain at all." I like hearing her talk about me, as if I matter.

Her cool hands touch my forehead—and press a damp washrag to my face when I vomit. She tells me of the nights she sat up with me in a steam tent in Blair Village when I had pneumonia, my breathing so heavy that neighbors could hear it through the walls. "With your asthma, you're always on the verge of it developing into pneumonia," she explains.

One day she takes me to a chiropractor. I'm surprised she still trusts them. He tells her my asthma was caused at birth when forceps crimped a nerve behind my ear. He does something to my back that makes cracking sounds but doesn't hurt much. After just one treatment he pronounces me cured, and writes about it in a journal. Later, after I fall down and hit my head, the asthma flares up again and the chiropractor has to repeat his miracle cure.

A few months later, when I keep saying "No!" my mother reaches out to slap me, and I fall over and hit my head on the floor. "That's what finally cured you," she insists. "Your asthma stopped, and I never had to take you to the chiropractor again."

Illnesses play into the family myth. After the visit to the cemetery, when Mother told us the story of Hannah and Samuel, she said, "God saved you for a purpose. I'll do everything I can to preserve you boys because I gave you to Him. Your lives are sacred now, and God has great plans for you." With each illness, each hospital visit, each close scrape, the myth grows.

I FEEL TORN inside, torn between the gentle mother who hovers by my bedside when I get sick and the mother who punishes me when I least expect it. Sometimes her anger bursts without warning, like a summer thunderstorm. I can't run to her without first checking her mood signs. At night when she tucks me in, is she cuddling, or clinging? Am I?

From the neighborhood kids I hang around, I discover that our family is different. Other kids talk about Mom and Mommy; our mother doesn't like those informal words. I never had a blanket to drag around or a stuffed animal. I never had a pacifier, and if I tried sucking my thumb as a toddler, Mother put cayenne pepper on it. "Are you sucking your thumb again?" she would say. "Little babies do that. Are you a little baby?"

I want to be noticed. I stand on top of the sliding board and shout, "Look at me! See how high I am, Mother!" But it seems she mostly notices the bad things. She tells other parents what a stinker I am, how I spit out tomatoes, and cringe when I see a needle. Often she brings up one particular incident that makes me look stupid.

It happened during one of the afternoon Bible clubs Mother

teaches in people's homes. A couple dozen squirmy kids pile into a living room for an hour or so, sitting on furniture and the floor to sing songs and listen to her lessons, which she illustrates with colored flannelgraph figures on a fuzzy board. A good storyteller, my mother can make the Bible come alive.

Mother teaches with great energy and maintains order. If a kid acts up, she threatens, "I'm gonna talk to your mama," or maybe, "The Lord wants you to be quiet—he told me so!" Bible clubs always end with treats of vanilla wafers and Kool-Aid, as well as prizes for Bible memorization, and a surprise "hot seat" with candy taped under it. I'm not eligible for the hot seat or the prizes, but I take pride in being the teacher's kid.

Her reputation spreads. Soon she joins a group called Bible Club Movement and teaches these Bible clubs four or five afternoons a week. Because she can't afford a babysitter, I end up attending every one of them as a preschooler. Bored by the repetition, I look for ways to entertain myself.

One lazy afternoon during snack time I decide to stick a raisin up my nose. It is much easier to get a raisin up your nose than to get it out, I discover. The dried raisin absorbs moisture and swells, blocking the nostril. I pinch the other nostril closed and blow. Nothing. I dig at it with my finger, which only pushes it farther up. In the end, I have to confess.

"What are you doing with a raisin up your nose?!" Mother demands.

I freeze, caught misbehaving again. "I don't know. It just got there."

The helpful hostess fetches an array of tools—toothpicks, tweezers, a spoon, a fork, a knife, a skewer—and Mother goes to work. The other kids stand around and smirk. Soon the inside of my right nostril is a pulpy, bloody mass, and all Mother can do is stuff it full of Kleenex and drive me to the emergency room. There, a friendly intern uses some kind of instrument that gets the raisin right out.

It seems I am always doing things like that, either out of boredom or on a double-dog dare. Almost always I get caught and punished.

Every kid I know gets spanked. Most of them live in fear of the threat "Wait till your father comes home!" Since we have no father, Mother fills in. "I'll blister your behind," she yells. When we protest, she tells us that she's taking it easy on us. "I got it much worse from my own mother," she says.

Marshall earns a sound thrashing for saying "son of a gun," a phrase on the no-no list, and another for fidgeting in church. I get one for drawing on my Sunday School paper instead of listening to the sermon. Both punishments are carried out in the church hallway, where, to our embarrassment, everyone can hear. At home, whippings come for slamming the screen door, not cleaning up our room, lying, fighting each other, talking back—the normal crimes of boyhood.

Sometimes she chooses a BoLo paddle, a wooden toy shaped like a Ping-Pong paddle. To me, it seems wrong, using a toy as a weapon. She experiments with other things, too: belts, switches from the yard, a flyswatter. The flyswatter hurts the least, but leaves insect goo on my legs.

She talks as she hits. "How many times do I have to tell you? Don't you talk back to me! I'll make you sorry you were ever born." The words fall like bricks.

I pretend-wail, trying to get her to stop. "I'll give you something to cry about," she says, not stopping. Then comes the confusing opposite: "I'll keep hitting until you quit crying."

I try arguing. I tell her I want to die, 'cause then I'd go to Heaven and tell Daddy how mean she is. She shoots right back: "I wish I would die, too. I'd go to Heaven and tell him what you did wrong."

Her favorite line is "I hope when you grow up that you'll have ten just like you. Then you'll know, then you'll see."

SOMETIMES MARSHALL AND I join as allies, and sometimes we turn on each other. As the elder, Marshall usually has the advantage. "You're in trouble! You better get home right now. She's MAD!" he announces with a *Ha ha you're in for it* look.

My worst betrayal of Marshall involves a book that both Aunt Kay and Mother have made us solemnly promise not to read. It tells the story of the Shakers, a religious cult of people whose members don't marry or have sex. Every time I pass the bookcase, that book hisses at me like a cobra. At night Marshall and I discuss what kind of juicy stuff must lurk between its covers.

One day I catch Marshall slumped down behind Mother's bed, not just sampling but devouring the book. I nurse the secret for several weeks until he does something outrageously unfair. Then I tattle. Mother exchanges a look with Aunt Kay, and they both praise me for doing the right thing.

Inside, I know I have slid to a new level of disloyalty to my brother. I have a bad taste in my mouth and a sick feeling in my gut. For a while Marshall no longer trusts me, and shuts me out. I feel all alone, like no one's on my side. I promise him I'll never squeal on him again. As far as I know, he never does get punished for reading the book, and I keep my promise not to betray him like that again.

We get labels slapped on us. Marshall is *lazy,* the curse of the gifted child. In the second grade, before I enter school, he confides to me that he walks to school terrified every single day, because he hasn't done his homework. "My scalp tingles, my head hurts, I sweat. I just know the teacher will call on me."

"Why don't you do the homework?" I ask.

"I don't see the point," he says. Sure enough, he crams the night before a test and still gets the best grade in the class. He accepts the *lazy* label and does not change.

I have a label, too. I learn it one day while sitting with a storybook in my favorite corner as Mother irons clothes in the next room. I can smell the heat coming off the iron and the sour smell as it hits an old cotton shirt. She is talking on our telephone with its long, twisted cord, her neck bent sideways to hold the phone against her shoulder. "Oh, you must mean Philip . . ." she says to the person on the other end. "He's the slow one. It's his brother who's quick and smart."

When she sees the hurt expression on my face after the phone call, she tries to explain. "You took your time at everything," she says.

"Walking, talking, tying your shoes. Even being born. You were almost a month late before you decided to make your grand entrance."

I have a different reaction to her judgment than Marshall does. I determine to prove her label wrong. I know the tales about people such as Cinderella—or Joseph in the Bible—who get picked on, yet one day come out on top. *Stick it out, Philip. You'll find somebody to notice you. You'll beat Marshall in something someday.*

MARSHALL IS AT once my hero and my rival. Because he spends most of his time reading books, he rarely gets into trouble. At the age of seven he announces that he wants to grow up to be a missionary, just like his father, and from then on Mother treats him specially. She thinks of him as her "good son." That makes me want to throw up. I know that he's sloppier around the house, that he doesn't do his homework, that he once forged her name on a paper from school. He's just too smart to get caught.

"It's not fair!" I complain. "You let him stay up later, and last week he went to Frank's house and watched TV! I never get to do anything fun."

"You'll have your chance," she replies. "He's older"—as if that explains anything.

When Marshall does something, I want to copy him. After seeing him ride a bicycle without training wheels, I spend the next few weeks begging Mother to take the training wheels off my bike, too, so I can ride like Marshall. With much huffing and muttering she fumbles with the pliers and rusted nuts until she works them off. After about five minutes on a wildly swerving bike, I realize I have made a mistake and plead with her to put them back on. Sensing trouble, Aunt Kay volunteers to replace the training wheels.

A month later I'm ready to give it another try. "Are you sure?" Mother asks, and I nod. Same humiliating result. Again Aunt Kay reattaches the training wheels.

The third time I bring up the subject, Mother warns me, "If these wheels come off, they're not going back on. Do you hear me? We're not doing this again." For several days I try to master the balancing act, and each time I end up in the dirt with the bike on top of me. Screwing up my courage, I ask her to replace the training wheels. She dries her hands on her apron and marches me with my bike to the dirt road, stripping leaves off a freshly picked young branch as she goes. My stomach knots.

"I'll teach you to ride a bike," she says. "Now, get on that seat!" She hits me with the switch and I mount the seat and lurch forward. No matter how loud I yell, she keeps swinging the switch, even when I start to tilt sideways. My only escape is to pedal forward, and I do so, screaming, with tears and snot streaming down my face.

Years later I retrieve the memory and look at it, like an old scar. I describe to Mother the love-hate feelings for bicycles that I had to overcome. "It should have been a joyful time, a triumph of childhood," I tell her. "But it was a dark joy. So often when I wanted to feel pleasure, I felt pain instead." By then I've learned about her own harsh childhood and wonder if she'll be sympathetic.

She stares at me as if perplexed. "Well, you learned to ride a bike, didn't you?"

DURING MARSHALL'S FIRST two years at school, I'm home in Ellenwood with two adults, so the odds are stacked against me. I always get caught. Then one day it dawns on me that Mother doesn't really know everything and Aunt Kay doesn't have eyes in the back of her head. *There's a part of me they don't know. They can't read my mind.*

I work on the ability to keep a secret. As long as I keep my mouth shut, and don't give anything away, a secret will remain hidden. Not telling things gives me a new kind of control. Nothing makes the adults madder than stonewalling, I find.

"What were you doing with those kids all afternoon?" Mother asks at dinner.

"Nothing, we were just playing," I say.

Aunt Kay chimes in, "I can tell from your face that you're hiding something."

I think about something else, anything, to keep from telling them about the BB-gun competition. I hold their eyes, trying not to blink. They stare back, searching my face for some hint of what I might be concealing.

This tactic earns me another label. "You're a sneak!" Mother says, a label I don't mind as much.

When spanking doesn't work, Mother and Aunt Kay make threats. Mother's strongest threat goes like this: "If you don't behave yourself, I'll call the men in white coats from Milledgeville to come get you." Milledgeville is the home of Georgia's insane asylum. Sometimes she chuckles as she says it, though I can't be sure. Can kids be "put away," like you put away a bad dog?

My worst act of treachery comes after one of Aunt Kay's threats. "If you don't straighten up, I'm going to send you to an orphanage," she says, echoing my mother's warning. For a few days I weigh which is worse, the insane asylum at Milledgeville or an orphanage.

I tell Mother about Aunt Kay's threat, in part to get her sympathy and in part to hear if it's true. I get more than I bargained for. Mother says the best thing she has ever said to me. She puts her hand under my chin, looks straight at me, and says, "Honey, no matter what happens, I will never, ever send you to an orphanage."

I believe her. I have located the bedrock. Bad as I am, I will never be put away.

What I don't know at the time is that Aunt Kay has agreed never to use corporal punishment on us, leaving that to Mother. She reached for the orphanage threat in a moment of desperation. Later, Mother discusses the matter with her pastor, who advises her that Aunt Kay must leave.

Soon this good woman, my champion, who has given us several years of her life, starts making plans to move to Kentucky, all because of me.

Maybe I am a sneak. I can't trust anyone—starting with myself.

It is easier to live in the world without being of the world than to live in the church without being of the church.

—Henri J. M. Nouwen

CHAPTER 7

CHURCH

Church defines my life. Our family attends services every Sunday morning and evening and also on Wednesday nights for prayer meeting. Plus, I'm expected to show up for Vacation Bible School, youth activities, "revivals," and whenever else the doors open. The church tells me what to believe, whom to trust and distrust, and how to behave.

My first church was a classic brick structure with a white steeple pointing skyward. "Your daddy sometimes preached there," Mother would remind us, "and that's where we had his funeral." However, a few years after his death that church split over the issue of whether to paint the outside bricks white, so she found another Southern Baptist congregation to join.

"It's much larger," she tells us in advance. "Nearly a thousand members." Colonial Hills Baptist occupies most of a block in a residential neighborhood in the town of East Point, not far from the

Atlanta airport. On our first visit, I gawk at all the rows of theater-style seats lined up in the sanctuary. The separate Sunday School building looks bigger than Marshall's elementary school. Here is where we will spend our formative years.

Every week I breathe in the church's aroma, a mix of women's perfume, floor wax, leather Bibles, sweat-stained wood, and a burnt smell from the heating registers. No candles or incense, of course—we're Baptists. Tiny lights twinkle from a world map painted on the left wall, one for each missionary the church supports. From the right wall gleams a set of organ pipes, by far the showiest part of the sanctuary.

Our pastor, Paul Van Gorder, has a degree from Bob Jones University but no seminary training. A handsome man with dark wavy hair, he attracts a crowd despite being a Northerner, from Pennsylvania. We can tell he "ain't from around here" by the way he pronounces certain words. He says *Gahwd* for "God," *Holy Spilit* for "Holy Spirit," and *ah-men* instead of "amen." Sometimes he speaks in language just like the Bible's: "We shall tarry a while longer until Jesus returns."

I'm too young to follow his sermons, but they must be good, because the nationwide *Radio Bible Class* program has chosen him as one of their main speakers. We take pride in our pastor, famous enough to be on the radio and sometimes even television. Many people, including my mother, take notes as he speaks, and some mark up their Bibles with different-colored inks. When Brother Paul says "Open your Bibles to Haggai," the sound of thin pages being turned rustles through the sanctuary. In our church, everyone knows how to find a minor prophet such as Haggai.

FOR MOTHER, SUNDAY is the highlight of every week. Other women talk about what wonderful work she's doing with her Bible clubs, and ask if she can possibly squeeze one more into her schedule. She introduces Marshall and me as her sons. "They can be a handful sometimes," she says with a laugh, and humbly accepts the compliments that follow. "I just don't know how you do it all, Mildred."

Mother believes children should act like adults in church, so I have to find ways to kill time. I test mental telepathy by staring at the teenage girl two rows ahead of me. Can I get her to turn around and look? Or I study the members of the choir, who sit in rows behind the pulpit. The fat man with a birthmark is nodding off—in church! That woman in a beehive hairdo looks stupid with those cat's-eye glasses. I daydream: *If a Communist invades our church with a machine gun, who in the choir will he shoot first?*

Marshall and I invent games during the hymns. The song leader has the ladies sing the second verse and the men the third: "Let's hear it now, men. I want you to really belt it out!" Marshall pokes me with his elbow, hoping to trick me into singing at the wrong time—with the ladies. Or we alternate every other word: Marshall sings *When,* I sing *the,* his turn *roll,* my turn *is,* his turn *called,* my turn *up,* his turn *yonder.* We page through the hymnbook looking for weird names among the writers, such as Augustus Toplady. None, though, can top P. P. Bliss.

It's funny, but all the talk about soul and spirit in church makes me more conscious of my body. In warmer months, when I wear a suit with short pants, splinters from the wood prickle my legs. I practice winking, popping my knuckles, anything that helps pass the time. I make tight fists, digging my fingernails into my palms. I hold my breath as long as I can, watching the clock's second hand. I squeeze the armrest hard, trying to make the veins pop out on my arms, like a weight lifter's.

Sometimes Mother catches on and reaches over to pinch me. "Pay attention to the sermon!" she whispers, loud enough for others to hear. A few humiliating times she drags me out by the wrist and spanks me.

Whenever possible, I try to sit near blind Mr. Baker, who relies on a German shepherd to lead him around. We kids have been told not to pet the seeing-eye dog unless Mr. Baker gives us permission, so I make it a goal to befriend the kind man. I envy his dog, who's allowed to sleep during the service. The poor thing must be bored all the time because he always has to obey his master. He can't even be petted without permission.

Everything changes when Mother agrees to teach a ladies' class during the church hour. She paroles us to other women, who find ways to entertain us. From humongous pocketbooks they pull out key rings, change for the offering, and goodies such as butterscotch candy and Juicy Fruit chewing gum. These women have different smells than I'm used to—vanilla, apple blossoms, hair spray—and a few even smell like cigarettes. One Sunday I'm assigned to a woman whose husband, a former sailor, pulls up his sleeve to show me a tattoo of a bosomy woman, possibly the first tattoo I've seen and definitely the first one in church.

I especially love sitting by Mrs. Horton, who wears a chain of furry animals across her shoulders—a "mink stole," she calls it. The dead mink have hard, glittery eyes and narrow mouths full of mean-looking teeth. Each animal's mouth clamps down on the butt of the animal in front of it. Their fluffy tails and tiny black feet hang down, begging to be played with.

As the service drones on, Mrs. Horton draws faces on my hand—an adult, drawing in church!—in such a way that if I wave my fingers the eyes wink. She puts her arm around me and gently squeezes me. She gives me a peppermint, which I move to put in my pocket until she whispers, "It's OK to eat it now." It feels like a sin, candy in church, but that makes it taste even better. She lets me drop money in the offering plate and keep a dime for myself. For the first time ever, church becomes fun.

SUNDAY EVENING SERVICES are more relaxed, and often Colonial Hills brings in guest speakers for a "youth night." Gospel magicians make doves appear and people disappear. A scientist from Chicago hooks himself up to a generator and shoots a million volts of electricity through his body. Miniature lightning bolts spark from his fingertips, and when an assistant tosses him blocks of wood, they burn in his hands, filling the church with a fireplace smell. No one, however, can compete with Paul Anderson, "the strongest man in the world," who from a squatting position lifts a giant balance scale with eight teenagers standing on it, four to a side.

Afterward, we retire to a large room next door for refreshments, where Mr. Wharton is in charge. Even though he's an office clerk, with pasty skin and a wandering eye, he quickly becomes a favorite to us kids, because he has his very own cotton-candy machine. He pours sugar into a tube in the center of what looks like a stainless-steel washtub and flips a switch. *Presto!* All I have to do is hold out a paper cone, and sticky strands of pink cotton candy magically appear, winding their way around the paper and my fingers.

My most memorable Sunday evening service takes place when Dr. M. R. DeHaan, a radio star from Michigan, visits for a weekend conference. It's like the World Series of church. We arrive early for a parking place, and still we have to walk a long way. So many new-comers show up on Sunday night that Marshall and I get permission to join the teenagers in the usually closed balcony. I feel as if I'm in a sports stadium, looking down on all the balding heads and wom-en's hats, with the choir and preacher way off in the distance.

On the main floor below, hundreds of fans are rippling, like rag-ged ocean waves. They're flat pieces of cardboard stapled to what looks like a Popsicle stick, and you wave the fan in front of your face to create a breeze. The front side of the fan has a picture: Christ at Gethsemane or the Good Shepherd or maybe a photo of our church. The opposite side has an ad for a funeral company.

Teenagers sitting nearby decide to edit the funeral ads. To *air-conditioned chapel* they add, "Keeps the body from smelling." Next to *ambulance service* they print, "Oops, too late," and by *24-hour oxygen* they write in "Just when you don't need it." We spend most of Dr. DeHaan's sermon vying to come up with the best slogans. Marshall suggests an overall motto for the funeral home: "We always let you down."

After the sermon, our pastor announces that we'll be collecting a "love offering" for Dr. DeHaan. As the ushers spread throughout the sanctuary, one of the rowdier teenagers drops a couple of M&M's onto the main floor below us. A few minutes later, he proposes dropping a straight pin on a bald man's head. Just then, another teenager "accidentally" knocks an overflowing offering basket off the ledge. Paper bills float through the air, swept up and down by ceiling fans, and scores of coins roll around noisily on the slanted wooden floor below. Some coins find the heating grates and dive through with a loud *plink*! The pastor scowls mightily and deacons rush up the balcony stairs to restore order.

That's the last time we sit in the balcony.

COLONIAL HILLS HOSTS two hallmark events each year. During the annual missionary conference, foreign flags hang from the balcony, dressing up the church. In five-minute time slots, the missionaries take turns telling us about their adventures overseas. I perk up when they describe things like eating monkey meat and working with pygmies. Some of them show slides, which always end with a sunset.

After the service, the missionaries stand beside booths in the back of the sanctuary, which have displays of blowguns, stuffed crocodiles, butterflies, and even a few shrunken heads. I learn about geography and foreigners from those booths. As I view the displays and talk to the missionary kids, suddenly I'm glad my parents never made it to Africa. I have nightmares about that continent's bird-eating spiders, and snakes that hide in the roof and drop on sleepers, and something called a guinea worm that crawls around under your skin.

On the final night, people make Faith Promise Pledges. Colonial Hills supports 170 missionaries, and each year its members raise bucketfuls of money. A man on the platform operates an adding machine with a long roll of paper. As ushers collect pledge cards, the pastor announces them: "Here's a pledge for one hundred dollars. I know this person is giving all they can, sacrificially." Then he booms, "And all of God's people say..." and we thunder back,

"Amen!" Occasionally we hear a thousand-dollar pledge and everyone claps and says "Hallelujah."

For several years I have saved pennies in hopes of buying a new bike when I turn eight. Just before the missionary conference, I tell Mother that the Lord is leading me to give my coins to the missionaries instead. She has me put them in a bag, 865 pennies and a handful of silver dollars, and on the final night she prompts me to walk up to the platform and hand them in person to Brother Paul. When I do so, he stops me, puts his hand on my shoulder, and announces to the whole church, "This young boy is giving all these pennies to the missionaries instead of buying a new bike! Praise the Lord!" Everybody claps, and I have never felt prouder, or more holy.

An expert in "the end times," Paul Van Gorder also organizes an annual prophecy conference. Because we believe that Jesus will return soon and the world will end, our church takes prophecy seriously. We study the Bible for clues to the future. During the conference, large banners hang across the platform: canvas sheets stitched together and covered with drawings of science-fiction-looking creatures. These drawings depict visions from the books of Daniel and Revelation, and speakers wielding long pointers explain how the various toes and horns and eyes and scorpion tails represent various world powers.

Russia makes it onto the charts. One speaker holds up a newspaper report on Russia's plan to breed horses in preparation for a coming war that will be fought on horseback. He says the Antichrist will arise from a newly united Europe and lead million-man armies from the north to descend on Israel, set off nuclear bombs, and bring about the battle of Armageddon. "Where's Gog and Magog, as mentioned in the book of Revelation?" he asks, and pauses for effect before tapping a map on the chart. "If you draw a line straight north from Jerusalem, you'll hit Moscow, Russia!" A woman behind me gasps. As I listen, part of me wants to be raptured before the Great Tribulation, while part of me wants to stick around and watch the fireworks.

Our church talks a lot about current events. In 1959, the year I turn ten, Colonial Hills hands out hundreds of copies of *If America Elects a Catholic President,* a book "Dedicated to the thousands of Christians who have suffered for Jesus' sake at the hands of Romanism." Despite the scare, John F. Kennedy gets elected and, as far as I can tell, Christians don't suffer any more than usual.

As the civil rights movement gets under way, lifelong Democrats become Republicans overnight. And after the president sends troops to make schools in the South admit Black students, tension fills our church. Where will they force integration next, we wonder—restaurants, motels, *churches?* Colonial Hills opens a private school as a haven for whites who don't want to attend integrated public schools.

Only once have I seen Black people at a church service. When the famous speaker Dr. DeHaan visited—the one time I sat in the balcony—he insisted that some of his Black supporters be allowed to attend. I counted six Black people in church that weekend, sitting together in a roped-off section.

One week in Sunday School, I hear about the "Curse of Ham." The teacher reads us a weird passage in Genesis 9 that tells of Noah, drunk and naked, cursing his grandson Canaan for some vague sexual sin. "The lowest of slaves will he be to his brothers," declared Noah. According to the teacher, Canaan's father was Ham, and the word *Ham* means "burnt black," so in this passage God was condemning the Black race to a future of slavery. No one bothers to point out that a drunken Noah, not God, pronounced the curse, and that it applied to Canaan, not his father, Ham.

On occasion Lester Maddox visits our church. Maddox is the closest thing to a celebrity that I know. Church people like to eat at his fried-chicken restaurant, the Pickrick Cafeteria. Mother has taken us there a few times, and I remember filing past the "Make a Wish for Segregation" wishing well by the entrance. The restaurant sells T-shirts, a Lester Maddox "Wake up America" alarm clock, and souvenir ax handles like those used by cops to beat civil rights demonstrators. The store displays three sizes: Daddy, Mama, and a smaller

Junior version that looks like a policeman's billy club. Each week
Maddox runs ads in the Atlanta newspapers denouncing the federal
government for threatening to take away his property rights. At the
church's Men's Brotherhood meeting, he announces that he'll close
the restaurant if the feds make him serve Blacks. Sure enough, he
does—and a few years later gets elected governor of Georgia.

In 1960 civil rights activists announce plans to integrate Atlanta's
churches. Our church recruits lookout squads, who take turns pa-
trolling the entrances against "troublemakers." The deacons print
up cards to give to any demonstrators who might try to sneak in:

> Believing the motives of your group to be ulterior and foreign to
> the teaching of God's word, *we cannot extend a welcome to you* and
> respectfully request you to leave the premises quietly. Scripture
> does NOT teach "the brotherhood of man and the fatherhood of
> God." He is the Creator of all, but only the Father of those who
> have been regenerated.
>
> If any one of you is here with a sincere desire to know Jesus
> Christ as Saviour and Lord, we shall be glad to deal individually
> with you from the Word of God.
>
> (Unanimous Statement of Pastor and Deacons, August 1960)

When no demonstrators turn up, the church eventually softens its
stance and permits a few Black families to attend—especially students and faculty from the all-Black Carver Bible Institute, where
my father once taught. The dean of students at Carver sends in an
application for his daughter to attend kindergarten at the church's
private school, hoping she can get a quality Christian education. His
request is denied. Around the same time, a Carver student, Tony
Evans, likes the church's Bible teaching so much that he applies for
membership.

Tony Evans's request sparks a big debate over whether Colonial
Hills is ready for integration. One member asks in an open meeting,
"Is it the policy of this church to exclude from membership and
from its school Black brothers and sisters in Christ?" The audito-

rium goes quiet. Finally the head deacon, red in the face and with his neck veins bulging, bangs down the gavel and pronounces, "This meeting is adjourned!" The church doesn't mind a few well-behaved Black people attending. They just can't become members or enroll in the school.

WHEN A SUNDAY School teacher begins rewarding us with ribbons and shiny metal trophies, I become a model Christian. I volunteer to read the lessons aloud, memorize the recommended Bible verses, and lead the class in prayer. Marshall cheats. The teacher holds a contest to see who can invite the most people to a special youth service. One guy invites 150, and half of them show up. Marshall makes 240 phone calls—only, as soon as the other party answers, he hangs up, waits a few seconds for the dial tone, and *then* pretends to invite them. He makes me promise not to tell and wins the trophy.

Church services usually end with an invitation. With every head bowed and every eye closed, we listen to the pastor or evangelist make a plea for the unsaved to accept Christ. "You don't get to Heaven by being good. Or even by going to church. There's only one way, my friends, and you can do it right now. Maybe someone here today is not sure you're going to Heaven. Dear friend, now is the day of salvation. Raise your hand if you want it. Yes, yes, I see that hand. Bless you. Yes, all over this auditorium . . . God bless you, yes, yes."

Like a circling mosquito, the speaker's words seem to come closer and closer, and my guilt surges up. "Are you sure your sins have been washed away? Maybe you're thinking, 'Preacher, I will someday, but not yet. Let me have my fun for a while, let me sow my wild oats.' Or you young people, 'Maybe after school's out this summer . . .'" Fear closes in around me, squeezing my heart and lungs.

The organ strikes up, and together we sing the invitation hymns. "Earnestly, tenderly, Jesus is calling / Calling, O sinner, come home!" Just like the Billy Graham crusades on the radio, these invitations end with "Just as I Am." We sing all seven verses. The third verse is the one that gets to me:

> Just as I am, though tossed about
> With many a conflict, many a doubt,
> Fightings and fears within, without,
> O Lamb of God, I come, I come.

Nothing plagues me more than the question of whether I am *really* saved. I've said the Sinner's Prayer so many times that I can spell it backward. I go forward and get prayed over by church elders while I keep my hands clasped together and my eyes squinched shut. I do it again, several times, afraid salvation is like a vaccination that may not take. Still, I can never silence the nagging questions: *Do I really mean it? Is it genuine?*

I remember how Mother offered me to God, as Hannah did to her son in the Bible, and I know I will never measure up. No matter how often I pray, "God, help me be more holy," I always lapse into my old trickster patterns. When a new kid introduces himself in Sunday School as Doug Turnipseed, I make fun of his name. He never returns, and I presume it's my fault. Another time, I join my friends in teasing a simple-minded girl with bad vision, sneaking up to tap her on the shoulder and then running away, just to frustrate her.

Guilt feels like acid in my stomach. *How can I know for sure that I'm going to Heaven?* I look to my brother, Marshall, who has taken the solemn step of baptism. Maybe that's the key. I ask Mother and she says I'm not ready. "You haven't reached the age of accountability," she says, but she won't pin down when that is. I wait, torn between acting as the good Sunday School kid who earns trophies and the smart-aleck kid who is nothing but a sneak. Once I pass that hazy age of accountability, the odds of my going to Hell will surely increase.

A song from Sunday School perfectly captures the dread I live with:

O be careful little eyes, what you see,
There's a Father up above
And He's looking down in love,
So be careful little eyes what you see.

Other verses extend the anatomy: "O be careful little ears what you hear . . . / O be careful little hands what you do . . . / O be careful little feet where you go . . . / O be careful little mouth what you say."

I know about a father up above, for Mother has used that as a threat. My own father, I know, can see every time I pick my nose, every time I sneak behind her back and disobey, every time I tell a lie. God, a Super-Father, is much scarier, equipped with X-ray vision, an eye with no eyelid. Somehow I miss the "looking down *in love*" part.

I yearn to take Communion, which is supposed to wash away sins. But Mother makes me wait for that, too, and the waiting builds suspense. Colonial Hills only holds a Communion service once a quarter. Each time, I listen to the crunch of crackers being chewed and watch the little glass Communion vessels magnify people's tongues.

"What happens when you take Communion?" I ask Marshall after one of the quarterly services.

"It's no big deal," he answers. "It's just grape juice, not wine. And the crackers are like the saltines you eat when you're sick, only they don't have as much salt."

He's right. When Mother finally lets me "partake of the elements," I rest the cracker on my tongue, letting it go mushy rather than chewing it. I hold the juice in my mouth for a while before swallowing it. When the Communion tray gets passed around afterward, I replace my glass in one of the small round holes, like Chinese checkers. The holy feeling soon wears off, and not much changes. I must still need to be baptized.

Finally, when I turn ten, Mother decides I am ready. I gloat around Marshall, who had to wait until his eleventh birthday. First, I sit through a nervous meeting with Brother Paul Van Gorder in his book-lined office. He leans back in his leather chair across the desk from me and asks, "What does baptism mean to you, Philip?"

I recite the correct answer that I've practiced. "I want to make public the change that happened inside me when I accepted Jesus into my heart."

"I believe God has great things in store for you, Philip," he says. "Baptism is sacred. It's permanent, no turning back. Don't do it unless you're ready to commit yourself for life." I swallow, and it feels like something is stuck in my throat. I pretend strength, nodding that I'm ready.

Our church schedules baptisms during the Sunday evening service. Behind the platform, curtains hide a baptistry inset in the center wall, and on baptism nights the curtains open to reveal a step-in tub with a painting of the Jordan River in the background.

Four of us get baptized the same night. After the sermon, the choir starts singing a hymn, and we four make our way to the dressing room. We are all barefoot, and the pastor gives us each a white robe. Though the room is not cold, I shiver as I pull the robe over my T-shirt and white pants.

Brother Paul reviews the instructions. "Grab hold of my hand and don't let go. Don't worry, I've got you. I'll pull you up. Just relax." I tell myself to relax, but I don't know how.

The solemn ceremony begins. I watch from the side as two women disappear under water and come up with dripping hair and the thin robes plastered against their white clothes underneath. It's strange to see grown women go limp in the pastor's arms. One woman is crying, with black marks streaking down from her eyes.

I smell mold from the baptistry and hear a buzzing in my ears. My heart is sliding around in my chest. *What if people can see through my clothes? What if I lose my grip and slip and drown?* I keep thinking I have to go to the bathroom, even though I just went. I concentrate on holy thoughts instead.

Brother Paul nods to me, and I step into water that's cold enough to make me suck in sharply. I try to hold my breath and control my chattering teeth. "In obedience to the command of our Lord and

Savior, Jesus Christ, and upon the profession of your faith in him, Philip, I baptize you in the name of the Father, the Son, and the Holy Spirit. Amen."

Suddenly I am underwater, my eyes shut tight, feeling a strong hand against my back and another pinching my nose, my own arms crossed in front of me. Then I break through the water and gulp in air. It's over, just like that. I move toward the steps on legs that feel jointless.

"Now walk in newness of life," the pastor says, and half-pushes me up the steps.

We read to know we are not alone.

—William Nicholson, *Shadowlands*

CHAPTER 8

LEARNING

Early on, I sensed the mysterious power of words. But what was their secret? Back when Aunt Kay lived with us, she and Mother would speak in a kind of code. Aunt Kay spelled out the letters one Wednesday night as we drove home from church: "Should we stop for some *i-c-e c-r-e-a-m*?" I had heard this code before: minisounds that somehow made sense when strung together—made sense to adults, anyway.

Books used the same code. I would look at the pictures in my children's books, pointing to them in glee as I recalled the scenes they depicted. But adults could stare at the black marks, spilled like pepper on a page, and repeat the story using the very same words I'd heard before.

"Mother, what's this?" I pointed to the black marks.

"That's the word for dog. See the picture?" She put her finger on three of the marks, one at a time: "*D-o-g* spells *dog*." I asked the question—*What's this?*—over and over, pestering her as she ironed or washed the dishes or read her Bible. With each answer I stored away another piece of the code.

If I bothered her too many times, she'd refuse to tell me any more clues that day. "Wait until you get to school. That's their job." I kept at it, wearing her down. The mystery code must be important, I figured, because adults can unfold a dull gray newspaper, do nothing but move their eyes, and somehow know that it will rain tomorrow or that the Russians have tested a new rocket.

Shortly before my fourth birthday, I cracked the code. We had a few gold 45-rpm records cued to some of my favorite stories, such as *Little Black Sambo,* who melted a tiger into butter, and *The Little Engine That Could,* who made it all the way up the mountain. As the man with the scratchy voice read the story I knew so well, I traced the black marks with my finger, lighting up when I hit a word I recognized. When the dog Nipper on the record barked, *Arf Arf,* I knew to turn the page.

On the breakthrough day, I turned off the record player, and still I could follow the story. Though I stumbled on some words, I picked out enough of them to grasp the meaning. Words shot from the page directly into my head, and the jolt gave me goosebumps. *I can read!*

From then on, I played less and read more. "He has his nose in a book all the time," Mother told her friends. I read hungrily, like one of those shrews in our garden that ate double its weight every day. But while the shrew spends its life belowground, reading gave me wings. It let me time travel to England or Africa or Robinson Crusoe's island. Or to Alaska: Jack London's *Call of the Wild* and *White Fang* made my heart hurt. I could barely read through my tears as the wolf dog lay near death.

I worked hard to keep up with Marshall, who spent rainy weekends sampling the fat volumes of the *Book of Knowledge* or *The World Book Encyclopedia.* Marshall had read every fiction book in his grammar-school library. "Here's a goal for you," he said. "Try reading a hundred books before you enter first grade." I eagerly accepted the challenge.

Much of what I read went right over my head. In my books,

schoolteachers *boxed the ears* of ornery students—I imagined a boxer in a crouch jabbing at an ear over and over, or a teacher smacking both ears at once with her hands, like cymbals. How do you *gnash teeth*? I wondered. I giggled over descriptions of a woman *doing her toilet*. I kept reading, even things I didn't understand.

As A FIVE-YEAR-OLD, I decide I'm ready for the most daunting book of all, the Bible. Mother has a fantastic Bible, black leather, with tiny half-moons of gold marking each of the sixty-six books inside. It smells like a baseball glove, and she treats it like one, reverently. I believe that its pages contain all the secrets of the universe. The Bible has its own vocabulary, I find: words such as *begat, mammon, thrice, abomination*.

I like stories from the Old Testament, the thick part of the Bible. We don't read fairy tales in our home, and there's no need since the Old Testament is just as exciting and also true. Daniel taming the lions, his friends strolling around in a fiery furnace, Elijah slaying the prophets of Baal, Samson torching the tails of foxes, David knocking off Goliath—with television and comic books banned from our house, the Bible's characters serve the role of superheroes.

Soon Marshall and I ferret out the racy parts of the Bible. "Hey, listen to this," he announces one day. "You know those two women who were fighting over a baby before King Solomon? They were *prostitutes*!" I don't know that word, but clearly it means something to Marshall. He tells me that the phrase "He that pisseth against a wall" is just a weird way of saying "male." We point out these passages to our friends in Sunday School, and it draws a laugh. During boring sermons, we turn to the juicy passages in Song of Solomon.

Sometimes the Old Testament makes me laugh, and sometimes it makes me tremble. How do you love a God you fear? I feel strangely attracted to the scene of Abraham sacrificing his son Isaac at God's request. I don't question God—only heretics do that—yet I can't help wondering about God's way of making a point. Did Isaac ever again trust his father, or God?

I take some comfort in learning that God had a soft spot for Jacob, the sneak who manipulated his older brother, though I still feel guilty about my own deceitful streak.

Always, the story of Hannah abandoning her son to God looms in the background.

EVEN BEFORE FIRST grade I have already gotten a taste of school— a private "Colored school" in the basement of the principal's home. Some sixty kids attend Miz Henley's one-room academy, which covers kindergarten through the eighth grade. Many times I've accompanied my mother as she teaches Bible classes there. Mother explains that Atlanta's segregated schools are so bad that Black parents pay extra money for their kids to learn from Miz Henley.

Miz Henley runs her outfit like an army boot camp. She smacks any student whose attention strays and takes a cane to those who misbehave in class. When my mother walks in, everyone stands up and chants, "Good mornin', Miz Yancey."

On winter days, students huddle around a woodstove, their yellow raincoats steaming with a rubbery smell. At break time all the kids surround me, as if I'm some exotic creature. I notice the different skin tones, from honey-colored to a dark shade my mother calls "*black* black" or "just as black as can be." I'm surprised to find that the palms of their hands are baby pink, like mine. A few shyly ask to touch my own skin, which suddenly seems dull by contrast.

Miz Henley's discipline makes me nervous about entering school myself, but Mother assures me that public school teachers don't hit their students with a cane—not in white schools anyway.

Because of my November birthday, Mother has to apply for special permission for me to enroll in school as a five-year-old. When opening day finally arrives, she drives me to a squat orange-brick building two miles from our home. Marshall leads me to my classroom, where rows of one-armed desks face a teacher's giant desk. Some cutout letters on the bulletin board spell out "Welcome, First Graders."

I can hardly sit still, so full of anticipation. "Hello, class, I'm your teacher, and my name is Miz Honea," says a smiling woman who wears her hair in a ponytail. She speaks with a liquid Southern voice. "I want to learn all your names, so, to help me out, I have a seating chart. Please gather your things and move where I tell you."

As a Yancey, I end up in the very last seat in the very last row, miles away from Miz Honea. I feel hurt, for already I have fallen in love with her. She writes her name with white chalk on the blackboard and tells us that it rhymes with *pony*, not *money*. That night I compose poems about "Miz Honea who rides a pony."

Within a few days it dawns on me that I already know everything she plans to teach us. When she passes out thin books about Dick and Jane and their dog, Spot, I'm incensed to find that these books substitute color illustrations for perfectly ordinary words like *squirrel*—as if we don't know the word. Turns out, not every kid does.

Bored, I now look for ways to entertain myself: fidgeting, drawing, rolling the pencil around under my foot, finger-tracing the grain of the wooden desk, trying to catch a fly bare-handed, pulling the wings off a dead yellow jacket.

When she catches me shooting the wrapper of a drinking straw at the girl seated in front of me, Miz Honea orders me to come forward. She draws a circle on the blackboard and instructs me to keep my nose in that circle, as punishment for misbehaving. That lasts a few minutes, until I discover I can play tic-tac-toe on the blackboard, or turn my head and make faces at the other kids. Miz Honea schedules a parent conference with my mother, who recommends spanking me with a BoLo paddle.

"I could never do that," Miz Honea says, and I melt under her mercy. Instead, she calls on me to stand in front of the class and lead a reading exercise.

Halfway through that first-grade year, we move from the country to a place with lower rent in Forest Park, a suburb that has no forests and only one park. I turn shy in the new school because all these students already know each other. Meaner than country kids, they stick out their tongues, use bad words, throw spitballs, and make fun of anyone who does homework. When the teacher asks a question, nobody raises a hand to answer.

The kind teacher takes me under her wing, giving me special projects that I go over with her after school. One day she brings me to see the principal, Mr. Lewis, who has only one arm. I try not to stare at the limp coat sleeve dangling at his left side. "This young boy has unusual reading skills," my teacher informs him. After I read some things aloud, Mr. Lewis jumps up, says, "My seventh graders could use some inspiration," and leads me by his one hand to the seventh-grade classroom.

When we enter the room, the teacher steps aside and Mr. Lewis takes over. "Boys and girls, I want you to listen to this first grader, who can read better than some of you. Go ahead, Philip, read this story from their book."

Panic-stricken, I stare at the big kids rolling their eyes and poking each other. "The first word is *Jeremy*," coaches Mr. Lewis, jarring me back to reality. Everybody laughs. I read the story from the seventh-grade book and soon learn that I have just violated a basic rule of school: Don't look too smart and don't show anybody up. The rest of that year, seventh graders flick me in the back of the head and taunt me.

At the end of the year, Mr. Lewis phones my mother. "I'd like you to consider letting Philip skip the second grade," he says. "The boy is bored. If he goes directly into third grade, he'll have to work hard to catch up, and the challenge might be good for him."

MY NEW TEACHER, Miz Rose, smells like her name. She wears glossy red lipstick and nail polish the same color as her lips. I fall in love all over again and am thrilled when she keeps me after class for extra tutoring. Students who went through second grade have learned to write something called cursive, while I only know how to print. At six, I am the youngest and smallest kid in the third grade.

Just before Christmas, Miz Rose gets pregnant and a bossy substitute teacher arrives. On her first day she gathers us all in a circle and asks for a reading volunteer. I raise my hand, and she gives me a nod. I start reading as fast as I can and breeze through a couple of paragraphs until she interrupts. "Stop! Enough already."

"What's your name?" she asks. I tell her. "Philip, quit showing off. Reading is not a speed test. The goal is to communicate. Now go back, start over, and this time read slowly." My cheeks heat up, and I feel an ache in the back of my throat. I repeat the paragraphs, this time pausing and pretending to stumble over words. "Much better," she says.

The joy of learning seeps away, and I spend more and more time with my head on my arm, sweating in the overheated classroom.

Field trips become my favorite part of school. On a tour of the Atlanta airport, I tell my seatmate on the bus about flying to Philadelphia as a baby and sitting on a millionaire's lap. Unfortunately, I also say, "Wouldn't it be great to see a plane crash!" picturing fire engines and ambulances with lights flashing and sirens blaring as they speed across the runway. The substitute teacher overhears me, and while everyone else visits the control tower and the observation deck, I have to sit alone on the bus with a fat, sleepy driver. Through grimy bus windows I watch the planes take off, following the white streaks left in the sky as they disappear.

Partway through my third-grade year, we move again because Mother can't afford the heating bills, and I enter still another school. Now we are living in something called a duplex, which is really half a house.

I survive the third and fourth grades and, after another move, enter fifth grade in yet another elementary school. This one, Kathleen Mitchell, proves to be the best of all. The principal, a roly-poly woman, stands at the door and hugs each student as we enter. I spend all of fifth and sixth grades there—two whole years at the same school.

MITCHELL ELEMENTARY OPENS my eyes to science, which worries Mother. "Be careful," she says. "They'll tell you stuff about evolution and dinosaurs that contradicts the Bible. You can't believe everything they teach in school these days."

In the world outside, the United States and the Soviet Union are looking for ways to destroy each other, and so both governments have poured money into science education. Ultramodern, my new school has the novelty of closed-circuit television. If our teacher doesn't know much about, say, nuclear fallout, then an expert lectures us from a studio room while we students sit at our desks and watch him on a TV monitor.

During one of these lectures, we see a film clip and learn a bouncy song:

> There was a turtle and his name was Bert
> and Bert the turtle was very alert.
> When danger threatened him he didn't get hurt,
> he knew just what to do!
> He'd duck! And cover.
> Duck! And cover . . .

The expert says that if Russia drops an atomic bomb on us, we should move in from the windows, look away from the bright flash, and climb under our desks with our arms over our heads. This will help us survive nuclear war. Over the next few weeks, when an alarm sounds, we practice ducking and covering, like Bert.

The school keeps searching for ways to excite interest in science. A man who calls himself Mr. Science puts on my favorite all-school program in the auditorium. He dips a banana in liquid nitrogen and smashes it to pieces, like glass, on the floor. He causes a miniature tornado to form inside a glass cylinder to demonstrate how weather works. After the show we swap stories about lightning. One kid claims he knows of a boy struck by lightning as he stepped from a metal boat to a metal dock. "He plumb disappeared, just like that," the kid says, snapping his fingers. "Lightning got him. They went diving and found nothin' but a melted belt buckle."

Biology attracts me most. I keep an ant farm at home, impressed by how busy the creatures stay, all cooperating as if they share a common brain. I buy Mexican jumping beans, cradling them in my hands to warm them so I can feel the vibrations inside. With a knife I carefully cut one open to find a little worm—life within nonlife.

I buy a see-through plastic model called The Invisible Man and spend hours painting the liver, kidney, stomach, and other organs with model-airplane paint, using the layered illustrations in the *World Book* as my color guide. I covet The Invisible Woman, but am too embarrassed to buy one, with those plastic breasts sticking out.

IN THE SIXTH grade I encounter my first male teacher, Mr. Roth, who is also the first Jew I have ever met. He acts much like my non-Jewish teachers, only he cares little about science. He prefers English. Peering out from hooded eyes beneath his bushy eyebrows, he leans back in his chair and quotes poetry. My interest in words revives.

One day Mr. Roth gives us a homework assignment. "Find as many different words as you can by using letters from the word *entertainment*," he says. That night, I come up with forty-three: *eat, ate, tent, meant, main, taint,* and so forth. When I arrive at school the next day I learn that Julie, a girl with long brown hair who plays the violin, has compiled a list of eighty words.

Since the school bus has dropped me off early, I run to the library and speed through the dictionary, letter by letter, scanning the pages for short words that might qualify. Many of them, like *en* and *em,* are new to me, and I have no idea what they mean. Success—I now have 130 words on my list!

Back in the classroom, Mr. Roth invites me to the front of the class to review my winning list. As I call out each word, students suggest a definition. Julie, the runner-up, sits with a big unabridged dictionary to check the obscure words. The class detects a few repeats and questionable additions, but most of my words pass scrutiny—until my morning's haste begins to show. When I call out *teat,* the boys all giggle. When I call out *enema,* the entire class explodes in laughter, and Mr. Roth suspends the exercise.

Later that year, he reads us the poem *If,* by Rudyard Kipling. I've never heard anything so profound. Part of it goes:

> If you can wait and not be tired by waiting,
> Or being lied about, don't deal in lies,
> Or being hated, don't give way to hating,
> And yet don't look too good, nor talk too wise:
>
> If you can dream—and not make dreams your master;
> If you can think—and not make thoughts your aim; . . .
>
> If neither foes nor loving friends can hurt you,
> If all men count with you, but none too much;
> If you can fill the unforgiving minute
> With sixty seconds' worth of distance run,
> Yours is the Earth and everything that's in it,
> And—which is more—you'll be a Man, my son!

Even though I can't describe what the poem means, the words themselves stir me. Somehow I grasp that if you can control the inside of yourself, nothing on the outside can get to you. I want that kind of control.

When I tell my uncle Winston about *If,* he offers me five dollars to learn the whole poem. I do: it's the first literature not from the Bible that I've ever memorized.

WE MOVE AGAIN, just as I enter seventh grade. I have to adjust to another new school, my fifth in six years. Our school system has no junior high or middle schools, and so while I finish off my elementary years, Marshall enters high school as an eighth grader. As nomad kids, we both occupy the bottom of the pecking order. By now I am wearing eyeglasses and Marshall has the indignity of bifocals. Now I'm not only "Curly" and "Fancy Pants Yancey" but also "Four Eyes."

I sign up as a patrolman, with the task of escorting younger kids across the street when the red light changes to green. My classmates scorn such a do-gooder job. They torment a girl who has six fingers and a boy they call "Tin Man" who wears a metal corset because of childhood polio. When I protest, they swarm around me. "Hey, who do you think you are, a policeman?" "Hey, Four Eyes, I'm talking to you. You don't like it?" "Hey, you little squirt, watch out—you're gonna get it!"

And I do get it. The class bullies ambush me on the way home from school. Three boys knock me down and kick me as I try to cover my head. I see stars, just as pictured in the comic books. I break free and run home, the sound of blood pulsing in my ears. I dread going back to school.

Two things save me. First, I beg my brother to walk me home after my school patrol duties. He's in the middle of a growth spurt, and when the bullies approach, he says, "I'm Philip's brother, and if you pick on him, I'll pick on you." No one dares take on a high schooler. I see Marshall through new eyes: my rival has become my protector.

The second turning point happens during an intramural baseball game when I surprise everybody—especially myself—by turning a tricky double play at second base. Suddenly my tormentors are cheering me on, slapping me on the back, yelling, "Nice play, Yancey." I can't believe that's all it took.

Mr. Epp, my seventh-grade teacher, is my second male teacher in a row. He has large biceps and a bronze tan and wears his hair in a crew cut. The girls start dressing up and wearing makeup to school. When we boys find out he once played minor-league baseball, he achieves the status of a god.

Mr. Epp must know I have no father, because several times he calls me aside, puts his arm around me, and asks me to help with a class project. I would walk barefoot to downtown Atlanta if he asked me.

For men and women are not only themselves;
they are also the region in which they were born, the city
apartment or the farm in which they learnt to walk, the games
they played as children, the old wives' tales they overheard,
the food they ate, the schools they attended, the sports they
followed, the poets they read, and the God they believed in.

—W. Somerset Maugham, *The Razor's Edge*

CHAPTER 9
TRAILER TRASH

Sometime during my elementary school years, the truth hits me that we are poor. That's why I've had to change schools so often. Mother finds a place with lower rent, we move, and a year or so later that rent also goes up, and we move again.

We live in scruffy neighborhoods of bungalows covered with asphalt-shingle siding. Every so often a family on our block falls behind on rent payments, and they come home from work or the grocery store to find all their belongings piled out by the curb. The rest of us turn away from the sight, as you do when you see someone naked.

I know military kids—"army brats," they call themselves—who say moving from place to place makes you tough. Not me. It feels like a kind of amputation. Each time, I think or at least hope: *This new school will be different. My teacher will like me; I'll suddenly be popular; no one will know my real age.* Each time, I have to start all over again and seek out new friends.

You can easily spot the poor kids in the school cafeteria, because we can't afford the luxury of a cooked lunch. I drool at the smell of sloppy joes, which other kids mock as "train wreck." Instead, I bring sandwiches from home: canned pineapple one day, tuna fish the next, then banana, dried beef, or bologna. Mother wraps them in wax paper and stuffs them in a brown paper bag that I reuse until its top edge gets too greasy.

At the time, *Queen for a Day* is a popular TV program, one I occasionally catch at my grandparents' house. The host, Jack Bailey, begins by asking, "Would *you* like to be queen for a day?" and then the women contestants share their pitiful stories. One has a child crippled by polio; another just lost everything in a house fire; a third has been abandoned by her alcoholic husband. After hearing each story, the audience votes for a winner by applauding. Bailey crowns the new queen, drapes her in a red velvet robe, and gives her a dozen roses and some expensive gifts, such as a refrigerator and a washing machine.

Watching, I think, *We're worse off than some of those people.* Mother often reminds us that we're living on $120 per month from her widow's Social Security check, plus a few contributions from supporters at her home church in Philadelphia. "Why don't you apply for the show?" I ask her. "Think of the prizes you could win."

"No, this is just the way it is," she replies. "Besides, they'll have to pay taxes on all those prizes."

Mother seldom complains, though she gets anxious toward the end of the month when money runs low. "I'm serving the Lord," she says, explaining why we can't afford new clothes. "That means we must make sacrifices."

THE SUMMER I enter seventh grade, Mother asks how we'd feel about living in a trailer, or "mobile home," as she calls it. "They make some beautiful ones these days," she says. "That way, we can own our home and not have to keep moving."

"Yeah, and maybe we can get another dog," I say, excited by the prospect.

A few days later we go shopping. Mobile homes, like cars and Christmas trees, are sold on lots. A young salesman in a white shirt and tie greets us, ushers us into one of the more luxurious models, and begins jabbering. "This one has a built-in dishwasher! And notice the beautiful cabinetry in the kitchen. Like a palace, really. Look at the chandelier over the dining-room table, with that lovely bay window to enhance the view as you eat. The manufacturer has spared no expense, believe you me."

As he talks, Mother holds her chin in her right hand, stares at the ground, and gives no sign that she is listening. To the salesman, her approach probably seems like stonewalling, but I recognize it as pure terror. She freezes every time she shops for a major purchase.

Marshall and I dash from one trailer to another, comparing models. "Hey, look, this one's twelve feet wide, and it has a raised kitchen and dining area." *That's nothing, that one over there is seventy feet long and has three bedrooms—we won't have to share.* We drag Mother from one mobile palace to another, pointing out the features. In the end, she decides on the smallest and cheapest one on the lot. With a $3,500 mortgage we get a home that no one can evict us from.

The aluminum trailer, cream-colored with blue stripes, eight feet wide and forty-eight feet long, will be our family home for the next five years. When we move, we'll take it with us, like a snail toting its shell.

Once inside, I like our trailer home. It has a fresh, new-car smell, and the fake-wood paneling, linoleum floors, and built-in cabinets outclass anything in the houses we've rented. Marshall and I divide up the drawers in the tiny bedroom that we share. The designers have managed to fit a washing machine into the space across from the folding-door bathroom, so we no longer have to frequent the laundromat. All the appliances—washer, stove, refrigerator—are shiny and pink, and they come complete with instruction manuals.

Outside is a different matter. For most of that summer, we're parked in a treeless trailer court on a busy street, surrounded by city asphalt. Men in stained T-shirts and women in bathrobes and slippers slam doors and yell at each other, arguments that can be heard at least five trailers away. Scab-picking little kids roam the court on tricycles in their underwear, shooting water pistols at each other. When they get spanked, their howls reverberate from trailer to trailer. We hear TVs blaring all day and all night.

Mother insists we can't afford air-conditioning, and I have never felt such eyeball-burning heat. The trailer traps the sun's rays like a giant bread warmer, and I hear clicking sounds as the metal roof expands. At night I keep flipping my pillow over in search of a spot not drenched with sweat. The only relief comes with rain, which thunks on the roof like hail.

"How much more would an air conditioner cost?" I ask Mother.

"Don't worry," she assures us, "we won't be here long. We'll have a nice lot once our name comes up on the waiting list." And just in time for the school year, a space opens in a better trailer park. A truck hitches up our home and takes off down the highway. We follow the movers to a shady lot amid ninety-seven other trailers on Jonesboro Road, where the truck guys back the trailer into position and jack it up onto concrete blocks.

I soon meet the trailer park's most renowned resident, Gypsy Joe, a Turkish-looking professional wrestler who wears his hair in a ponytail. Gypsy Joe has one of the largest trailers, parked in a prime lot near the entrance. Sometimes my trailer-park friends let me watch him on their TVs as he wrestles against such legends as Haystack Calhoun, Gorgeous George, and Freddy Blassy—fat, hairy men dressed in bikini shorts. We know the wrestlers fake a lot and take dives, but it's a tough way to make a living, and in our park Gypsy Joe reigns supreme.

Marshall and I hang out with the trailer-park boys, who smoke cigarettes in the woods and explore the smelly sewage-treatment plant next door. My favorite is a tough little kid named Neil, who always has a runny nose and dirty hair. Neil tells me his parents are divorced, the first time I remember hearing that word. While his mother stays inside drinking, Neil has the run of the neighborhood. He likes to stand in the middle of the street and yell "Car, Car, C-A-R, stick your head in a jelly jar!" as a car slams to a stop in front of him, and then run away from the angry driver. I have only seen Neil scared once. He fled to our place to hide from his father, who had just smashed the windows of a locked car with a beer bottle. Neil's mother was sitting in the driver's seat, blasting the horn and screaming for help.

One day my new friend Larry pounds on our door, breathless. "Marshall, Philip, come quick! You gotta see this." He leads us to a trailer that's been pulled over on a dirt pad away from all the others. "A man died in there. I seen the ambulance guys take him out. He's been dead seven days, they guess, and his guts—they exploded all over the place. The smell could kill you. They sprayed something in it, but it still stinks to high Heaven."

Larry proves right about the rotten-sausage smell. I spend the better part of the afternoon holding my nose and peering through jalousie windows at the mess inside. On the dining-room table sits a plate with half-eaten fried chicken and french fries, along with some whiskey bottles. A rumor spreads among us kids that the man drank eleven pints of whiskey and his stomach blew up. There are stains and marks on the walls and floors that look suspiciously like blood and dried organs. To my ten-year-old mind, it's the highlight of the summer.

TRAILER-PARK KIDS INTRODUCE me to a whole new level of fun. We fight battles with muscadine berries, which leave a bright purple splotch on the enemies' clothes. When parents complain about the stains (which also happen to smell like wine), we switch to pods from the sweetgum tree, Sputnik-shaped weapons that leave no marks but sting like a wasp when they hit.

We nail together tree houses and form private clubs with secret passwords. One kid can burp the entire alphabet, letter by letter. Another talks like Donald Duck, and his brother can touch his own nose with his tongue. As a rule no girls are allowed, with the exception of a scrappy eleven-year-old blonde named Linda. We call her

"Sharpy Toenails" because she files her nails to a point in order to jab other kids while riding her bike.

Sharpy shows me how to start a fire by focusing the sun through a magnifying glass on some old leaves. A tiny white image of the sun settles on a leaf, a wisp of smoke appears, the edges of the leaf turn black, and suddenly an orange flame springs to life. I practice on anthills, focusing the glass on an exit tunnel as the red ants charge out, only to curl up, scorched, and tumble down the hill.

Larry has a collection of model rockets. He starts with miniature Nike Hercules rockets powered by rubber bands and graduates to fabulous launches powered by chemical explosions. The rocket leaps skyward with a great *whoosh,* and we all run in the direction where it might land, hundreds of feet away. We experiment with animal payloads—a grasshopper, a beetle, a tiny frog—and most survive, though they act a bit wobbly.

Courage is our most admired quality. We play "chicken" with fireworks, seeing who can hold a sparkler longest as the lick of fire sputters down toward the fingers, or how many seconds a daredevil can hold a cherry bomb before tossing it clear of danger.

The trailer-park gang toughens me up during my seventh-grade year. I no longer have to call on my big brother for protection. I have friends of my own. We are the skinned-kneed assault troops, the rocket-shooting, fire-making, muscadine-throwing lords of the trailer park.

I FEEL A kind of perverse pride about living in a trailer, just as I do about being fatherless. Kids at school know which of their classmates live in the park on Jonesboro Road and scorn us as "trailer trash." But I've never had such loyal friends at school or church, so I wear the label as a badge.

Sometimes I'm envious when we visit families who live in air-conditioned houses with intercom systems and pool tables and garage doors that close at the press of a button. I fantasize about a room of my own, where I could do homework at a desk instead of hunching cross-legged on a top bunk. Yet their lives seem dull compared to mine, with neighbors like Gypsy Joe and the man whose stomach exploded.

Although Mother's income falls well below the official poverty line, we have enough food, a faithful dog, and a crooked basketball hoop without a net. In addition, Marshall and I feel a pull toward two other pursuits, neither of them appreciated by our trailer-park neighbors: books and classical music.

Books connect me to a larger world: the Civil War, Mount Everest, Indians in the Wild West, knights and castles in Europe, the scary animals in Africa and the bizarre ones in Australia. Whenever I have to accompany Mother to a gathering of adults, I make sure I bring a book along. Adults sit around discussing the same old things; books, like a flying carpet of the mind, transport me to new places.

So does music. At the grocery store, Mother has accumulated enough points to earn boxed sets of Long Playing records from the Longines Symphonette Society. I carefully remove an LP from its paper sleeve, making sure not to touch the grooves with my fingers, and place it on the spinning turntable. It hisses for a few seconds as I lower the needle, and then the machine produces sounds that I never knew existed. For a moment I am suspended in pure beauty, a state utterly unlike the shabby surroundings of my life.

The problem is, I live in a home with Marshall. In elementary school his band and orchestra teachers raved, "We've never seen a child with such musical gifts. He's extraordinary." I would pick up a reed instrument, such as a saxophone or clarinet, and struggle to make a sound, any sound. Within a few minutes Marshall would be playing scales and melodies. How did his lips know to do that?

In his sixth-grade year, the marching-band director needed horn players, so he quickly taught Marshall to play the tuba, which required a new set of mouth skills, "buzzing" the lips in a large cupped mouthpiece. Later that year the school's orchestra conductor recruited my brother to play the sousaphone, the largest of all brass instruments. The contraption wrapped around him like a python with a giant mouth yawning open just above his head. For a time, I had to share my bedroom not only with Marshall but with this loud monstrosity. I protested every time he removed the mouthpiece and shook out the spit onto our bedroom floor.

Hearing about Marshall's natural ability, a generous woman at Mother's church in Philadelphia offered to pay for his music lessons, and my brother narrowed his interests to trumpet and piano. This set up a running conflict with our mother: "People are sacrificing to pay for your lessons, and you're too lazy to practice! You're wasting their hard-earned money."

Fortunately, Marshall has already downsized to the trumpet by the time we move into the trailer. Right away he earns a chair in the high school orchestra, as an eighth grader. I attend the opening concert, which calls for the performers to wear black pants or skirt and a white shirt. Marshall's pants have a hole in the right knee, which he thinks he can hide by folding the program over it. No such luck. The first-chair trumpeter asks him, "Why in hell are you wearing pants with a hole in them?"

He may be lazy and wear ragged clothes, but Marshall has musical talent that makes my jaw drop. His fingers hover over the piano keyboard like hummingbirds, darting down to bring forth just the right sound. "You can only control two things on a piano," he lectures me: "volume and tempo. The pitch is built-in. So it's important to apply precisely the right pressure to each individual finger."

He plays a short piece, taking turns to emphasize each finger—now the thumb, then the little finger, then the others. No matter how hard I try, my playing sounds clunky compared to his. I'm happy just to hit the right notes.

PARTLY IN SELF-DEFENSE, I turn to the violin. With a gift from the Philadelphia benefactor and the last of my saved-up silver dollars, Mother and I visit a music shop in downtown Atlanta. Among the gleaming trumpets and flutes, the string instruments look sedate and serious—more my style. The violin, an elegant figure eight of an instrument carved from a tree, seems both natural and classy. I plunk down $167 for a German-made violin. "You'll be pleased," the salesman says. "It comes from a famous violin-making town."

I chose the violin thinking it would be easy to learn since it has only four strings compared to eighty-eight keys on a piano. I couldn't have been more wrong. The violin has twelve different positions up and down the fingerboard, all unmarked. How do I know exactly where my fingers should come down on, say, position eight? "Practice, practice, practice," says my teacher, Mr. Lortz, who plays in the Atlanta Symphony.

Mr. Lortz only takes students on Saturdays, when I could be exploring the woods or working on a curve ball. Instead I stand in a windowless practice room, with a violin chin rest irritating my neck and sweat pouring down my back, listening as Mr. Lortz informs me what I am doing wrong—namely, everything. I can tell by my teacher's pained expression that his sensitive ears hurt worse than anything I am feeling.

My violin lessons come to a merciful end when a thief breaks into our home and steals the instrument. By then I've noticed that the violin itself is probably fake. The label inside reads "Made in Mittenwald, West Germany, 1944." Even I know there was no West Germany in 1944.

That leaves the piano. Somehow we manage to squeeze a clanky old upright into the living room of our crowded trailer. It had served well beyond its time in a church, where some Sunday School cherubs painted it lime green and decorated it with Donald Duck decals. It's missing some keys, and the sustaining pedal works but not the soft pedal on the left—unfortunate, as a soft pedal would be welcome in our close quarters.

On this instrument my talented brother performs. Marshall tells me that concert pianists are at a disadvantage compared to other soloists, because they usually play on unfamiliar instruments. I glance over at our abused piano decorated with cartoon characters. "And the familiar instrument is an advantage?" I say.

Using the gifts from Philadelphia, Mother hires an advanced

piano teacher for Marshall and consigns me to Mrs. Wiggins, a jolly, white-haired woman who sits on the bench beside me and sings along in a quavery soprano as I play. Every time I reach for a low bass note I bump her ample bosom with my elbow. Embarrassed, I pause and blushingly start the piece over, but she never moves out of the way.

At home, Marshall practices Brahms and Tchaikovsky, while I work on "Mary Had a Little Lamb," "Twinkle, Twinkle Little Star," and "Shine, Little Glow-Worm." He laughs at my clumsy attempts at trills and mordents. "C'mon, it's easy. Here, watch this . . ."

I never do master the piano. Mainly, I remember the hours of sitting in a sweltering trailer, fumbling with the slick keys as sweat dribbles from my armpits, my knees, my elbows, my face. If I shift positions, the wooden bench grabs my sweaty legs. If I turn on a fan, the pages flop around and I have to reposition them behind hymnbooks. My efforts disprove the theory that practice makes perfect. I practice diligently and barely progress; Marshall rarely practices and can play anything from memory.

I have only one recital, a humbling affair in which I, Mrs. Wiggins's star pupil, royally flub my piece. I play it at double the normal speed, mechanically, without luster, and with an obvious memory gap in the middle. "You played brilliantly," says my always-cheerful though not-always-truthful teacher as she hugs me after the recital. "You just had a little letdown in the middle. That happens to the best of pianists."

Mother says very little. Marshall says nothing, though his facial expression betrays what he's thinking.

THE TRAILER GIVES us no privacy, and we seem to displease Mother more with every year that passes. Marshall still doesn't take school seriously, and I hang around with dodgy kids she disapproves of. We each find a private world to recede into.

When Marshall faces a school exam or fights with Mother, he retreats to the piano, the one place he can express emotion without getting punished for it. I learn to read his moods by the music he chooses—from soothing Chopin or Mozart to stormy Rachmaninoff—and watch his face as he plays. He enters a world that only he inhabits, no one else, and listens to a language that speaks to him alone.

I find solace in the woods. When I feel harassed at school, or when tension mounts inside the trailer, I head into the forest, with Mother's cry—"How many times do I have to tell you not to slam the door!"—fading away. Unlike my family, the wilderness cannot talk back. When I leave the cramped trailer and its noisy surroundings, I cross the threshold into another, calmer world, one that asks of me nothing but attention.

Something inside me comes to life on these walks. My uncle Winston has given me a Kodak Brownie Hawkeye camera, and I take it with me on forays into the woods. The camera fits my preferred role as an observer. Life goes on around me; I'll just record it. Hunched over the small viewfinder, I feel safe, in control.

I walk through the dense undergrowth until I find a decaying log, where I rest in the shade and breathe in the moist green smell. Soon the forest grows accustomed to my presence. The longer I sit still, the more birds I hear. I listen to those named for their sounds: bob-*white*, whip-poor-*will*, chick-a-*dee-dee-dee*. I relish the sense of being alone with nature, knowing that of all people in the world only I am hearing these sounds in this place. The tranquil mood feels vaguely religious, what I should be feeling in church but rarely do.

In the spring, spontaneous beauty arrives in my own backyard. Flowering vines cover the abandoned cars and refrigerators and junk piles, and our dingy trailer park now shimmers with color. Wildflowers sprout alongside the cracked asphalt roads. Wild azaleas grow underneath the trees, and wisteria blossoms drape the green pines with a waterfall of lavender. I pity my friends who prefer sitting indoors watching a grainy picture on television.

One day while hiking in the woods, I hear sounds coming from an abandoned shed. I find the shed now carpeted with hay, and before me stands a creature as magical as a unicorn. My eyes are dazzled.

It's some kind of tiny horse, with a golden coat and a long white mane that spills over its eyes and across its back. It has stubby legs and a short neck, and barely reaches my knees.

A sound startles me, a cracked and raspy voice such as I have never heard. "Looking for something?" it says.

A man wearing leather boots, jeans, a plaid shirt, and a cowboy hat comes into view. Each time he speaks he lifts his hand to a scarf around his neck and hisses like a bellows. "Are you . . . ssss . . . from . . . ssss . . . around here?" I must look alarmed, because he holds out his free hand and says, "Hi. . . . ssss . . . I'm Gus."

Gus explains that after a throat operation he has to speak through a device that plugs the hole in his neck and picks up vibrations from his vocal cords. "And this here's Tiny. She's my miniature Shetland pony."

I tell him I live nearby and I like to explore in the woods. Gus hisses, "Well, then, let's just keep this secret between us, OK, pardner?" He gives me a sugar cube and Tiny licks it from my hand with her rough, warm tongue.

From then on, I keep a carrot or an apple in my pocket, and as soon as school lets out, I head for the shed. I comb Tiny, walk her around on a leash, and never tell a soul about her. Like a faithful dog, Tiny watches me with her dark eyes, and listens to whatever I say, cocking her ears and nuzzling my pockets. Inside, I feel a kind of tenderness almost like joy.

I head back to the trailer. Drawing near, I can already hear Marshall and Mother arguing about music lessons.

PART THREE
ROOTS

In order to be prepared to hope in what does not deceive,
we must first lose hope in everything that deceives.

—Georges Bernanos (in *Reason for Being* by Jacques Ellul)

CHAPTER 10
SOUTH

The year I'm attending seventh grade, 1961, the National Book
Award goes to Walker Percy, a novelist from Mississippi. When a
reporter asks him why the South has produced so many great writers, he replies, "Because we lost the War." His answer applies to a lot
of questions about the South. Winners may forget. Losers don't.

Atlanta has reminders everywhere. Marching bands play "Dixie"
at high school football games. State buildings fly a Georgia flag that
incorporates Robert E. Lee's battle flag. Historical plaques about the
Battle of Atlanta dot the city, and I often ask Mother to pull over
and let me read them. To the east hulks the granite bulge called
Stone Mountain, with its massive carving of three Confederate heroes.

A loyal Southern boy, I devour books about the Civil War. About
as many soldiers died in it, I learn, as in all the other wars in which
the United States has fought *combined*. The Confederacy began the
war outnumbered four to one and ended it with one-third of its

soldiers dead. The North's strategy of draining Southern blood, regardless of the cost, ultimately worked.

With only ten thousand residents, Atlanta was not even the capital of the state in the 1860s; Milledgeville had that honor. But key railroad lines converged in Atlanta, and General Sherman knew that if he cut those supply routes, he would strangle the Confederate armies. Sherman wrote to his wife, "I begin to regard the death and mangling of a couple thousand men as a small affair, a kind of morning dash." He torched the city, reducing stately homes to the charred chimneys his men called "Sherman's sentinels." Then began his March to the Sea, which cut a wide swath of devastation across Georgia.

I remember reading the bitter eyewitness account of an elderly woman who was five years old when Sherman's army came through her family's farm in Georgia. The soldiers ordered everyone out of the house, helped themselves to supplies, then killed all the animals and burned the storage barns and house, leaving the family with nothing but the clothes on their backs. "You never forget an experience like that," she said.

In my adolescence, a hundred years after the war, feelings still run deep. "Those damn Yankees" has been shortened to one word known to every white Southerner: *damnyankee.* I've grown up under the Southern myth of the "War of Northern Aggression": Honorable gentlemen fought valiantly against overwhelming odds and lost to brutes who invaded their land and left it charred and bloody. Southern armies were led by virtuous leaders such as Stonewall Jackson, who avoided fighting on Sunday, and Robert E. Lee, who set a record for the fewest demerits by any West Point graduate. Lee's opponent, Ulysses S. Grant, set a record for the most demerits, and spent much of the war drunk.

Like every white schoolboy in those days, I have been taught the doctrine of the Lost Cause: that the South fought over the principle of states' rights, not slavery. The right of states to make their own decisions was guaranteed by the Constitution, after all. As one of my teachers said: "Think about it—only thirteen percent of South-

erners owned slaves. Would we fight a war over that? And North-
erners were just as racist, and more hypocritical. They operated the
slave ships and profited from the products of slave labor."

I remember collecting a set of toy Civil War soldiers as a child. I
threw away a few of the blue ones to give the grays an advantage. In
my grandmother's living room, I scrunched up the rug to create hills
and valleys like the ones around Atlanta and talked my brother into
taking the Northern side. Unlike history, my battle produced a re-
sounding Rebel victory.

Every year or so I ask my mother to take me to the Cyclorama,
"the world's largest oil painting," which re-creates the Battle of Atlanta with paintings and life-sized figures arranged in a circular
building. The strains of "Dixie" and the sight of my city ablaze always bring me to tears.

Though our family rarely eats out, we hear from church friends
about several of Atlanta's most popular restaurants, which keep
alive traditions of the Old South. Aunt Fanny's Cabin features Black
waitresses dressed as plantation slaves who sing gospel songs to the
diners, while young boys in slave costumes display the menu on
signboards hung around their necks. Nearby, white diners crowd
into Johnny Reb's Dixieland to hear a nightly performance of "The
Battle of Atlanta," in which the Black waiters and busboys celebrate
the "final charge of the Confederacy" with a chorus of whoops and
Rebel yells.

In school I write book reports and papers on the Civil War and its
heroes. On our family trips to Philadelphia, I talk my mother into
taking detours to battlefield sites. My most moving moment comes
at Cemetery Hill in Gettysburg, envisioning Pickett's Charge. I've
written a school paper on the battle, and now I'm standing at the
very spot where the tide turned against the South. Up until then, the
Rebels had been hounding the enemy, chasing them all the way into
Pennsylvania. After Gettysburg, the high-water mark of the Confederacy, came a relentless grim decline.

The last Civil War site I visit is the room in Appomattox where
Robert E. Lee finally surrendered. I listen to the guide tell the story

as if it were a great triumph, the exact opposite of what I've learned in school. I feel a sudden cold-hot shock as he describes the scene that ended the war. A sliver of confusion about the Lost Cause enters my mind that day, and afterward I never want to visit another battlefield.

You have to live in the South to understand it, I decide.

OCCASIONALLY, MOTHER TAKES us on summer drives through the rural Georgia countryside. She knows some church people who have moved away from the big city of Atlanta, and on these visits I get a taste of the real South. My first view of a cotton field startles me: the crop looks exactly like clumps of snow caught on dry twigs. Sometimes we see the ruins of an old plantation chimney pointing skyward in the middle of a field, a stark reminder of how things used to be.

Every county seat we drive through looks the same: a square of mom-and-pop shops and diners surrounding a brick courthouse. Farmers in bib overalls loiter around the courthouse, talking and chewing tobacco while their wives shop for groceries and clothes. They lean back in cane-bottom chairs and complain about things they can't control—family, weather, the economy, their ailments. They distrust politicians of any stripe. "They's all crooked, ever' one. They don't care a possum's tail about the people. They're in it for the money. The gov'mint oughta jes' get off our backs and leave us be."

If we stop for a snack, the locals turn to stare at this woman and her two sons who don't belong. Even so, I like the way perfect strangers act as if they have all the time in the world when you ask them a question. No one seems tense and hurried, like city people. They address Mother and me with "Yes, ma'am" and "Yes, sir." The South sugars everything: watermelon, grits, iced tea, even its language.

I learn about my region by listening—which I've always preferred to talking. Southerners have perfected the art of storytelling, and by remaining quiet I get an earful. Everyone seems to have a relative who shot a cousin for messing with his daughter, or knows about a Pentecostal preacher who slashed her drunk husband with a pair of scissors. Whatever happens of interest works its way into a story.

Visit a clinic for advice about a skin rash, and you may hear the doctor's account of someone in the next county who showed symptoms similar to yours. "This one woman, she had blisters like that all over her backside. And I mean *all* over. Lord, have mercy! She was big as a queen-sized bed—we could hardly get her dress unzipped—and I couldn't for the life of me figger out how she got somethin' that looked like poison oak back there. I called a specialist over at Grady Hospital and asked him if he'd ever seen the like . . ."

The juicier the story, the better. "You read in the papers about that guy who killed both his parents? Beat all I ever saw. Must've been the drink got to him. He was so bad to drink that his wife left him—I don't know, five, six times—but she always come back. Well, one night he took hisself a gun and up and shot both his ma and his pa. He laid down and slept 'til about noon. When he woke up, he tried to make it to look like a robbery and called the cops. They smelled a rat, and got him to confess. Imagine, doin' that to his own people. What's this world a-comin' to?"

I listen from another room as my mother's best friend tells about her sister–in–law, who headed up a hospital's anesthesiology department. "She was a lesbian, even though she was married to my brother. She'd been to an asylum once for some sort of treatment. Anyway, this one guy—everybody knew him, the town drunk—he came in a-cussin' up a storm. She told him if he didn't stop she'd sew his mouth shut. And by God if she didn't do just that. She put him down and took a needle and sewed both his lips together."

She pauses for effect before continuing. "Well, you just cain't do somethin' like that, I don't care who you are. The hospital hated to lose her, so they gave her a choice: either you go back to the asylum for more treatment, or we're gonna take away your medical license, there's no two ways about it. She didn't show up for work the next day or the next. On the third day a cleaning woman at the hospital smelled somethin' funny and opened a closet and there she was, dead as a doornail. She'd given herself an overdose—they found the needle. The family was mad as hornets because she willed everything to her woman lover."

I soon understand where country-music songwriters get their material—just by listening to raw Southern life.

Religion comes up all the time. I go to the grocery store with my mother and the checkout clerk asks in a nasal voice, "What church y'all goin' to, honey?" Everybody goes to some church—although when one of my relatives becomes a Mormon, the others react as if he's turned Communist. I twist the radio dial and count twelve stations playing hymns or sermons. Billboards and barns are painted with various religious slogans. *Prepare to meet thy God. Christ died for you—can you not live for him? He loved you so much it hurt* (this one has red paint, like blood, dripping off the letters).

Death ranks right at the top of what people talk about. A relative falls ill and the countdown starts. "They cut him open, and they was nothin' they could do, so they just sewed him up. He looks like graveyard death already. When I touch him, his skin feels clammy as a toad. He won't last long—I give him two weeks, a month at most."

The other end of life gets equal notice. Joining Mother on one of her visits, I sit in a living room where toddlers seem to be the chief form of entertainment. Conscious of being the center of attention, a child runs around tossing a ball and hitting his little sister. The women seem captivated by the drama playing out before them, which to me looks very ordinary. "He's a wild child, that one, the spittin' image of his daddy. You think you're somethin', Billy-John, don't ya? You sweet thing you—come over here and give Meemaw a kiss. Give me some sugar."

I learn from these conversations that, from birth to death, people *matter* in the South. They are the main topic of concern, not the economy or foreign policy or scientific discoveries. Somehow I know that if our house burns down or we run out of money or I get hit by a car, this would be the place to live. Southerners look after their own.

• • •

IN THE EARLY 1960s, the civil rights movement gathers steam and now nearly every conversation circles back to race.

As a true son of the South, I am born and bred a racist. My grandfather tells me that an ancestor, William Lowndes Yancey, led a group known as "the fire-eaters," who called for the South to secede and thus helped start the Civil War. "Yep," he continues, "and until Emancipation my own granddad kept a few slaves on a plantation someplace called Rough and Ready, Georgia. I've still got the official letter ordering him to set 'em free."

This fact makes a heady impression on me, a kid from the slums. He also tells me that, after Emancipation, some of those enslaved workers, who had no surnames, took on the name Yancey. That night I thumb through the Y pages of the Atlanta phone book, searching for Black-sounding names like Willie Mae and Deion, wondering if my ancestors used to own theirs.

I've been taught in school that most slaves lived contentedly on the plantation. After all, why would an enslaver mistreat the very workers he depended on for his livelihood? The Children of the Confederacy published a sort of catechism that asks, "What was the feeling of the slaves toward their masters?" Good Southern kids parrot back the answer, "They were faithful and devoted and were always ready and willing to serve them."

Each Christmas as we sit at my grandmother Yancey's table, Black employees from my grandfather's truck-body shop appear at the back door. They knock and then stand there awkwardly until my grandfather gets up and drops a couple of silver dollars into their hands as a Christmas bonus. Some of them I know, such as Buck, an illiterate blacksmith with webbed fingers, who signs his name with an "X." Leroy, the muscular foreman, always gets the biggest bonus. He stands on the back porch shuffling his feet, and says, "Jes' come to wish y'all a Merry Christmas, Mistuh Yancey." Grandpop smiles and goes inside to retrieve six silver dollars, one for each member of Leroy's family.

We're relaxing in the living room at the Yanceys' one night when the TV news covers a civil rights protest in Atlanta, which leads my grandfather to reminisce about the race riot of 1906. "I'd just turned eighteen. Some rumor spread about Black men raping white women. Well, a mob of white folks got together and started a big riot downtown. I think they lynched several dozen Black men. Some of the rioters cut off fingers and toes as souvenirs."

I haven't heard this story before and don't know how much to believe. "Were you there in person?" I ask.

He nods. "I saw it with my own eyes. My dad told me to stay away, but I disobeyed. I rode the streetcar downtown the day after the biggest riot. Bodies were still hanging from the streetlamps— Negroes had been strung up live and used as target practice. The gutter was red with blood. I'll never forget that sight."

Nobody knows what to say until my uncle Winston, who has been listening, speaks. "And they want you to believe everything has changed. Our family doctor is the highest-ranking member of the Ku Klux Klan in Georgia. Everybody knows it, though of course he never mentions it. He was a high school classmate of your dad's. Heck, you wanna see the power of the KKK, you can drive right now up to Forsyth County, just north of Atlanta. You'll see a sign posted at the border: 'Nigger, don't let the Sun set on you in Forsyth County.' And they mean it."

I flinch at the *N*-word, forbidden in our house. My aunt Doris, like many polite Atlantans, carefully avoids it, too, though just barely. "I got me a little Nigra to fix my roof," she says. Or, "I don't know how old that patient was. It's kinda hard to tell with Nigras, you know."

Uncle Jack proves to be the most racist of my relatives. After Congress passes the Civil Rights Act of 1964, he packs up his family and moves to Australia, which at the time has a "whites-only" immigration policy.

TO MY SURPRISE, my Philadelphia relatives are no less racist. My uncles warn of "darkies" buying a row house a few blocks over.

"They're already invading the parks and swimming pools," my uncle Bob grouses. "Soon they'll take over this whole part of town." He says that when he served in Korea, even with his eyes closed he could tell when a Black soldier walked into a tent. "They smell different. That's why dogs don't like 'em."

On our car trips to Philadelphia, I wonder where Black people eat, use the restroom, or spend the night. In Southern states, we never see whites and Blacks in the same restaurant or motel. That would be illegal. Mother assures me they have their own places—*The Negro Motorist Green Book* lists them all—but I see very few "Colored Motel" signs along the highways.

Apart from visits to Miz Henley's school, I rarely come into contact with Black people. We play in segregated parks, go to separate barbershops, and attend different schools and churches. By law Black kids cannot swim in a white swimming pool, and a Black doctor or nurse cannot treat a white patient. Some pet cemeteries even have a separate section for the cats and dogs of Black people.

Atlantans share the same overall space, but without touching, as if on an invisible checkerboard of black and white squares. Tall buildings downtown designate one elevator for Negroes, freight, and baggage; the nicer ones are reserved for whites. Public buildings usually have three restrooms: White Women, White Men, and Colored. Drinking fountains are labeled White or Colored, often with cold water available only for the whites. A friend of mine from church told me that as a child he kept twisting the knob for the Colored fountain, expecting colored water to come out.

Rich's, the city's most prestigious department store, sells clothes to Black customers but won't allow them to try on the clothes, so as not to offend its white patrons. The store also bans Blacks from its restaurants. During my seventh-grade year, Martin Luther King Jr. joins a series of student sit-ins, forcing Rich's to change.

The route to my grandparents' house takes us through Black neighborhoods. I stare out the car window at the streets and front porches teeming with life. Old men sit in rocking chairs, chewing snuff and spitting the remains into tobacco tins. Women sit beside them shelling butter beans or quilting. The sidewalks, where any exist, are a playground for hopscotch and jump ropes, or form the boundaries for street ball.

I breathe in the smells: barbecue, fresh grass clippings, cigar fumes, and also one acrid burnt smell I don't recognize. "It's hair," my mother says. "They're using heated metal combs and pressers on their hair to make it straight, like white people's." On bus trips to downtown Atlanta, I start noticing ads for skin whiteners and hair straighteners. "A clear, whiter skin is the stepping stone to popularity, love, romance, and business success" reads one.

My own hair has never been straight, which attracts the ridicule of my schoolmates. "Hey, where'd you get those curls, huh? You got some Black blood in you?" It's a serious matter. According to state law, based on the one-drop rule, a person with a tiny fraction—just one drop—of Black blood is classified as Negro.

Black people give us someone to look down on and feel superior to. My family has lived in government projects and in a trailer park. We may qualify as "poor white trash," but at least we are white. Even compliments have a racist undercurrent: "He's right smart, for a Black man . . . She's real pretty, for a Black girl."

Every few months Mother hires a woman named Louise to help with chores, such as cleaning the stove and defrosting the refrigerator. Imagine, someone lower on the ladder than us! Mother treats her well, but Louise never eats with us. She insists on taking her lunch break while standing up, in the kitchen. Once, Mother went to Louise's home for dinner, and even there Louise ate in a separate room. She explained, almost apologetically, "Ma'am, no offense, but I ain't never ate at a table with a white woman before."

ONLY LATER WILL I learn another side of the South, which the child-me missed. I read eyewitness accounts of slavery by Frederick Douglass and others who describe a cruelty I can barely comprehend. I wince at Civil War soldiers' descriptions of corpses rotting in trench mud, of limbs sawn off with nothing to dull the pain, of a

Georgia prison called Andersonville in which more Union soldiers died of starvation than had died in the North's five bloodiest battles combined.

Something seems to crumble inside me as I read these accounts, which stay with me like an afterimage. The Confederate army no longer seems so honorable, the Lost Cause no longer so just. The war may have loosened the shackles of slavery, but more than a century later the spirit of racial hostility lives on. I feel engulfed by a sense of revulsion, not only at what I once believed to be true but also at myself. Growing up, I swallowed the myth.

Guilt denied never goes away. The South casts the war, as it casts almost everything, in religious language. Historian Shelby Foote tells of a Confederate monument in his hometown dedicated to "the only nation that lived and died without sin." On one of my childhood pilgrimages I visited the Richmond grave of Jefferson Davis, which has this inscription carved in stone: "Blessed are they which are persecuted for righteousness' sake for theirs is the kingdom of heaven." That is the myth of the Lost Cause that I believed as a boy and through my adolescence.

General Grant, who had seen the worst that war has to offer, expressed a different view at Appomattox—sadness "at the downfall of a foe who had fought so long and valiantly, and had suffered so much for a cause, though that cause was, I believe, one of the worst for which people ever fought." As a Southerner, coming of age for me included a dawning awareness that we were living with a story that was self-deceiving, a lie. The resulting tension planted something deep in my soul, a nagging sense of betrayal.

I couldn't put together the contradictions of my homeland. A religion-soaked place with so much gossip about cheating friends, child abuse, rape, drinking, and violence. A friendly, hospitable people who viewed outsiders with suspicion. An honorable people who defended that honor with violence. A defeated people who took out their anger on a race even more beaten down.

As I grew older, a crack opened up in what I had always been taught to believe, the first of many cracks to come.

They, certainly, did not think themselves unusual,
in their own eyes; they were like everyone else, and their conduct
seemed to them, so far as I can judge, highly natural,
just what anyone else would do under the circumstances.

—Mary McCarthy, *Memories of a Catholic Girlhood*

CHAPTER 11
PHILADELPHIA

At the end of every summer we drive to Philadelphia to visit my mother's family, the Diems. There, I gain a glimpse of my mother's life and upbringing.

The drive takes two days, and Mother constantly worries about traffic. "We haven't hit any yet, but wait till we get to Richmond. . . . Well, that wasn't so bad, but wait till we get near Washington . . ."

On the trip, we splurge by eating in restaurants. "You can choose anything you want," Mother says, taking out an envelope full of cash she's been saving all year. Marshall orders his favorite dish, veal cutlet—for breakfast, lunch, and dinner. The day's highlight comes in late afternoon, when we search for a motel within Mother's budget. Marshall and I lobby hard for one with a swimming pool, and sometimes we win.

In the motel room, Mother drops our bags, heads to the bathroom, and removes a paper seal that reads, "Sanitized for your protection." We change into swimsuits and, after a dip in the pool, retire to the room, shivering in unaccustomed air-conditioning, and climb under the covers to enjoy the luxury of television. This is living!

As we near Philadelphia, the view outside the car windows gets uglier, but also more thrilling. Refineries belch flames in the air. Crossing rust-colored bridges, we peer down at the ships lined up in the dark water, waiting to touch land. We dip into tunnels coated with exhaust and shoot out the other side into blinding sunlight. Susquehanna, Schuylkill, Tinicum, Passyunk—the names on the highway signs sound foreign to our Southern ears.

FOR A KID from the leafy suburbs of Atlanta, southwest Philadelphia, where the Diems live, might as well be a foreign country. Each block looks like every other block: a line of two-story row houses, with front yards so small you can stand on the porch and spit a watermelon seed to the sidewalk. Pavement covers almost everything— the street, the sidewalks, the front steps—and the only trees I see are two-inch seedlings poking their way through cracks in the sidewalk. The streets have numbers, not names—70th, 69th, 68th, rather than Peachtree Street or Meadowlark Lane.

Around Labor Day those streets feel like molten lava. How, after driving two days in a northerly direction, could we have ended up in a place even hotter than Georgia? We always visit at the most miserable time of the year, because of a weeklong missionary conference at Mother's home church, Maranatha Tabernacle.

A few of the neighbors call me over. "Hey, kid, where you from?" When I tell them Georgia, they ask me to say something "in Southern" and make fun of how I talk. "What comes after nine?" they ask, and when I say *ten,* they laugh as if I've told a joke. "That ain't how you say it. It's *ten,* not *tin.*" When I say *y'all,* they laugh harder, slapping their knees and pointing at me as if I'm a stand-up comic.

Southwest Philly assaults the senses. Horns blare, police sirens wail. A truck rolls by with a vendor calling through a scratchy loudspeaker, "White corn, six for a dollar, Jersey cantaloupe, bananas . . ." At dusk, lights twinkle along the span of the Walt Whitman Bridge, and I can see orange gas flares pluming from smokestacks in New Jersey. Smells—sulfur from the refineries, roasting coffee, fresh-baked bread from the German bakery, sausages grilling in someone's backyard, a neighbor's cigar—mingle together. My nose works harder in Philadelphia.

On a foldout bed in a screened-in porch, I lie awake at night, squinting against the streetlights outside. My uncle Jimmy sits in the living room till midnight, watching two TVs and listening to a radio, all tuned to different sports shows. After he finally heads to bed, I worry about neighborhood gangs. I hear the clack of footsteps approaching, closer and louder, and hold my breath until they pass by. Just as I drift off to sleep, the milkman drops bottles into the metal box on the front steps, and all the nearby dogs bark at once.

The row house on 67th Street gets boring fast. A creaky wooden staircase leads to the upper floor, and Marshall and I slide down the bannister or bump down the stairs on our bottoms—*thump, thump, thump*—until Uncle Jimmy makes us go up and down the stairs thirty times as punishment, taking all the fun out of it. "That'll teach you," he says with a wicked laugh.

Food is unrecognizable. Instead of white bread, the Diems eat rye bread with seeds and a crust that bites back. They serve strange meats, such as liverwurst and scrapple. They slather mayonnaise on boiled potatoes and cook all vegetables to mush. For lunch, my grandmother serves a chicken salad lumpy with gelatin and gristle. As a Southerner, I'm shocked to see her serve iced tea made from an instant mix, *unsweetened*. My uncles flavor it with artificial juice from a plastic lemon-shaped container. I wonder how my mother survived childhood.

Uncle Jimmy walks around the house in a droopy, sleeveless undershirt, with his bear-fur chest half-exposed. He drinks ice water straight out of a yellow Tupperware container, and milk directly from the carton. Marshall and I gawk. Rules are different up here.

TWO ADULT UNCLES live in the tiny row house with my grandparents. I dread staying with these boors, who take delight in picking on Marshall and me. On the drive home after each trip, Mother gives more details about her family, filling in the blank spaces.

"Jimmy's troubles started in the Korean War," she says about her brother. "He fell in love with a Korean gal who worked as an interpreter for army intelligence. Jimmy wanted to marry her, and she got clearance to come over here with him, not so easy in those days. When he told your grandmother, she said, 'I'm not going to have one of those slanty-eyes in my family!' and he's never been the same since."

Almost completely bald, Jimmy has a thickly furrowed forehead and tired, deep-set eyes, which make him look menacing. Hairy round shoulders bulge out from his tank-top undershirt. Every weeknight he retires to the one-bulb bathroom and shaves with a straight razor, a chore that requires forty-five minutes and leaves specks of blood on his undershirt.

Uncle Jimmy responds to questions in a way that seems more retort than answer. If I ask whether the Phillies won last night, he says, "What's it to you?" If I ask him to turn down the TV volume at night so we can sleep, he says, "You and how many marines?" Then he repeats it several times. "Like I say, you and how many marines? Did ya hear me—you and how many marines?"

Jimmy wears a watch that doesn't work. When I ask why he wears it, he thinks for a minute and says, "It's right twice a day, ain't it?" Ballpoint pens lie scattered around the living room, but I can only find one that writes. Jimmy knows which one, though, and if I don't replace it in the exact spot, he corrects me. He demands that Grandmother serve him dinner promptly at 4:30 each day, in case he decides to go bowling that night. On Friday night he breaks the routine by going out for a Philly steak sandwich. "They know what I want as soon as I walk in the diner," he brags.

In time, life sours for my uncle when he makes his first visit to a doctor in years. I will later meet that doctor and hear his report firsthand. "So, I ask your uncle Jimmy to step behind the curtain and put on a gown. The room fills with a horrible smell, like a hamper full of dirty diapers. He comes out, and I swear to God his right leg is crawling with maggots. It has necrotic tissue, blood poisoning, gangrene, you name it. He probably has neuropathy from diabetes so he doesn't feel much pain, but how could you not notice a leg like that?! We sprayed Lysol, Pine-Sol, anything we could find, and the smell in my office still didn't go away for weeks."

The day after that visit, a surgeon amputates the leg just below the knee. Uncoordinated to begin with, Jimmy never really adjusts to a prosthetic leg. He clomps down those creaky stairs in the morning and sits in his chair all day, with a chamber pot for his toilet. No more bowling, no more driving. He watches sports on TV most of the day and reads three daily newspapers, cover to cover.

Whatever in life my uncle Jimmy misses out on, his younger brother, Bob, makes up for. Oversized, loudmouthed, blustery, he wears his prodigal-son reputation with pride. On our early trips to Philadelphia, the teenager Bob tormented me relentlessly. "Hey, I'm coming to Atlanta, so book me a suite in the General Sherman Hotel, OK, little Rebel?" he said, and laughed loud and long at the joke that will be repeated several times a day. "Oh, and if that one's full, try the Ulysses S. Grant Hotel."

He would twist my arm behind my back and say, "Repeat after me: 'The South lost the Civil War. I love Yankees.'" If I refused, he'd lock me out of the house, even in the pouring rain. I spent hours huddled under a tiny awning, shivering, upholding the honor of the Confederacy. "Hey Jimmy, I hear there's a Rebel running around here somewhere—have you seen one? No? Well, I guess we'd better keep the door locked. Can't be too careful, you know. We wouldn't want any Rebels in this house."

Uncle Bob claims he played professional football, though I can never find any record of his name on a roster. At his heaviest he weighed 325 pounds, and nobody messed with Bob Diem. "I got called for holding once and yelled at the ref, 'What do you mean, holding?' He said, 'Well, Bob, I didn't see you smash him in the mouth with your forearm, so I knew you must have been holding.'" He lets out a deep belly laugh. "My philosophy is, stick it to them before they stick it to me."

Bob's large ego matches his size. "This is the best thing you do, coming up here every year," he says, "because maybe some of my qualities will rub off on you. I'll make a man of you." When he learns I want to be a writer, he says, "Good. You couldn't find a better subject. My life story will make a bestseller."

My uncle relishes his role as the black sheep of the family. In the years to come, he will live out his reputation in ways that scandalize the rest of the family. He divorces his first wife and disowns his only son for being gay. A second wife commits suicide, shooting herself in the shower. He squanders any money he makes on gambling and files more bankruptcies than he can count.

I ask him one time, "Do you have any regrets?" He hardly gives it a thought. "Nope. I always did exactly what I wanted."

Like his older brother, Jimmy, Bob also has a tragic end. He takes poor care of himself and ignores his diabetes, even after losing a couple of toes. On Christmas Day 2009, the county sheriff, alerted by neighbors who smell something awful, breaks into his house. He finds Bob's body lying on his bed, where it's been for several days. Crazed with hunger, his pet Rottweiler has eaten off one foot and much of the other. The sheriff has to shoot the dog and then calls in a biohazard team. They find thousands of roach eggs: in the stove, in lights, in radios, in the ceiling fan, in any warm place.

I HAVE FEW memories of my grandfather, Albert Diem. Mother always speaks fondly of him. "He kept the family together, working two jobs to get us through the Depression. Then he did double shifts at the General Electric factory during the war. After all that, GE laid him off at the age of fifty-six."

I knew him as a thin, kindly man who sat in a Naugahyde recliner turning the pages of a newspaper with nicotine-yellow fingers. His doctor forbade him to smoke because of a heart condition, and Marshall and I reported to Mother whenever we caught him sneaking a cigarette on one of his walks around the block. Secretly, I liked watching the way bluish smoke curled up from his nostrils. *So that's what sin looks like,* I thought.

We were in Georgia when my grandfather Diem died. One day Mother got a postcard informing her that he was in the hospital. The next day, we were eating a pork-chop dinner in our trailer when the phone rang. Uncle Jimmy said three words, "Well, he's gone," and Mother started crying loudly, "Boo hoo, boo hoo," just like they do on television. She ran to her bedroom, and Marshall and I sat mute and bewildered, staring at our half-eaten meals.

After arranging to leave us with our Yancey grandparents, Mother caught a train to Philadelphia for the funeral. No one met her so she took a cab to the house, where she found the family gathered around the dining-room table arguing about how much money to spend on the casket.

My grandmother Sylvania was the main force in the Diem family. As a child I feared her, with her filmy eyes and white chin hairs and clicking dentures and a dour expression on her face. Her lower lip protruded and her cheeks got in the way when she talked, which made her difficult for me to understand. I sensed she didn't much like children, especially noisy or active ones.

From Mother, I gradually learned Sylvania's own story.

She was born in 1898 into a working-class family, the eighth child of ten, and went by the nickname "Sylvie." Her father, William, a butcher and a coal stoker, earned enough to feed them all—until he started drinking. According to Sylvie, he was a "mean drunk." She used to cower in the corner as he kicked her baby brother across the linoleum floor, like a football. She hated him as only a child can hate, especially after she learned he was visiting her older sister's bedroom at night.

One day, after a loud argument with his wife, William announced that he wanted her out of the house by noon. The ten kids crowded around their mother, clinging to her skirt and crying, "No, Mom, don't go!" But nothing could soften their father. Holding on to her brothers and sisters, Sylvie watched through the plate-glass window as her mother walked down the sidewalk, a suitcase in each hand, growing smaller and smaller until she disappeared from view.

Some of the children soon joined their mother, and others were farmed out to live with relatives. Sylvie and the two youngest boys stayed with their father. Only seven years old, she took over the mothering duties, cleaning the house, cooking, getting her brothers bathed and dressed. All through childhood, she harbored a hard knot of bitterness against her father. When she turned fourteen, he kicked her out of the house, and for years she lived with other families, cleaning their homes to earn her keep.

As an adult, Sylvania reconnected with her brothers and sisters. Like her, they had dropped out of school early, either to work or to join the army. Eight of them settled in Southwest Philly, within a few blocks of 67th Street. All but one—a lifelong spinster—got married, started families, and tried to put the past behind them. Their father, William, had vanished. No one knew where, and no one cared.

Many years later, to everyone's shock, the father resurfaced. He had guttered out, he said. Drunk and cold, he had wandered into a Salvation Army rescue mission one night. To earn a meal ticket he had to attend a worship service. When the speaker asked if anyone wanted to accept Jesus as Savior, William thought it only polite to go forward with some of the other men. It surprised him more than anybody when the Sinner's Prayer actually worked. The demons inside him quieted down. He sobered up. For the first time in his life he felt loved and accepted—by God, if no one else. He felt clean, able to make a new start.

And now, he told his children one by one, he was seeking them out to ask for forgiveness. He couldn't defend what had happened, nor could he ever make it right. But he wanted them to know he was sorry, sorrier than they could possibly know. He had taken a job at an icehouse not far away and was forging a new life for himself.

The children, now middle-aged and with families of their own, were wary. Some expected him to fall off the wagon at any moment. Others figured he would ask them for money. Neither happened, and in time the father won them over—all except Sylvie.

LONG AGO MY grandmother Sylvania made a vow never to speak to "that man," which is how she referred to her father. His reappearance rattled her, and old memories of his drunken rages came flooding back as she lay in bed at night. She resented her brothers and sisters for forgiving him. "I don't believe in last-minute forgiveness after living a bad life," she said. "He can't undo all that just by saying 'I'm sorry.'" She told her children, including my mother, "I have no father, and you have no grandfather."

Sylvania's husband, Albert, had a softer heart. Several times he sent my mother, then a little girl, on a secret mission to the icehouse to check on her grandfather. William always insisted he was fine, although Mother noticed he was missing a few fingers from chopping ice.

William may have given up drinking, but not before alcohol had damaged his liver beyond repair. He fell seriously ill, and for the last five years of his life, he stayed with one of his daughters, Sylvania's oldest sister. They lived eight houses down the street from my grandmother, on the very same block. Keeping her vow, Sylvania never once stopped in to visit her ailing father, even though she passed her sister's place whenever she walked to the grocery store or caught a trolley downtown.

Pressured by her husband, Sylvania did consent to let her own children visit their grandfather occasionally. Nearing the end, William saw a young girl come to his door and step inside. "Oh Sylvie, Sylvie, you've come to me at last," he cried, gathering her in his arms. The others in the room didn't have the heart to tell him the girl was not Sylvie but her daughter Mildred, my mother. He was hallucinating grace.

When William died, my grandfather insisted that his wife, Sylvania, attend her father's funeral. As an adult, she encountered him only then, as he lay in a casket.

Hard as steel, Sylvania never apologized and never forgave. My mother remembers coming in tears to apologize for something she'd done. Sylvania responded with a parental Catch-22: "You can't possibly be sorry! If you were really sorry, you wouldn't have done it in the first place."

That scene would come back to me in later years, as I sought to understand the woman who is my mother.

The greatest burden a child must bear
is the unlived life of the parents.

—Carl Jung, *Alchemical Studies*

CHAPTER 12
MOTHER

Something happens during all those trips to Philadelphia. For the first time I begin to see my mother as a person in her own right—a girl named Mildred, a child and daughter, a sister, a teenager—not simply Mother.

Stories spill out as we walk around the neighborhood, past the GE factory where she worked and the stately brick high school and clapboard church she attended in her youth. I hear more accounts as we sit around the dinner table with her brothers, Jimmy and Bob, who delight in telling me details that make Mother say, "Oh, stop!"

The Diems' firstborn child, Mildred grew up during the Great Depression. She remembers bad clothes, bad food, and her mother's bad moods. Sylvania gave birth to five more children, each one another mouth to feed on her husband's meager income. In the crowded row house, kids were always underfoot. Sylvania would lie on a couch with a rubber ice pack on her head. "Keep it down!" she'd shout. "I have a splitting headache."

More than once, she grumbled, "Why did I ever have you kids? You've ruined my life." Some nights she gave them whippings just to make a point: "I know you've done something wrong even if I didn't catch you in the act."

As I probe Mother for memories of her childhood, I hear no happy ones. "It wasn't easy" is all she'll say. She must have been unusually naïve. She learned about deodorant when a friend slipped her a note with a drawing of a container and three scrawled words, "You need this!" Once, her prankster brothers talked her into soaking her hand in a pail of water and then grabbing the metal chain that hung from a basement light fixture. The electric shock worked far better than intended, and they had to knock her free of the chain with a body block.

World War II defined my mother's high school years. Many of her classmates quit their studies to join the army, some of them never to return. Sylvania insisted that after graduation the Diem daughters had to get a job and live at home, handing over their weekly salaries. When Mother begged to go to college so that she could study to become a teacher, Sylvania shut her down: "Never mention that idea again. If you go to college, all the others will want to go."

Without telling anyone, my mother plotted a break from the family after her twenty-first birthday. She lined up a place to stay in downtown Philadelphia, with a family she'd met at church. For a sheltered, timid young woman, it was an audacious move. One of her sisters noticed her packing clothes in a suitcase and alerted the parents.

The next morning, she walked into her parents' bedroom to kiss them, as if she was headed to her regular job. She wore a hat, which confirmed their suspicions that something was afoot. Sylvania roused herself from bed and said, "Mildred, if you walk out that door, you're never welcome back." Not bothering to respond, my mother retrieved her suitcase and walked to a trolley stop.

Free at last, Mildred began a new job and enrolled in college classes on the side. Before long, the family she was living with invited a sailor for Sunday dinner—the man who would become my father. They had a storybook romance, carried on through love letters and weekend leaves.

As soon as my father received his discharge from the navy, the young couple got married. Their pastor required a private counseling session before the ceremony, and only then did my mother learn how babies are made. "What he described was so appalling, I nearly backed out of the wedding," she later admitted.

She did not back out, and over the next four years she moved west to Indiana and Arizona, then southeast to Atlanta, and birthed two sons. She looked forward to fulfilling her lifelong dream of serving as a missionary in Africa—a dream dashed by the onset of my father's polio, the act of faith to remove him from the iron lung, and the miracle that never came.

ON ONE VISIT to Philadelphia, I ask Mother if she learned any good qualities from my stern grandmother Sylvania. She thinks for a moment and says, "Responsibility. You do what's expected of you." As an adult, Mildred Sylvania Diem put that lesson into practice.

In December 1950, her future blank with grief, Mother began a new life in Atlanta with Marshall and me. As a first step, she learned to drive. Next, she began teaching the Bible in private homes. A few churches and individuals sent in donations, and our little family scraped by. I often heard comments like: "Your mother's a spiritual giant. Imagine, raising you two boys and carrying on that workload. She's an angel straight from God."

Once we were well along in school, Mother decided to pursue a goal she'd been harboring: to finish college. She signed on with a fledgling Bible college that agreed to grant her credit toward a degree for every course that she taught. She studied hard, learning enough to instruct the small classes of three to five students. Through that educational barter system, she earned a bachelor's degree, then a master's of theology. "I learned more from teaching than I ever did as a student," she says, looking back.

To help with finances after we bought the trailer, she agreed to drive a van twice a day, transporting children to and from a day-care center. Evenings, she typed up the sermons of a professor at Columbia Seminary, to be compiled into books.

Despite Atlanta's strict segregation, a new opportunity soon arises: she gets invited to teach Bible classes in an African American home. Word of my mother's teaching spreads, and soon she's conducting classes in other Black neighborhoods. In one apartment complex they begin calling her "Miss Jesus." She mocks the Black students' dialect and some of their customs, yet she seldom turns down an invitation, often traveling alone at night to areas where she is the only white person not wearing a police uniform.

Mother comes away with a host of generalizations about race. "We always start the meetings real late. They have no sense of time, you know. They go by CPT—Colored Peoples' Time—some inner feeling they have. That's just the way they are.

"They have a whole different understanding of right and wrong, too," she continues. "A Black man told me, 'You gotta understand. If we find out a woman's been cheatin' on us, we beat her or kill the other guy involved. We can't help it.' You see, it's a cultural thing with them."

My mother, who refuses to fly on an airplane ("If God wanted us to fly, he would have given us wings"), never gets any closer to Africa than the African American communities of Atlanta. I never hear her express much disappointment. She has transferred her missionary hopes to us, her sons, whom she devoted to God at her husband's graveside.

During one of Colonial Hills's conferences, she invites a missionary couple over after church to tell us about their time in Africa. Hoping to please her, I talk about going to Africa as a missionary veterinarian. "I want to take care of the sick lions and elephants," I say.

Marshall lives to regret his declaration, as a seven-year-old, that God wanted him to be a missionary. Mother holds that pledge over

him like a sword. "You'll never make a missionary with that attitude," she says when he does something to displease her.

MOST KIDS KNOW little about what their dad or mom does at work.
Not Marshall and I—we have no time off from the God-business.
We tag along to Mother's Bible clubs and teaching assignments, and
are expected to believe as firmly as she does.

Although nearly everybody is religious in the South, Mother has
more stringent standards. Out of two hundred conversion decisions, she claims, only one of them proves genuine. We are *different*,
she believes, wholly dedicated to God in a way that others aren't.
They talk about avoiding the things of the world; we actually do it.
They sing about the Second Coming; we expect it any day.

Mother has strong opinions about denominations. She doubts
that Catholics are Christians at all. Presbyterians and "those Whis-
keypalians" are beyond the pale. Methodists have lost their fire, and
their churches are "more like lukewarm social clubs than houses of
worship." Even Southern Baptists are suspect, because you can see
deacons standing on the front steps of the church smoking cigarettes. Also, some Baptist organists play softly during the pastoral
prayer, which means they probably have their eyes open.

Our home looks like a Christian gift shop. Every plaque and wall
calendar features a Bible verse, and the magazine rack is stuffed with
titles like *Voice of Prophecy*. Missionaries' prayer cards cover the front
of our refrigerator. At breakfast each day we pull a verse-to-memorize
card from a plastic Bread of Life container in the shape of a miniature
bread loaf. On the wall hangs our only artwork, a reproduction of
Warner Sallman's famous *Head of Christ*. Its airbrushed Jesus appears
a bit sad, his eyes raised upward as if looking for help.

We grow up listening to religious radio nonstop. I think Mother
just feels better with someone talking about God in the background.
Marshall and I practice mimicking the angry, heavy-breathing Southern preachers and their warbling-soprano wives. The rants by Carl

McIntire against godless communism keep us on edge. Predictably, Dr. M. R. DeHaan's *Radio Bible Class* comes on every Sunday morning just as we are sitting down to a breakfast of fried eggs. I don't really listen to his sermons, but for years afterward every time I hear his gravelly voice, I smell fried eggs.

When very young, we say a prepared blessing—"God is great, God is good. Let us thank him for our food"—but after a certain age we have to come up with our own. I pray for pets and neighbor kids. I peek through squinted eyes and thank God for the meat, the potatoes, and each vegetable, except tomatoes. Marshall cracks up when I end a prayer with a rhyme I've picked up somewhere: "Amen, Brother Ben, shot a rooster, killed a hen. Hen died, Ben cried, then committed suicide." Mother does not think it funny.

We are so immersed in spiritual talk that one time, when the phone rings, Marshall answers it with, "Our Father who art in Heaven," rather than "Hello."

At school we discover just how different we are from other kids. We don't cuss or go to movies, know no music written in the past fifty years, and own no television. We spend much of our spare time doing church activities. And on Sundays we aren't allowed to swim, fish, or play ball.

I don't mind most of the rules. In fact, I feel set apart, dedicated, even morally superior. We have the truth, after all, unlike most of our friends. I excel at church, and soon Mother's friends are calling to ask me to pray for a lost wallet or watch. "That boy's prayers get answered," they say, and I swell with holy pride.

Mother informs everyone that both Marshall and I plan to be missionaries. In the seventh grade I screw up my courage and tell her that first I'd like to try playing minor-league baseball for a few years. She snorts disapproval.

FOR A LONG time our family life is calm, like the silence before an earthquake. And then, just as Marshall enters high school, the warning tremors begin.

Suddenly, everything we do seems to enrage our mother. I get lost in the woods and return home a little late for dinner. Marshall forgets to tell her about a band concert he's playing in over the weekend. The atmosphere becomes icy, and she acts like we've committed the unpardonable sin. "I hope you have ten kids just like you!" she yells. We've heard that line before, and I wonder if she learned it from her own mother, Sylvania.

She who endured so many whippings as a child turns easily to corporal punishment. As the eldest, Marshall bears the brunt of her fury. "I'm going to get Mr. Bonds from church to blister you with a hickory stick. He'll knock some sense into you!" Or even, "Do you know what they did to disobedient children in the Old Testament? Read Deuteronomy. They stoned them to death!"

Marshall provides plenty of fuel for her ire. In school he has earned the reputation "Does not live up to potential." Although his IQ tests at 151, he rarely completes homework assignments and doesn't bother to study for tests. His music teachers hail him as a prodigy, but he practices his instruments only when he feels like it, which is seldom.

My guard goes up one day when I walk in after school and see Mother ironing. The hot smell of pressed cotton wafts through the trailer. Rather than gently smoothing the creases, she is slamming the iron down like a hammer. Her face has a twisted look, and all my senses go on alert. *What did I do wrong? Or is it Marshall again?* I creep past her to my bedroom. I know she sees me, but she says nothing, and neither do I.

Wordlessness fills our home. The three of us don't say anything that evening. At dinner I listen to the sounds: the clatter of stainless steel on Melmac plates, the clink of glasses, the gristly noises of chewing and swallowing, a ticking clock. She looks at us harshly, as if she can read on our faces something to dislike. Marshall and I lock eyes, coconspirators at brooding.

It becomes a kind of game. When one of Mother's dark moods hits, we stop speaking. How long can we keep it up?

We maintain the silence as long as a week, always aware the explosion will come. When it bursts, the words echo off the trailer walls. Her voice starts out low and works up until it's high and taut as a violin string. "You think you're so smart," she tells Marshall. "Let me tell you something, mister. You have another think coming. You're lazy. Good for nothin'. You only think of yourself. You're a slob. Just look at your closet. You think I'm your slave? I tell you what I'm gonna do, and I don't mean maybe. I'm gonna take all your clothes and throw them out in a mud puddle. Then maybe you'll appreciate what it's like to live with a slob."

Marshall defends himself. "Yeah, but like I told you, I'll clean the room this weekend. I'm in high school now. It keeps me busy."

He's only stoking the fire. "Don't you sass me like that! You think I don't see that sneer? And don't 'yeah' me. It's 'Yes, ma'am'—*Do you hear me?* If there's one thing I demand, it's respect, and if I can't teach you, I'll get someone in here who can."

I slide down in my seat, trying to be inconspicuous. With my homework spread out before me, I grip the edges of the dining-room table hard enough to feel the pulse in my fingers.

The fight drags on, and eventually I retreat to our bedroom at the back of the trailer. Lying in bed that night, I can't fall asleep. Is that a sob I hear coming from her bedroom down the hall?

Marshall never ducks. He always takes her on—and always loses. Her yelling drowns out his arguing. Watching how they clash, week after week, I decide on a different tactic with Mother. She already thinks I'm a sneak, so why not be one. I will turtle down, hide my feelings, avoid all conflict. I won't see things or hear things. I will become invisible.

Marshall and I face a common foe. In our bunk beds at night, we talk about her. In the past we dared not question the woman who, as everyone reminds us, has sacrificed her own life in order to rear us. After the many explosions, after days of silence at the dinner table, doubts steal in. We can't put together the two people who are our mother: the angelic one everyone else sees and the volatile one we live with.

Certainly, no one could accuse our mother of "unspiritual" behavior. Unlike some women in our church, she has never worn a pair of slacks, nor does she wear nail polish or makeup, not even lipstick. She never fails to have lengthy personal devotions every morning, and she teaches the Bible for a living. What chance do two adolescent kids stand against such an authority?

Mother claims she hasn't sinned in twelve years—longer than I've been alive. She follows a branch of the holiness tradition that suggests Christians can reach a higher spiritual plane, a state of moral perfection. The pastor of her Philadelphia church uses a glove to illustrate the point. "The Holy Spirit lives inside you like my fingers in this glove," he says. "It's not you living now; it's the Spirit of God in you." Her bookcase is stocked with books describing this state, called the Victorious Christian Life.

Sinlessness guarantees she will win every argument with us, her sons, at least in her mind. It also guarantees that—like her own mother—she sees no need to apologize, ever.

As we're lying in our beds one night, Marshall reveals something that makes my blood run cold. "I hate her," he says. "Always have. Even when I was your age, ten years old, I wanted her to die. I had this foolish notion that if I touched her lightly in the same spot a million times, an open sore would develop and she'd die. I tried it, every time I passed her."

"What happened?" I ask.

"She just said, 'Quit hitting me!' and that was that."

OUR THREE-PERSON FAMILY isn't working anymore. I have no way to put into words the changes going on, but something is tearing me inside. I want to run up to someone I recognize in church and say: "Please, please can you help us? I need someone to know what's happening at home." Then I remember my mother's reputation and realize that no one will believe me. She's a saint, the holiest woman in Atlanta.

In church Mother wears a beatific smile and has a glow about her. She attends every service, takes notes, meekly submits to male authority. When people praise Marshall for playing the piano or trumpet, she nods with parental pride. Yet I've never heard her compliment him after a musical performance, or me after a good report card. "I don't want you boys to get proud," she says.

I start to worry about her. Out of the blue she says things like "It's just too much," leaving me to guess what's wrong. "I can't take it anymore!" she says one day. "I don't know if it's worth going on living." I stare at her, wondering if my mother is coming unhinged. When I make plans to visit a friend, she says, "Go ahead if you insist. But if you do, I probably won't be here when you get back. I may be with the Lord." *Now* what am I supposed to do?

I sense that Mother has concerns I know nothing about. "Money doesn't grow on trees, you know!" she says, too loud, when I see something I like in a store. I can tell that repairmen, plumbers, garage mechanics, and car salesmen are ripping her off, yet when I try to bring it up, she lashes out. "I'm telling you, son, the man told me those front-wheel-drive cars are no good. And he's nobody's dummy. You think you know more than him?" I learn not to challenge Mother.

It's the 1960s, and to her it must seem as though the world is coming apart, scattering danger everywhere. Mother leaves tracts around the house with provocative titles: "Satan's Music Exposed," "Hippie Peace Symbol and the Cross of Antichrist," "Skimpy Skirts and Hippie Hair." She has so much to oppose. Hippies. The Antichrist. Communism. The Illuminati. Intellectualism. The occult. Her thick-headed sons.

Whatever's bothering her works its way into her body. After a blowup with Marshall one night, she claims that a blood clot has gone through her heart. A few weeks later, she has trouble moving her left arm. "I think it's a broken muscle," she says.

Eating becomes a chore. "It's something left over from the desert fever in Arizona," she explains. "It attacks your liver. You're supposed to eat lots of macaroni and cheese and candy—especially chocolate—but you don't really want to, you're so stuffed-feeling." I ask what might taste good. Wrong question. "Eat—how can I? I'm sick! If I even try to think about food, I want to throw up."

Knee problems develop. Convinced one leg is an inch shorter than the other, Mother gets a shoemaker to build up her left shoe to compensate. Now she stands lopsidedly and walks with an unnatural gait, torquing her back. An orthopedic surgeon agrees to remove a vertebra and repair a disk.

Another doctor gives her cortisone shots for pain in her shoulder. She refuses to let him X-ray it, though: "I'm claustrophobic. If I go into one of those machines, I can't breathe!"

After she falls in the trailer, Marshall accompanies her, with a suspected broken arm, to the hospital. The doctor calls him out into the hallway and says, "I can't find anything wrong with your mother, but she won't leave here unless I do something, so I'll put a cast on it. Don't worry, she's fine."

Mother seems content only when something goes wrong physically—and for her, "content" means miserable. Some days she lies in bed with a washcloth over her head. "My nerves have about had it. I can't eat anything. Maybe it's an ulcer acting up. I need to get away somewhere, but I've got nowhere to go. Leave me alone, child. I have a headache!" I flash back to the stories she told of her own mother, lying on the couch with an ice pack on her head.

On days like that, I tiptoe around her bedroom, and for dinner warm up some fish sticks or a potpie. Back, feet, sinuses, neck, migraines, vertigo, stomach, joints—the ailments always seem to flare up at a crucial time: when Marshall angers her, just before a holiday, when I go on a school trip. I have no way of knowing which pains are real and which are imagined, and no clue how to help an ailing woman who happens to be my mother.

Mothers are supposed to make their children well when they're hurt, not the other way around. I wonder, *Is my mother unraveling, or is that just how women are?* She should have had daughters. They'd know what to do.

I volunteer for after-school activities to avoid spending too much time at home, yet even then I have to rely on Mother to pick me up. Sometimes I stand outside the school for thirty minutes or an hour, waiting. After darkness falls, I see only headlights driving by. Maybe she's had an accident. Maybe she drove off the road on purpose, ending it all, as she sometimes threatens. Soon guilt floods in. How can I possibly think such thoughts?

My brain spins. What will my life be like as an orphan? Will the state of Georgia assign me to a new, temporary mother? *If she's not here within the first fifteen cars, she's not coming.* I count to fifteen slowly, like a child playing hide-and-seek. When her car doesn't appear, I set another goal. I walk to the end of the school driveway and back. Again. And again, counting the headlights that pass.

She always shows up. I know better than to mention how long I've been waiting.

Yet each month she writes letters to her supporters using spiritual, upbeat language. I find one lying around, and read:

> I've been doing some reminiscing lately over my life and the way the Lord has worked in it, and it just amazes me. When you serve the Lord life never is boring, and you don't always know what is coming next, but as you look back you can see the direction of the Lord in each step. He has promised to lead and guide us "step by step" and He has faithfully done that.

She quotes verses about triumphing in Christ, the joy of the Lord, and being content in whatsoever state you're in. She reserves all the darkness, all the anger, for us, her sons.

ONE SUMMER DAY, I have to get away from the heat in the trailer. No one is talking there anyway.

I walk a few blocks to a public swimming pool and change in the locker room, depositing my clothes in a rusty metal basket and pinning its number tag to my swimsuit. I slip into the chlorine-smelling water, duck under the surface, and force myself to open my eyes underwater. After I get used to the burning sensation, my vision clears.

When I open my mouth, bubbles float to the surface. As I exhale, I sink slowly to the bottom of the pool, where I can watch the headless bodies of all the people kicking around me. I hear the odd, slushy sounds of shouts and laughter from above. I am alone in the midst of a crowd, watching. I let the feeling of calm, of safety, flow through me until the air runs out and I have to shoot to the surface.

There is a terrible kind of cruelty,
no matter how well intended, in demanding the denial
of self when there is no selfhood to deny.

—James Fowler, *Stages of Faith*

CHAPTER 13
ZEAL

The summer I graduate from seventh grade, Mother accepts yet another job, teaching at a Christian camp in Kentucky. We throw some clothes in a suitcase and drive from Atlanta to a rustic site nestled in the hollows of Appalachia.

For the next six weeks, Marshall and I live with several dozen other boys in a ramshackle cabin that smells of canvas and turpentine. The first afternoon, barefoot, I learn the hard way to avoid the splinters and nailheads poking up from the floorboards. At night, I turn over in my bunk bed and let out a yell—"Ow!"—waking the entire cabin. I have caught my nose on a nail protruding from the wall, ripping one nostril and causing a terrific nosebleed.

The boys' outhouse has six holes cut in a rough bench with no hinged seats—yet another splinter hazard. I take a deep gulp of outside air before entering, and try to hold my breath inside. If nature calls after dark, I sprint across the grass, hoping not to step on a snake or a scorpion, and then sit on a hole freshly webbed by a spider.

A camper in my cabin has accidentally dropped a flashlight down the hole. Until the battery wears down, a pale yellow light shines through the chinks in the outhouse walls. No one volunteers to retrieve it.

To the other campers I must seem like a city slicker. These are tough, rangy kids with missing fingers, barbed-wire scars, and blank spaces where teeth should be. They quiz me about skyscrapers, television, expressways, and passenger trains. The only trains they know are the ones that carry coal strip-mined from the hills. "Do you know any Negroes?" one asks. "I ain't never seen one."

The camp's leaders must have served time in the military, because they run the place like basic training. At six o'clock in the morning—*groan*—a staticky loudspeaker clicks on and strains of the hymn "Whispering Hope" echo through the hills. Half an hour later we campers stand at attention in the cabin for a check of lice and bedbugs and an inspection of our bed-making skills. Next comes a half-hour quiet time devoted to Bible reading and prayer, followed by fifteen minutes of calisthenics. Finally, we march in formation to breakfast and a daily schedule of indoor handcrafts and outdoor games, sandwiched around Bible lessons and missionary stories—my mother's contribution.

On Friday night, after a roast-beef dinner, we gather around a fire to toast marshmallows on straightened coat hangers. The stars, undimmed by city lights, prick bright holes in the cobalt blue sky above. After leading a few hymns, the camp director reads from the Psalms, poems that speak of mountains and streams and animals. I think about the creatures that might be out there, watching us.

One of the counselors asks, "Would anyone here like to share what God has done in their hearts this week?" We scuff our feet in the dirt. Kentucky kids, with no experience in public speaking, are slow to respond, and they keep it short.

"I jes' need to live for the Lord when I git back to my family. It's easier here around y'all."

"Some things I know gotta change. I cuss too much, for one thing. I smoke like a chimney. And without God's help I'll end up just like my dad."

"I been hangin' with the wrong crowd. I need to find me some new friends."

After each confession the camper who spoke tosses a stick into the fire, a sign of how he wants to blaze for Jesus.

TWO WEEKS IN, I'm totally bored by the routine. Marshall and I hear the same Bible stories and play the same games, but with a new group of campers. The only breaks occur on weekends between camp sessions, when we drive through towns with names like Flat Rock and Dripping Springs and visit some of the campers' houses. Most of them sit on concrete blocks, like our trailer, and have cardboard patches tacked to the outside walls.

On these visits I learn to pump water from a well, working the handle up and down until, with a sound like a cough, a flow of clear, cold water spurts from the spout. I try my hand at milking a cow, but nothing comes out, no matter how hard I tug. The cow stamps her feet and my country coach says, "You'd best let go 'fore she kicks yore brains out." He takes over, his hands moving smoothly from one teat to another, and streams of warm milk hit the bucket with a pinging sound. I breathe in the smells of warm milk and musty dried manure and the cow's grassy breath.

I gain new respect for people I had judged ignorant. I learn to reach under a hen and grab an egg so fast that the hen has no time to peck my arm. I watch a farm woman wring the neck of a chicken, swinging the plump body around like a lasso until suddenly she flicks her wrist and the bird's neck snaps. She swings an axe, and I watch amazed as the headless chicken, spurting blood over its white feathers, runs around the yard flapping its wings, as if nothing has happened.

Kentucky brings me close to nature. When a water moccasin swims toward two of us campers in a rowboat, a mere head visible with its flicking tongue and cloudy eyes, my companion calmly slaps an oar in the snake's direction until it changes course. I lie in bed at night and listen to the thrumming of frogs as they hit different notes, like an orchestra tuning up. I fall asleep to the soft call of whip-poor-wills, and jerk awake at the cry of a bobcat, identical to a baby's bawl.

Then, one day's adventure exposes something awful in myself. Hiking in the woods with a mischievous friend from the cabin, I see a box turtle dragging along in the dirt. It acts almost cartoonish, with tiny yellow-striped legs laboring to propel an oversized dome on its back. The head with its parrotlike beak bobs up and down as the reptile lumbers toward the bushes. I bend over to catch it, and just like that its head, legs, and tail retract. I poke here and there, trying to get a reaction, but the turtle knows better than to open up.

We find another turtle, and then another. We have stumbled upon a nest. Within a few minutes we catch seventeen of the box turtles. We line them up in a row, all hiding inside their shells, unmoving.

For some reason, my companion drops a large boulder on the end turtle and with a loud crack the shell breaks and red blood and shiny moist insides gush out. Hesitantly, I pick up the boulder and do the same to another turtle.

Something possesses us. Without saying a word to each other, we proceed to drop heavy rocks on all seventeen turtles, one by one, laughing as their shells split open. Perhaps scared by the noise, not one tries to escape. They die mute.

We walk back to the cabin in silence. All that summer I live with a private stench of shame. Such wanton cruelty in anyone else would appall me. Now, I am the guilty one. The scene clings to me like a second skin, damning proof of a self I have not known. I speak of it to no one, but inside me a dark hole yawns open, as if something has burst.

AT THE END of that summer, Mother makes the decision to move our trailer to the grounds of Faith Baptist Church on the eastern edge of Atlanta. She explains that she can no longer afford the monthly trailer-park rent, so she has agreed to head up the church's Christian-education program in exchange for a free parking space for our trailer. "We'll never get away from church," I complain. "We'll practically live in one!"

We go from the 1,000-member Colonial Hills, too conservative for the Southern Baptists, to the 120-member Faith Baptist, too conservative for any denomination. The sign out front spells out the church's identity in a many-pointed star: "Independent, Fundamental, Bible-believing, New Testament, Blood-bought, Born-again, Dispensational, Premillennial, Pretribulational." The church's motto? "Contending for the Faith!"

Faith Baptist occupies twenty acres, the site of a former pony farm. A truck hauls our mobile home to a spot that some of the churchmen have rigged up with electricity, water, and sewer. In the process, the movers poke two holes beneath the trailer's kitchen window, which workmen cover with strips of shiny metal. The front of our aluminum home now looks like a grinning face with two front teeth missing.

The congregation meets in a small brick building, its inside walls bare of any decoration. Our pastor, Brother Howard Pyle, comes from a proud family of fundamentalists, all graduates of Tennessee Temple University. He has flaming red hair, a surplus of zeal, and an eagerness to follow in the footsteps of his four preacher brothers. The Pyles and their three daughters live in a large house on the church property, directly across from our trailer.

Church life centers on the preacher, and Brother Pyle uses that fact to full advantage. Shaking his right index finger at us, he preaches fiery sermons in a strained rapt voice. Over the next four years, I attend hundreds of services—Sunday morning, Sunday night, and Wednesday night prayer meeting—and hear hundreds of sermons, most of them describing what we should guard against: sin, Hell, the devil, temptation, the wiles of the evil one. Most services end with an altar call for salvation, even though the congregation rarely includes a visitor and all of us regulars have already gone forward at least once. No one seems to mind. With such high stakes, you can't be too careful.

Our new community seems more akin to the folks in Kentucky

than to the middle-class crowd at Colonial Hills. A one-eyed hairdresser who can't shake the nicotine habit. A plumber with an abundant sprout of nasal hair. A garbage-truck driver. A middle-aged mother who often requests prayer for her alcoholic husband. I wonder, *What brings these people back week after week to hear about wickedness and failure?*

Music helps lighten the tone. We have an energetic song leader who waves his arm in ¼ time, like the pope blessing a crowd. Accompanying him at the piano, Marshall soon dazzles our humble congregation. He breaks into runs and trills that make that tired old instrument sound as if Jerry Lee Lewis himself has stopped by.

One Sunday in the middle of the service, the church door flies open and someone yells, "Fire!" We all run outside, and find orange flames licking the roof off the pony barn, which we use for Sunday School. Fire trucks roar up with sirens blaring, the deacons scurry about moving lumber and attaching hoses, and all of us church members look on as the flames climb the air and heat bakes our faces. Then we file back into the sanctuary, smoky with the scent of charred timbers, and listen to Brother Pyle deliver an impromptu sermon on the fires of Hell, which he describes as seven times hotter than what we have just witnessed.

"Think about that fire," he says, "causing pain far beyond the worst burn you've ever had. That's a pale picture of what Hell will be like—seven times hotter, forever and ever with no second chance." I try to wrap my eleven-year-old mind around eternity, and fail.

Hell, though, I can easily imagine. I live every day in fear that God will send me there. The prospect leaves an acid taste in my mouth and a tense feeling in my stomach. Whenever I start feeling safe, the scene with the turtles comes back.

EVERY FALL, FAITH Baptist erects a circus tent on the grass field beside the pony barn and holds a week of special "revival" meetings. Since we live on the church grounds, Mother expects us to attend services every night of the week. Our first year, a preacher named

Jack Hyles drives down from Indiana to preach on "Thirty-Nine Steps to Effective Soul-Winning." Another year, the firebrand Bob Jones Jr. leads the revival, stirring things up when he denounces Billy Graham as a compromiser.

A Texan named Lester Roloff draws the most enthusiastic crowds to the big white tent. Roloff owns his own plane, which he flies to speaking engagements. Like a cowboy, he wears boots and a bolo tie, and he speaks in a bass voice with a Texas drawl. Roloff got his reputation by ranting on the radio against homosexuality, communism, television, alcohol, tobacco, drugs, gluttony, and psychology. He did so in such strident terms that he had to leave the Southern Baptist denomination and become an Independent Baptist, just like us. Now he runs group homes for troubled teenagers, where, in his words, "parent-hating, Satan-worshipping, dope-taking immoral boys and girls" are turned into "faithful servants of the Lord."

You never know what you'll get when Lester Roloff starts preaching. A health fanatic, he claims most problems can be cured by faith, fasting, and food. He scorns most pills, except "the gos-pill," he says, and urges us to follow the diet found in Leviticus, along with a few of his own additions. "Even rats and roaches won't eat that worthless white bread," he claims. "You don't believe me? Leave a piece out for them. They know it's full of chemicals and poison, and they won't touch it." In a major sacrifice for a family raised on Wonder Bread, Mother follows his advice and converts us to the brown wheat variety. Soon we're also eating grapefruit for breakfast, but I draw the line at Roloff's favorite snack, carrot juice.

One thing about a Roloff revival service: nobody falls asleep. In the middle of a sermon, he'll suddenly come up with an unrelated pronouncement—such as "Dancing feet don't hang on praying knees!"—and begin a blast against lukewarm Christians who dance. "Do I hear an amen? Amen!" Then he bursts into song in an off-key voice like Johnny Cash's: "Wearin' out my shoes / Tellin' God's Good News / Ringing doorbells for my Lord / Ringing, ringing, ringing doorbells / For my Lord!"

Within a few years, however, Lester Roloff gets in trouble with the state of Texas over his group homes. He has often bragged about the strict rules: no television, doors locked from the outside, radios tuned to his station only, mandatory daily church attendance. At a court trial, sixteen girls testify that they have been whipped with leather straps, handcuffed to drainpipes, and put in isolation cells as penalties for failing to memorize a Bible passage or make a bed.

"We are under attack," Roloff says in his defense. "The Communists, Masons, atheists, humanists, evolutionists, and other godless sickos want to destroy the family. Parents beware, the government wants your child!"

As authorities haul him off to jail, he shouts defiantly, "Better a pink bottom than a black soul!"

I SPEND MY summers at a Bible camp and the rest of the year living on the grounds of a hard-line church. I inhale religion. Yet as I prepare to enter high school, I feel more anxious than holy.

I have yielded to the pressures of altar calls. I have felt the shiver of pious pleasure on hearing a revival speaker say, "Yes, Jesus, thank you, Jesus," as I make my way forward to get born again *again* or to rededicate my life to the Lord. I know how to give my testimony in a soft, sincere tone and can pray in a way to beckon amens, and sometimes tears, from those around me.

Alone, though, in the little privacy I have on the top bunk in our cramped bedroom, doubts nag at me. My prayers address God as "Our Heavenly Father," but with no earthly father to compare him to, I don't know what that means. I hear a woman pray at church, "Lord, be gentle with me, just be gentle. But, dear Lord, use whatever it takes with my kids, even if it's suffering. Break them." Maybe God is like my mother—a superperson who both loves me and schemes to break me.

"Say or do nothing you would not want to be saying or doing at the moment of Jesus's Second Coming," Mother admonishes me. She tells of a time in her youth when a friend invited her to a movie. She was tempted at first. "Then I thought about what would happen if Jesus came back while I was in that theater! What could I say to him?"

I lie awake at night reviewing everything I've said or done recently. Tossing a baseball at a net backstop for an hour. Joining my brother in the silence wars around the dinner table. Sneaking a look at my uncle's dirty magazines. What would cause me shame if Jesus returned today?

Mother's prophecy magazines—*Midnight Call, The Chosen People, Fruits of Zion, Israel My Glory*—report an increase in famines, earthquakes, and catastrophes, sure signs of the end times. Communism is spreading like a virus, fulfilling the prophecy about "wars and rumors of wars." Russia has hydrogen bombs more powerful than ours.

Every day a gruff voice comes on the radio, introducing the *20th Century Reformation Hour*. "Friends, it's Carl McIntire. Have you heard that Khrushchev claims to want peace?

> Khrushchev was a man of peace and this we all recall
>   A piece of this, a piece of that until he has it all."

McIntire has just lost his campaign to keep Hawaii from becoming our fiftieth state. "Think of it—in our own nation, a perfect nest for spies from China! Communism is at our doorstep."

There is so much to fear.

EACH YEAR I make a New Year's resolution to read through the entire Bible, checking off the little boxes on a printed guide—three chapters a day, five on Sunday. Some years I achieve the goal; more often I bog down in the Prophets. Marshall and I practice saying names of the Bible's sixty-six books in order, as fast as we can: "GenesisExodusLeviticusNumbers...." My record is seventeen seconds, better even than Marshall's. "That doesn't count," he argues. "You slur your words together."

Faith Baptist is a King James Only church, loyal to the English translation of the Bible published in 1611. We don't trust any of the newfangled versions because, as Brother Pyle says, most of them have translators who are liberals. We get a full dose of venom against the Revised Standard Version when a preacher named Peter Ruckman visits Faith Baptist. He regales us with stories of his colorful past—Zen Buddhism, alcohol abuse, working first as a disc jockey, then as a drummer for dance bands—before Pastor Howard Pyle's brother converted him to fundamentalism.

From the pulpit, Ruckman mocks the Revised Standard Version, which he calls the Reviled Standard PerVersion. He reads a few passages from that edition and sails the Bible out toward the pews, where it falls with a thud. Next he tosses an American Standard Version, which he says is "more of the same godless, depraved crap." Though Ruckman's antics offend some church members, including my mother, we stick with the King James Version just to be safe.

Faith Baptist fosters a minority complex, a feeling of us against the world. Others may see us as a radical fringe but we take pride in living in a way that outsiders—Hollywood, Washington, DC, *The New York Times*—cannot possibly understand. A phrase from the Bible's book of Titus sums up our identity: "a peculiar people, zealous of good works."

In order to avoid any appearance of evil, the church frowns on such activities as roller-skating (too much like dancing), bowling (alleys often serve liquor), mixed swimming, and reading the Sunday newspaper. Movies are forbidden, and television is suspect. A few girls wear makeup and mild lipstick, always discreetly, but they never wear slacks on church property. My mother shuns makeup and all jewelry, except for a single strand of pop beads.

Every so often a woman who doesn't know the code enters our church with a fancy hairdo, bright-colored lipstick, open-toed shoes, and shiny red nails. She exerts a force like gravity. The men keep stealing glances, and the women with scrubbed skin and hair buns frown and shake their heads in disapproval. My hormones have not yet kicked in, and I don't fully understand the need for all the safe-guards. I gather that bodies represent danger, and on the danger scale, female bodies must rank near the top.

All these rules are meant to protect us from the sinful world outside, and in a way they succeed. Marshall and I might sneak off to a bowling alley, but we would never think of touching cigarettes, liquor, or drugs. I have no time for worldly activities anyway. I am always at church.

THE YEAR I enter high school, I feel a subtle but seductive tug in a different direction. A growing part of me resists the image of a redneck fundamentalist. I feel an urge to experience life, not avoid it. I don't reject the faith—not yet, anyway. Rather, I find myself swinging like a pendulum, sometimes striving to be the best Christian around and sometimes wanting to give up in despair.

Charles Sheldon's classic, *In His Steps,* rocks me. The novel imagines what happens when a pastor dares his church members to ask before every major decision, "What would Jesus do?" His congregation takes up the challenge. A woman turns down a marriage proposal because her suitor lacks direction in life. In order to help the needy, a rich woman buys property in a seedy part of town. A publisher discontinues his newspaper's Sunday edition.

I think long and hard about how I might follow in Jesus's steps. Then one Sunday Brother Pyle preaches a sermon on idolatry, and I start wondering if I have idols. My prized collection of seven hundred baseball cards comes to mind. It's the envy of my friends, and includes an original 1947 Jackie Robinson as well as Mickey Mantle's rookie card. I spend hours organizing the cards by team, position, and stats—time that could be put to spiritual use. Definitely an idol.

After prayer and anguished indecision, I resolve to destroy the idol by giving away most of my precious collection to a neighbor down the street. Expecting a divine reward, I feel betrayed when several days later my neighbor auctions off the collection for a tidy sum. I try to console myself: "Blessed are they which are persecuted for righteousness' sake."

When we last visited Maranatha Tabernacle in Philadelphia, I heard the doctrine of perfection that Mother has been teaching. The pastor urged us to go through the "love" chapter in 1 Corinthians 13. "Self-sacrificing love *never* gets impatient . . . *never* gets jealous . . . *never* boasts . . . *never* gets conceited . . ." and so on. Love "is *always* kind, happy in the truth, and generous. It overlooks faults in others, believes in the best in others, and is *always* long-suffering and victorious."

"Now, substitute Jesus every time you see the word *love*," the pastor said. That worked just fine. "Next," he added, "go through and substitute yourself: '*I* am always patient and kind. *I* never envy nor boast nor think an unkind thought.'" I saw immediately that I had a long way to go to attain this Victorious Christian Life.

Mother buys into this theology one hundred percent and maintains she's reached that higher plane of life. I have to bite my tongue to keep from reminding her of that sermon on love when she flies into one of her rages. As for myself, I sincerely want to follow Jesus's steps, but then I tell a lie or do something stupid the next day. I feel attracted to holiness and repelled at the same time, like two magnets brought together. "Be ye therefore perfect, even as your Father which is in Heaven is perfect," Jesus said. I want that ideal, yet always a little voice inside ridicules how far I fall short. It works on my soft conscience like a poison.

I've read biographies of Christians who were tortured for their faith, such as Watchman Nee, a Chinese pastor who spent twenty years in a Communist prison. If Communists ever subjected me to torture, I know exactly what I'd do. I would fall, sniveling, at their feet and deny my faith.

PASTOR HOWARD PYLE is an entrepreneur. After we've lived at Faith Baptist for nearly a year, he asks Mother to head up the teaching at a new youth camp he's developing with his brother Norman at a facility near Conyers, about twenty-five miles east of Atlanta. It means canceling her work at the Kentucky camp, but she accepts. I'm soon delighted with the upgrade. As we drive on the grounds, I notice manicured athletic fields and a large swimming pool. I'm most impressed when I learn that the cabins have indoor bathrooms.

The Pyle brothers try their best to impose order on the campers: no card playing, lights out at ten, separate swim times for boys and girls, no hand-holding or kissing, no shorts (for girls), no radios, mandatory quiet time and attendance at all meetings. But in contrast to the Kentuckians, these city campers compete to break as many rules as possible, not to accumulate good-behavior points. They short-sheet each other's beds, cover the urinals with transparent plastic wrap, and play secular music on contraband radios.

The camp brings in speakers from Bob Jones University who prove to be funny and entertaining. Local athletes stop by to lecture the boys on how tough and masculine Jesus was. Musical groups make appearances, too, including a trio of blond sisters who sway as they sing. I fall instantly in love with all three. As they sing, I pick out one of the sisters and stare at her, trying my old church trick of channeling my admiration directly through thought waves. Of course, I'm too shy and awkward to actually speak to such a goddess.

Each week we gather for a required sex talk. For an hour, one of the counselors tries to hold the attention of teenage boys who are poking each other and laughing at inappropriate places. We learn that sex before marriage is like grabbing a peanut-butter sandwich instead of waiting for steak. The proper question is not "How far can I go?" but "How far should I stay away?" Like Joseph in the Bible, we must resist even the appearance of improper behavior with the other sex.

The counselors talk a lot about lust. "How do you know when you're lusting?" one camper asks. The answer: "Look once, that's normal. Look twice, and you're borderline. Keep following that girl with your eyes, and you cross the line." I never want to stop looking. Am I a serial luster?

I lie low the first week or two at the new camp. But as I grow more confident in the new place, I adopt a goody-two-shoes routine of getting up early and having extra-long devotions on the front porch, where the counselor can see me. I pray in public at every opportunity and give testimonies. Sure enough, I win "Camper of the Week" and receive a plaque on the final night.

The last week of the summer, however, I start listening to the dark side. I climb a fence with a friend and do cannonballs in the algae-lined swimming pool after hours. I persuade a kid with diabetes to hand over the used syringes from his daily injections. As if the scene with the turtles has never happened, I give them to a science freak who experiments by injecting frogs with Mountain Dew and Coca-Cola. With each day of camp, I get ornerier.

Peter Ruckman, the man who tossed Bibles around in our church, is the featured speaker this week. Besides the evening sermons, which he illustrates with colored chalk as he speaks, he conducts afternoon workshops on various topics. We meet in the dining room, and this day he's chosen to speak about race.

It's the sixties, and the civil rights movement is making daily news in Georgia. Freedom riders and other protesters are demanding an end to whites-only schools, restrooms, and lunch counters. Ruckman uses his workshop to defend segregation, citing the same "Curse of Ham" theory that I heard at Colonial Hills. "Read Genesis 9 for yourself," he says. "God cursed Ham and his descendants to be servants. Campers, this is where the Negro race comes from."

Then Ruckman grins and moves from behind the pulpit. "Have you ever noticed how Coloreds make good waiters? Watch them sometime. They swivel their hips around the chairs and hold those trays high without spilling a drop." He does an exaggerated imitation, and the campers laugh. "Don't you see, that's the kind of job they're good at. But have you ever met a Negro who's the president of a company? Have you? Name one. Every race has its place, and they should accept it. We can get along fine as long as we stay separate and don't mix."

As it happens, I have become the pet of Bessie, the camp cook.

She's a large Black woman who loves kids, works hard, and sings while she prepares food. As Ruckman is talking, I see her refilling the salt and pepper shakers at the other end of the large room. She shows no sign that she has heard him, but I break out in a sweat just thinking about it.

LATER THAT AFTERNOON I check up on Bessie. She seems cheerful as a bird, so maybe she didn't hear what Ruckman said. Or maybe she wouldn't let me know if she had. I still feel queasy about the workshop. We talk for a while and she gives me three peanut-butter cookies fresh out of the oven, meant for dessert at the evening meal. I'm still munching on one when I walk outside and run smack into Brother Pyle.

He must have been gunning for me. He looks down at the cookies, flushes red, and accuses me of stealing them. I try to explain, but he won't listen. He points his finger at my chest, and his head gives a little jerk. "You're a deceitful troublemaker, an Achan in the camp, young man," he says. "You're trying to bring down the work God is doing here." I look at him with a blank expression that he must take as a sneer, because he stalks off.

That night, Friday, culminates the camp week, the last meeting before campers head home on Saturday. We hold evening services in an open-sided building that seats four hundred. Sometimes a summer thunderstorm rumbles through, unleashing a downpour that rattles the metal roof so loudly that the meeting has to adjourn. I pray for rain, not wanting to sit through another emotional revival service in my crotchety mood.

Friday night is the camp's final shot at converting the unconverted and heating up the lukewarm. We're tired and sunburned, aware that we will be returning to homes without swimming pools and foosball, and that school will soon take over our lives. In a word, we are vulnerable.

The speaker, Nicky Chavers, a student from Bob Jones, does his best. He plays off advertising slogans. "Are you a Brylcreem Christian? A little dab'll do you? Are you an Alka-Seltzer Baptist? Put him in the water and he'll fizz for half a minute?" He's witty and passionate and also long-winded. To my dismay, the rains hold off.

When time comes for the altar call, Norman Pyle takes over, and we start singing "Just as I Am." After the first verse Pyle says, "Maybe you've held out all week, determined not to give in. Friend, are you ready to meet your Maker? Are you ready to die? Why wait? You never know what tomorrow may bring." A few campers trickle forward as we plow through another stanza.

The invitation widens. "Now I want all of you who have rededicated your life to Christ this week to join these dear souls at the front. Make a public profession. I know it's not easy, so be courageous and show God that you mean it."

Then follows a call for those who have decided on full-time Christian service. Before long, fully two-thirds of the audience has come forward to kneel at the front. I glance wistfully at the corrugated roof overhead. Still no rain.

"If you just feel a need for someone to pray with you, we have counselors standing by," Pyle continues. More campers make their way to the crowded front. Finally, the clincher. "I have one last invitation. Now listen carefully. Any of you with unconfessed sin in your life—any sin whatsoever—God is calling you to come forward and confess it."

Campers stream down the aisles as he prompts us. "A careless word, perhaps . . . a flash of anger . . . a laziness in your spiritual life. Have you looked on anyone with lust this week? Have you thought ill of anyone?" The stream becomes a river as the pianist gallantly pounds out another refrain.

This is my sixth straight week at camp. Every other week I have gone forward at the final service. Tonight, my soul is calloused. Eventually only two of us remain standing in the large auditorium. I edge closer to my friend Rodney for moral support as the pianist begins yet another round of verses. Fellow campers kneeling down front glare back at us in irritation; we are delaying the late-night round of refreshments.

"I don't know, Rodney," I whisper, "I can't think of any sins to-night, can you?"

"No unconfessed ones," he replies with a tight grin. The two of us hold out until at last the speaker gives up, says a closing prayer, and calls it a night. When I walk out, my knees ache from standing so long.

PART FOUR

DISORDER

I am a slow unlearner. But I love my unteachers.

—Ursula K. Le Guin, *Dancing at the Edge of the World*

CHAPTER 14
HIGH SCHOOL

The gymnasium stands creak and groan from the weight of five hundred fidgety adolescents. "Welcome to Gordon High School," says the principal, Mr. Craig, a dapper man with silver streaks in his well-combed hair. He is wearing a suit, starched white shirt, and plaid bow tie. "You are about to experience the best years of your lives."

It feels as though we are entering the *scariest* years of our lives. In our Georgia school district, which lacks middle schools, we have gone directly from elementary school into high school, entering the eighth grade as lowly "subfreshmen." And because I began school a few months early and then skipped second grade, I am entering high school in 1961 at the tender age of eleven.

I glance at my fellow subfreshmen, slouched on posture-taxing backless seats. On the way to this assembly, we passed giants: cocky boys wearing athletic jackets and girls with breasts filling their tight sweaters. They looked at us diminutive newcomers with expressions of disdain.

The principal drones on for a while about General John Brown Gordon, whose portrait adorns the school's entrance. One of Robert E. Lee's most trusted officers, he took three bullets at the Battle of Antietam and yet continued fighting. In his honor, our school's sports teams bear the name Gordon Generals.

After quoting a few lines of Shakespeare, Mr. Craig introduces his vice principal, a football coach with a big chest, a thick neck, and a crew cut. The assembly's tenor changes as the coach reviews Gordon's dress code and rules of behavior: no facial hair or blue jeans, no smoking, no chewing gum in class, no physical displays of affection. "I hope we don't have to meet in my office," he growls, "but, buddy, you better not cross me, or I personally guarantee you'll be sorry." The tough kids snicker.

MY FIRST FEW weeks in high school, I have the sense of stepping into a wider, more dangerous world. Departing the church property for school each day, I cross a threshold to a place where troublemakers smoke cigarettes in the bathrooms and drop lighted M-80s and cherry bombs in the toilets. I try not to gawk at the *Playboy* pinups posted in some lockers, nor at the couples who flout the rules against public displays of affection.

Marshall, who has already spent a year in high school, briefs me on the various cliques. Jocks rule at the top of the pecking order, along with their cheerleader girlfriends. The hoods, or punks, cause most of the trouble. They're the ones who set off firecrackers in the bathrooms and who phone in bomb threats on the day of a big test. You can hear them coming by the *click-CLICK* of steel taps nailed to the heels and toes of their shoes, and I heed that signal like the rattle of a snake.

The hoods love to torment wimpy subfreshmen like me. "Hey, what you starin' at? Yeah, you—I'm talking to you! You don't think so? You callin' me a liar? You little queer, git over here, I'll give you somethin' to look at." I learn to hurry from class to class, head down, trying to be invisible.

Marshall advises me to find some friends among the *nerds,* bookworms who pose no threat. Yet he hangs out with Malcolm, a skinny little guy, barely five feet tall, who walks with a polio limp and wears the loudest taps in school. Malcolm dresses in black and greases his hair like the hoods, though they would never accept someone like him. Other students give him a wide berth, however, because he carries a switchblade and has proved his manhood by eating live grasshoppers. Also, he has an uncle high up in the Ku Klux Klan. It baffles me that he became Marshall's favorite companion.

Before long I witness a colossal clash when the number one hood takes on the number one jock, our school's golden-boy quarterback. A throaty roar—"Fight! Fight!"—spreads through the hallways as I'm heading to my next class. A hundred students rush in and form a circle to keep teachers away as the two duel over a girlfriend. I watch as the hood grabs the quarterback and bashes his head against a sharp water-fountain nozzle—one, two, three times—and the school hero falls in a pool of blood. The pretty blonde who inspired the combat crumples to the floor, her arms wrapped around her knees, sobbing.

I soon realize there are really only two groups in high school, winners and losers. I have no doubt which one I belong to. The high school yearbook runs large photos of the seniors dressed in tuxedos and formal wear. Slightly smaller photos show the juniors in sports jackets and dress-up clothes, and even smaller photos capture the sophomores and freshmen in school clothes. Subfreshmen are jammed together fifty-six to a page, as if pasted in by mistake from some elementary school.

My clothes alone tag me as a loser. "Are you Pentecostal?" a classmate asks me one day. "I just wondered, because you sure dress like one." Mother can't understand why I want different colors of socks when white goes with everything. Most of my clothes come as hand-me-downs from Marshall, loose around the waist and short in the arms and legs. We're both resigned to not fitting in, the price we pay for having a missionary mother. As far as I know, no one else at Gordon lives in a trailer.

Gym class becomes my least favorite hour of the day. President Kennedy has just launched a fitness program to help us keep up with the Russians, and the coach seems to have mistaken us sub-freshmen for Marine Corps recruits. We do calisthenics first for exercise and then for punishment: "Give me fifty push-ups, Yancey, and this time keep your butt out of the air!" Back in the mildewy locker room, seniors creep up behind the underclassmen and pop them with wet towels, hard enough to draw welts.

Phys ed is also teaching me what it means to be a male. The guys talk about nothing but sports teams and body parts, both the girls' and their own. If you don't laugh at their bawdy jokes, they call you queer. When the coach doesn't show up one day, the toughest hood takes over. "Watch this," he says, and proceeds to push a straight pin through his hand so that it comes out the other side. We act duly impressed. Next, he attracts a circle of onlookers and charges them a dollar each to watch him stick the pin through his penis.

At the end of the school day, the cool kids drive home, their cars squealing out of the parking lot. Music blares from the open windows, music unlike any I have heard. Chubby Checker, Elvis Presley, Ray Charles, Jimmy Dean, Frankie Valli—a generation gap of sound is opening up. To my ears, accustomed to classical piano, the new style seems wild and seductive. My church labels it satanic and ridicules its "jungle beat."

Along with other losers, I take the yellow bus to and from school. I sit on a cracked vinyl seat and hold the metal bar that makes my hands smell like rust. Bullies thrive on the bus. Stick your head out the window for air, and their spit comes flying back at you from a window farther ahead. Throughout the ride, they roam the aisle looking for prey. They are like dogs lunging at the end of a leash, and the bus driver, who holds the other end, doesn't seem to care. Maybe he, too, is afraid.

One afternoon the main bully sticks several straight pins through a pencil eraser and walks up and down the aisle whacking kids on the head. When he hits Marshall, my brother grabs the pencil from him and whacks him back. The bully stares at him, his dark eyes wide with shock, his mouth twisting into a wicked grin. "Now you done it," he says at last. He turns to his friends. "Boys, we're gittin' off at a different stop today. This punk here's made a serious mistake. He needs me to teach him a lesson."

At our stop the bully and six of his friends file out of the bus and surround my brother. Some of the neighbor kids stay to watch, and others run home. I race to the church grounds in search of adult reinforcements: "Come quick! They're ganging up on Marshall!"

When I run back to the bus stop, I expect to find my brother stretched out unconscious. Instead, I see the bully sitting on the ground nursing a bloody nose. Marshall stands to the side, looking more surprised than the bully, rubbing the knuckles on his right hand.

The next morning, my brother and protector has his choice of seats on the bus.

THE YEAR I enter high school, Georgia's education system ranks forty-eighth out of fifty states. Our move to the church property, however, has put us in DeKalb County, a school district that belongs among the nation's elite. The school offers a bewildering variety of courses, and I turn to Marshall for guidance.

He insists that I sign up for at least two years of Latin. "It'll teach you proper grammar," he says. The teacher has us stand up and conjugate verbs—*amo amas amat, amamus amatis amant*—as a kind of calisthenics, stretching our hands out high and working our way down to our ankles. She is passionate and ridiculous all at once, but she loves Latin, and by the end of that first year, she has us doing free translations of Julius Caesar's *Gallic Wars*.

I also enroll in Spanish, figuring it's a lot like Latin. At first we're taught by a timid woman who speaks in a whisper and seems terrified of her students. She frequently leaves us unsupervised in a language lab, listening to inane conversations over headphones. "¿Dónde está su casa?" "Aquí está mi casa." Those first weeks must scare the teacher into a new career, because halfway through the school year she quits. The new semester begins with us students sitting in the language lab and no sign of a teacher.

Suddenly a young brunette with a perfect figure appears at the door. The guys make comments and wolf whistles, thinking a saucy new upperclassman has arrived. She lounges against the door frame for a moment, then she cracks a sly smile and steps to the podium to announce, "Hello, I'm Marta Baskin, your new Spanish teacher." She tells us she learned the language in South America as a missionary kid—though she doesn't look like any M. K. I've ever seen.

Since I'm still trying to decide what subjects interest me, Marshall persuades me to take a history class from his favorite teacher, Cecil Pickens, the oddest character in the school. He has some syndrome that gives him an excess of collagen, like the India Rubber Man. He limps badly and looks deformed, with oversized lips and a face that twists into a perpetual squint. "Give him a chance," Marshall says. "He'll teach you to think outside the norm."

Mr. Pickens gives an assignment on the very first day: "Chapter one in your textbook is quite short. I want you to learn everything in it, and we'll have a quiz tomorrow." We practically memorize the chapter, and the next day's quiz has only one question: *Who is the photographer credited for the photo at the top of the chapter?* Nobody knows. "I said learn *everything*," Mr. Pickens chastises us. "Pay attention in this class."

Students either love or hate Mr. Pickens. One day, he disappears, and a rumor spreads that cops have picked him up drunk, with Communist literature in the back seat of his car. Mr. Pickens claimed he was simply exposing his students to other ideas, trying to get them to think for themselves. We never see him again.

On the first day of biology, I wake up to science. A tall, skinny man with an angular face steps in front of the class and introduces himself as "Doc," not Mr. Navarre. His classroom is a veritable zoo, with terrariums and aquariums lining the walls, watched over by a complete skeleton of the human body—in the jaws of which some impish student has placed a cigarette.

Doc begins the class by taking off his shoe, strolling over to one of the terrariums, and holding it in front of a two-foot alligator. *Chomp!* The shoe is smashed flat.

"Now, watch," Doc says. He reaches in the terrarium and puts one finger on the top of the gator's snout. "You see, this guy has muscles powerful enough to destroy my shoe, but those muscles only work in one direction. Biology teaches these things." He pauses for two beats, then adds, "And that can be important if you live near a swamp."

I may not live near a swamp, but I've always lived near woods. From that first day, I feel something stir inside me. Science is not some abstract exercise, like philosophy. It's a way for me to get better acquainted with the natural world I already love.

Doc regularly invites students to his home, which doubles as a natural-history museum, and there he rekindles my interest in insects. "Never underestimate insects," he says. "There are a thousand pounds of living termites—and roughly twenty million flies—for every person on earth."

I start carrying a butterfly net and a collection of small jars on my hikes in the fields and woods. In time I have enough specimens to fill two Styrofoam display boards. In the center of the butterfly board I place a spectacular luna moth, a pale green, luminous creature with large feathery antennae and sweeping tapered wings dotted with four eyespots. No one would believe that I plucked it alive off the screen door of our trailer.

The other board includes several praying mantises (a devil to mount), a fearsome rhinoceros beetle, some water striders, stink bugs, and grasshoppers, as well as my prize, an Eyed Elater click beetle that I pried out of a decaying log. Beneath each specimen I attach a tag noting both its common and Latin names.

I have a separate display of cicadas, my favorite insect. These creatures with bulgy red eyes have just made their appearance after thirteen years underground. They emerged by the thousands—no, millions—until the air vibrated with a clackety sound, something like the loose belt on a lawnmower. Then one day the sound ceased, and I collected the discarded cicada shells, almost transparent and flecked with gold. I marvel at these odd creatures, who waited longer than I have lived to make their entrance into the world, then laid their eggs and surrendered after barely a month aboveground.

My enthusiasm for science leads Doc Navarre to recommend me for a summer fellowship at the Communicable Disease Center (CDC), a research complex near Emory University. I fill out forms and write an essay on why I want to pursue a career in science. To my astonishment, I win one of six coveted positions. I have never felt so proud, and so out of my league.

On my first day at the CDC, I meet the other high school interns chosen from across Atlanta. "Tell us about your scientific experiments," a senior scientist asks us. A girl from a private school describes the insecticide she developed from an English ivy plant, which won her third place in the national science fair competition. The guy sitting next to me says that in the process of identifying insect-borne diseases, he's discovered an ingenious way to trap ticks.

"Really?" asks the scientist. "Tell me more. I send out highly paid workers to collect ticks. It's very labor-intensive. We drag a blanket through a meadow, and the ticks, who perch on the edge of a blade of grass with their claws out, grab hold. What's your method?"

The high school senior explains that ticks are attracted to carbon dioxide, which animals exhale when they breathe. "I leave a block of dry ice in a field," he says. "The next day it's melted to a much smaller size, and I can pick out scores of ticks preserved in the dry ice."

"That's brilliant!" the scientist exclaims. "We'll try it tomorrow."

When my turn comes, I mumble something about my insect collection and breeding experiments I've attempted with tropical fish and then slink down in my seat.

That summer fellowship gives me my first experience in the professional working world. The CDC has collected thousands of mosquitoes from a region in Texas where encephalitis has broken out. Most days I sit at a microscope, sorting mosquitoes into trays based on stripe patterns on their wings. Once separated by species, the mosquitoes are ground up, combined with horse serum, and injected into the brains of baby mice. Nine days later the infected mice will show signs of the disease, and then field staff can devise an eradication program for that type of mosquito.

The microscope assignment makes me feel important, though the sorting process itself gets tedious. Interns can also attend CDC seminars, which prove far more interesting. A rabies expert shows films of horses and dogs staggering around, foaming at the mouth, attacking a lamppost or a piece of lumber. After the film, another scientist etherizes a live rat infected with bubonic plague and dissects it right on the conference table.

By the end of the summer, I have decided on my career path: to become a microbe hunter, or perhaps an entomologist.

SOMETHING ELSE HAPPENS to me that summer, and it involves race.

Growing up in Georgia, I've heard all my life that Black people are not like us. They use worse grammar than whites. They think differently and act differently and always will. I've never had a Black classmate in school, and the churches I attend only reinforce my prejudice.

The year I entered high school, nine students integrated Atlanta's schools for the first time. Over the next few years, other schools in the area admitted Black students, yet not one has set foot on the Gordon campus. Although Black families have moved into the neighborhood, no parents dare to enroll their children in our high school. Why? We all believe that my brother's strange friend Malcolm, nephew of the Grand Dragon of the KKK, has single-handedly kept our school all-white.

Malcolm put out the word that the first Black student to integrate Gordon High would go home in a box. Somehow he got a list of the names of thirteen Black students who applied for a transfer to Gordon, and a few weeks later the KKK burned crosses in their yards. All thirteen changed their plans.

In the 1960s the Ku Klux Klan is still a force to fear. I remember as a child watching a funeral procession for an Exalted Cyclops or Grand Wizard or some such KKK bigwig. Needing to turn left across traffic, we had to wait until the entire motorcade passed. Dozens, scores, hundreds of cars slid past us, each one driven by a figure wearing a silky white or crimson robe and a pointed hood with slits cut out for eyes. "Don't stare," Mother said—but how could I not? The next day's *Atlanta Journal* reported that the funeral procession was five miles long.

I feel twinges of guilt about racism now and then. I wince when our pastor calls Martin Luther King Jr. "Martin Lucifer Coon." I try not to repeat racist jokes, even though they always bring a laugh. The summer I work at the CDC, however, I feel much more than a twinge—something closer to an electric shock.

A month before my fellowship, the mailman delivers a packet of materials designed to prepare us interns for the tasks we'll be performing. I pay special attention to the paper on bacteria-staining techniques because it's written by the man who will be my supervisor, Dr. Cherry. A timid high school kid, I have no idea how to act around a PhD in biochemistry from an Ivy League school. I get goosebumps just thinking about it.

Though I don't know much chemistry, I want to sound halfway intelligent around Dr. Cherry. So I diligently study the various procedures involved in his specialty: the Ziehl-Neelson acid-fast stain, Loeffler's alkaline methylene blue stain, the Wayson stain, and others way over my head.

When I show up for work the first day, I get a photo ID badge and am escorted to Dr. Cherry's office. The security guard knocks on the door, hears "Come in," and opens it. I nearly drop my pack of papers on the floor.

Dr. Cherry is a Black man.

In one second, something cracks inside me. I think back to the scene at camp when the visiting speaker did his imitation of waiters swiveling their hips around tables without spilling a drop. "Have you ever met a Negro who's the president of a company?" Peter Ruckman asked. "Every race has its place, and they should accept it."

Day after day I work directly with Dr. Cherry, a wise and gentle mentor. He wears bifocals and has a receding hairline. He patiently answers my questions about staining bacteria and sorting mosquitoes, even though I know he has several hundred employees to supervise. Sometimes he tells me about his children, who are in high school like me.

I wish I could somehow contact Peter Ruckman and introduce him to Dr. Cherry. My scientist employer is definitely not "serving in the tents of Shem," the fate of his race according to the Curse of Ham theory. All summer a crisis of faith smolders inside me. *The church has clearly lied to me about race.* And about what else? Jesus? The Bible?

I ride a city bus to my CDC internship, often the only white person on a bus transporting Black maids to the stately homes surrounding the Emory University campus. One day, a middle-aged, obese woman with sweat marks under her arms and stockings rolled down around her ankles climbs the steps, drops coins in the fare box, and lurches down the aisle with a three-year-old in tow. Just as they get to my row, the kid suddenly lets go of his mother, bends over, and vomits on the floor beside my seat. The woman curses, grabs his arm, and drags him to the back of the bus.

Disgusted, I check my clothes for vomit splash, and look around for another seat—an instinctive response. Yet I am caught off guard by what I feel next. Can I imagine this woman's life? No doubt she rides this bus because she owns no car. Every day she mops, dusts furniture, and cleans a house the likes of which she could never afford. She probably brought the child along because she has no one else to look after him.

I step off the bus, feeling something short of compassion but more than pity.

We are, I know not how, double in ourselves,
so that what we believe, we disbelieve, and cannot rid
ourselves of what we condemn.

—Michel de Montaigne, *Essays,* "Of Glory"

CHAPTER 15
SPLIT

At school, no one knows I live in a trailer by a fundamentalist church. The first week, after the bus dropped us off, I walked with a neighbor and classmate, Eugene Crowe, to his house. From there I hopped a low fence in the backyard and headed home across the church property. "Hey, would you mind if I took this scenic route?" I asked Eugene, and made it a habit. As long as I don't invite anyone else over, which I never do, my secret doesn't get out.

The trailer is a perfect symbol of my world at home and church: narrow, rectangular, cloistered, metallic. Everything else—the CDC internship, city buses, school activities, books, politics, my love of science—exists in some parallel universe. Nothing in one universe reminds me of the other, and yet each seems real and true until I step across the fence.

All through high school I navigate between the two worlds, home-and-church and *the world beyond*. Whenever I'm forced to bring them together, I feel a hot red rush of shame.

My sophomore year, the English literature teacher announces a field trip to the premiere of *Othello,* starring Laurence Olivier and Maggie Smith. "I arranged permission for you to miss afternoon classes on Friday," she says, and all the students cheer—except for me.

After class, I sheepishly approach the teacher. "Miss Chastain, I've got a problem. You see, my church thinks it's wrong to go to movies. They're not allowed."

She looks at me for a moment, chewing on her lower lip, then responds kindly. "I understand, Philip. I'm just sorry you'll miss the movie. Don't worry, I'll come up with another assignment for you." When the other students find out, they treat me like a pariah. And on Friday, thrilled to be cutting classes, they board the bus for a matinee while I stay behind in the empty classroom and write a paper on Chaucer.

Marshall, who's going through one of his spiritual phases, pressures me to join a school club called Youth for Christ (YFC). "We need to stand out as Christians," he lectures, responding to my eye roll. "You can be a silent witness in lots of ways."

As if to compound my shame, the YFC staff person encourages us to carry a big red Bible on top of our schoolbooks ("Why is it red? Because it ought to *be* read.") and to wrap our textbooks with splashy Youth for Christ covers. In the school cafeteria, true believers bow their heads and say grace in a way that others notice. I can't bring myself to do it, so I bow my head for a few seconds and scratch my eyebrows before opening my sack lunch.

On Tuesday afternoons a large bus with Youth for Christ painted in red letters on the side pulls up in a driveway across from the school, and our faithful troupe climbs on board. There's a beat-up piano bolted to the floor just behind the driver, and Marshall leads us in a few songs as the bus makes a circuit in front of the school before conveying us to someone's home for a meeting. I usually manage to drop something so that I'm bending down to pick it up as we pass the school entrance, lest anyone recognize me through the window.

On Saturday nights YFC holds a citywide rally in downtown Atlanta, in the plush auditorium of the High Museum of Art. Designed to keep godly teenagers from worldly activities, the rallies feature musical groups and speakers brought in to entertain and inspire us. Each week the director asks us to forgo the milkshakes and burgers we would normally enjoy after the rally. "Instead, I beg you to put your spending money in the offering buckets that our usherettes will now pass up and down the rows of seats."

Just like my church, YFC stresses the importance of talking to others about our faith. One speaker tells us: "Seventeen dedicated Communists conquered Russia. If every Christian in America converted just two people to Christ in a year, and each of those converts did the same thing, the church would grow exponentially. In a decade we'd have ten million new Christians, and in fifteen years one billion!"

I accept the personal goal of two converts per year. Too embarrassed to approach my classmates, I try knocking on doors and witnessing to strangers. "Hi. Could I ask you a question? If you died tonight, would you be ready to go to Heaven?" It never works out. They either say they're already going to Heaven or slam the door in my face.

At least I can pass out gospel tracts. I study a selection of them at church. One has a crude drawing of sinners having a good time while flames of hellfire loom in the background. Another leaflet has no illustrations, just a question on the cover—"What do you have to do to go to Hell?"—with the inside page completely blank. That technique doesn't work either: I can never figure out how to have a friendly conversation with someone when my main point is that they are going to Hell.

I conclude I must be a phony, a hypocrite. I know how to act in church and in YFC meetings. I know what I'm supposed to say and not say, think and not think. Yet once I step into a new environment— the world beyond—blood surges to my head and my legs go wobbly. Guilt over my failures compounds my shame.

My sophomore year, Marshall signs up for the YFC piano contest, and I sign up for the "preacher boy" competition. I work as hard on my sermon as on any term paper, memorize it, and practice it with gestures in front of the bathroom mirror. Sometimes I can't hold back the tears, wholly believing what I'm preaching. At the last minute, I withdraw from the contest. A good performance may win me a free trip to the national convention in Indiana, but how can I say the words if I'm not sure I really mean them?

BESIDES SHAME, THERE is fear. Not owning a television, we get our news from the shrill voices of Carl McIntire and Billy James Hargis, radio evangelists who spend more time talking about politics than religion. In their telling, every politician is a crook, every civil rights leader a closet Communist, every president a lily-livered coward. Roosevelt "sold us down the river" at Yalta. Now we are living under John F. Kennedy, who, McIntire insists, "will be the end of this country." Mother loves listening to them, though it keeps her in a constant state of anxiety. Marshall makes fun of these two "fear-mongers," as he calls them, which always starts an argument with Mother.

Mother claims that Bible prophecies are being fulfilled right before our eyes. European countries are joining together in a Common Market, and a computer in Belgium supposedly has all our names stored away in preparation for the Mark of the Beast. A rumor spreads one month that some Social Security checks mistakenly got mailed with the printed instruction "To be cashed only if number corresponds to number on forehead of cashee." One of Mother's books predicts that New Agers will acquire nuclear bombs and eliminate two billion people by the year 2000. Another warns that Catholics have stashes of guns hidden in their basements, with plans to take over the United States.

Church reinforces the fear. At Brother Pyle's summer camp, a Greek scholar speaks on "the guaranteed last sign before the Second Coming of Christ." I sit spellbound in the pew, waiting to learn the final clue to the end of the world. He cites a verse in 2 Timothy about "perilous" times to come. "The Greek word literally means *haywire* or *screwy* times," he says. "Can anyone seriously doubt that we're living in screwy times?" I leave feeling cheated, hoping for something more precise.

Khrushchev has threatened, "We will bury you!" and newsmagazines show maps of the red blot of communism spreading like spilled blood across the hemispheres. I've read that Communist invaders spare anyone who can speak their language. To make certain we have our bases covered, Marshall signs up for Russian classes and I study Chinese, so that one of us will survive an enemy assault from either direction. I've also read that Communists examine the hands of their conquered foes for calluses: smooth-skinned bourgeoisie they line up and shoot, while those with worker hands they set free. I rake leaves with a passion, spurning gloves in order to harden the resulting blisters into calluses. Already I am doubting that my handful of Chinese words and Marshall's Russian vocabulary will save us.

Fear mushrooms into near hysteria during the Cuban missile crisis. A television at school shows President Kennedy, grim and exhausted, announcing a naval blockade against the country determined to bury us. Gordon High holds a science fair every year, and now instead of inventing new chemical compounds or electronic gizmos, the winners compete to design the best fallout shelter.

The Department of Defense distributes a pamphlet meant to reassure us: "If a person receives a large dose of radiation, he will die. But if he receives only a small or medium dose, his body will repair itself and he will get well." But nothing can reassure those of us who live in Georgia, because we know Castro's missiles will obliterate us. A cynical poster has it right: "In case of nuclear attack, lower yourself under your school desk, put your head between your knees, and kiss your butt goodbye."

I have mixed feelings about President Kennedy. Despite the warnings from my church, he doesn't seem to be taking orders from the pope after all. I like the way he stands up to Khrushchev, and I can't avoid being swept up in the Camelot mystique: touch football on the

White House lawn, the "Ich bin ein Berliner" speech, his classy wife, Jackie, memorizing and reciting poetry for the president's birthday.

Then comes a day in November 1963 when I am sitting in Mrs. Pucciano's chemistry class staring blankly at the periodic table of elements. Mrs. P. is one of the first Catholics I have ever known, and some of her ten kids attend Gordon High. We hear the sound of students running—*running*—through the halls in the middle of class time, and as Mrs. P. goes to investigate, one of them yells, "The president's been shot!" She slams the door closed, hoping we haven't heard. We have. Mrs. P. asks us to close our books, remain silent, and perhaps even pray—until we learn more.

Within minutes the intercom clicks on with a voice we recognize as the principal's. The year before, the eloquent Mr. Craig was replaced by Mr. Jenkins, a football coach who is anything but eloquent. "Hello, is it on? OK. This is your principal speaking." He hits the microphone button a few times, causing bursts of static. There is a hush in the room. We are still, like deer on full alert.

"Some of you have heard the disturbing reports from Dallas," the principal begins. "The governor of Texas . . ."—with those words Mrs. Pucciano crosses herself and exhales a sigh of relief. Mr. Jenkins hits the button again and proceeds—"and the president, John Kennedy, have been shot." A few students let out audible gasps. "President Kennedy's wound is particularly serious in that it is in the head." We wait for more, but the intercom clicks off.

Mrs. Pucciano puts her head down on her desk, her shoulders shaking up and down. Some of the girls sob. And from down the hall we hear the muffled, ugly sound of students applauding and cheering. Of course we know why: over the last few years, President Kennedy has been sending federal marshals to enforce racial integration in the South.

Gordon High dismisses early that day, and the entire country seems to stop moving. The event is so momentous that two days later, a Sunday, Mother lets me hike over to Eugene's house after church in order to watch the news on his television. I walk in the door and Mrs. Crowe asks me if I'd like some iced tea. Before she even returns from the kitchen, I watch on live TV as Jack Ruby shoots Lee Harvey Oswald in the stomach.

The Greek scholar from camp was right. Our nation is going haywire.

WHATEVER GOODWILL I felt toward Kennedy does not carry over to his successor, Lyndon Johnson. Every time he opens his mouth, I cringe. "Mah felluh Amuricans," he says, sounding like a hick from the hills of North Georgia. He behaves crudely, picking up dogs by their ears and discussing foreign policy while sitting on the toilet with the door open. The election year of 1964, my junior year, I join the Young Republicans for Goldwater committee and volunteer as the state secretary.

On the Fourth of July that year, I attend a "Patriots' Rally Against Tyranny" held at the Lakewood Speedway. The rally features such notables as Alabama's governor, George Wallace, and Mississippi's governor, Ross Barnett, as well as Atlanta's own Lester Maddox. A crowd of eleven thousand Southerners wave miniature Rebel flags and cheer as the speakers take turns denouncing Washington for trampling states' rights.

I'm sitting on hot bleachers, fanning myself with the program, when the political rally veers toward race—and violence. A handful of Black men have attended, sitting together in one corner of the grandstands, in a conspicuous dark clump. When a speaker introduces Governor Wallace, three of them cup their hands around their mouths and loudly boo.

I see no one give a signal, but shortly after a rousing rendition of "Dixie," some Klansmen rise from their seats and make an ominous descent through the stands, surrounding the cluster of Black men. They begin beating them about the head and shoulders with their fists, and then with folded chairs. A half-dozen other whites join in, urged on by the crowd's yells. "Hit 'em! Kill 'em!"

The Black men huddle together, looking around in desperation for an escape route. At last, frantic, a few of them break free and start climbing a thirty-foot chain-link fence designed to protect spectators from the race cars. Their tormentors scramble to catch them.

The speaker's bullhorn falls silent, and we all turn to watch as the attackers pry loose the clinging bodies, as though removing prey from a trap. After a time, Georgia State Patrol officers wearing broadbrim hats and navy-and-gray uniforms saunter over and escort the bloodied Black men from the fairgrounds.

When the rally resumes, George Wallace takes the stage and delivers a speech written by Asa Carter, a KKK leader. He calls the Civil Rights Act of 1964 "the most monstrous piece of legislation ever enacted . . . a fraud, a sham and a hoax, this bill will live in infamy." The civil rights movement comes straight out of *The Communist Manifesto,* he says. "We must revitalize a government founded in this nation on faith in God!" The crowd shouts, "George! George! George!" as he circles the stage with his arms raised in a V for Victory symbol.

My mind still on the assault, I barely listen to the other speeches. A chill has settled over my skin, even in the July heat. I can't enter into the crowd's jubilation. The rally—indeed, politics itself—has lost its appeal, drowned out by the crowd's throaty yells and the crunch of the Klansmen's bare fists against flesh.

The rest of the summer, memories of that scene linger in the air, like a bad smell that won't go away.

DURING MY LAST two years in high school, I feel myself drifting away from family and church. School has opened up new frontiers. There, at last, I'm beginning to find success and acceptance.

With some trepidation, I try out for the school play *Inherit the Wind,* which tells the story of the Scopes Monkey Trial. The play mocks the fundamentalist icon William Jennings Bryan, whom my church views as a hero. I audition for the part of Elijah, an illiterate mountain man who sells Bibles to the townspeople of Dayton, Tennessee, and preaches hellfire and brimstone to the crowd outside the courthouse. The drama coach is thrilled. "I'm so happy to discover new talent!" she says, unaware that I have listened to many preachers like Elijah.

Next I join the debate team, which seems like another form of acting. You research a topic, passionately present arguments in favor of some plan, then switch sides and argue how ridiculous it is. In my second tournament, I end up with a better overall score than Marshall does, the first time I have ever beaten my brother at anything. When he sees that I rank higher on the team, Marshall drops out.

My junior year, I go on a weekend excursion with the school debate team to Athens, where the University of Georgia is hosting a state tournament. The school district pays for two nights in a motel, and we debaters make the most of it. We cannonball into the swimming pool, empty the vending machines, even smoke cigars. Late at night we drop quarters in the Vibro-massage beds just as our roommates are falling asleep.

The most memorable event of that trip takes place on the drive home, as we wind along the roads of eastern Georgia. I am riding in a car with the new sociology teacher, our chaperone, who has untrimmed hair and a bushy mustache, a rarity in those days. He owns only three ties and two sports coats, and sometimes wears the same clothes to school five days in a row. He also drives the ugliest car in the school parking lot.

In that rattletrap car packed with five eager young debaters, Mr. Bradford tells us why he lives so frugally. "Do you realize," he says, "that one-fourth of the people in the world earn less money in a year than I spent on the watch I'm wearing right now?" His left arm moves across the steering wheel to display a gold watch worth about thirty dollars.

I have never thought of myself as rich. After all, I live in a trailer. But Mr. Bradford, fresh from an assignment with the Peace Corps, goes on to describe daily life in some of the world's poorest countries. I am startled speechless.

He turns his head toward the back seat, his eyes locking on me. "And I bet you can't guess what I did before the Peace Corps. I was a Southern Baptist evangelist." We all laugh.

For a few minutes, Mr. Bradford says nothing. I concentrate on the scenery outside, still absorbing what he's told us about his time abroad.

Finally I ask, "So, why'd you become a teacher instead of an evangelist?"

He responds energetically, as if he's been waiting for the question. "Well, I'll tell you why. When I got back to the United States, nobody in the church cared much about what I saw overseas. People were more concerned with chasing the American dream. I couldn't get the Peace Corps scenes out of my mind, and one day I decided I could no longer live with the hypocrisy. The time had come to speak my mind.

"I happened to be the scheduled speaker at my church's Wednesday night service. So, after a full day's work on the farm, I marched down the aisle and took my seat on an upholstered chair on the platform. Thing is, I hadn't changed clothes, and I was still wearing my smelly overalls. My work boots left a trail of mud and manure down the aisle. That sanctuary had a new odor in it, and members of the congregation began whispering to each other.

"My sermon took only five minutes to deliver, and went something like this:

You act shocked. You laugh as though I were a costumed clown. I tell you, *you* are wearing the costumes. Seventy-five percent of the world's people are dressed like me. Half the world went to bed hungry tonight. You stuffed yourselves, fed the dogs—and still threw away a good meal.

Something is wrong with a country that lets grain rot in the silos while bodies rot away in other nations. And this church—no one dressed like me has been welcome here. No poor person has spoken from this platform. What's more, you don't care. When I leave tonight, I'll be remembered as the oddball, the misfit, the clown. You won't think of yourselves as the strange ones. But you are. The strangest thing of all is that you don't even realize it."

With that, our teacher proudly informs us, he walked out of the church. He had said his last prayer and read his last Scripture.

FOR THREE YEARS I've thought a career in science would be my future. The final two years of high school, however, the power of words gradually overtakes me.

I felt its tug as a freshman, when the elegant principal, Mr. Craig, made stops at our introductory English class. The teacher always asked him to recite some Shakespeare. Mr. Craig would clear his throat and close his eyes, then rocking slowly back and forth quote line after line of the most beautiful language I had ever heard. The class always fell quiet, and not just because he was the principal.

Now I am studying Shakespeare in English literature classes. We read *Julius Caesar, Romeo and Juliet,* and *Hamlet.* Sometimes we joke about lines like "Friends, Romans, countrymen, lend me your ears . . ." Every so often, though, the magic of the language sweeps us out of our petty little worlds and pulls us toward something grander.

In my advanced literature classes, other books wield a different power: *1984, Animal Farm, Brave New World, Catcher in the Rye, To Kill a Mockingbird, Siddhartha.* They draw me out of the church bubble I live in and—like Mr. Bradford's Peace Corps stories—expose me to ideas and realms I haven't known before. I feel like a virgin reader, and a subversive one, wondering if it's sinful to read such books. I am encountering backgrounds wholly unlike mine, and it makes the blood buck in my veins.

When I read a good book, I have the almost mystical sense that all of it has happened to me. Or, rather, I *want* it to happen to me. I read Chaucer and wish I was one of those pilgrims swapping bawdy stories on the road with friends and strangers. I read *Return of the Native* and fall in love with love. I read Hemingway and want to enlist. I read Salinger and long for the courage to act out the insolence that simmers inside me.

For the first time I see my fundamentalist faith as it looks from the outside. Shirley Jackson's story "The Lottery" takes me back to Old Testament accounts of drawing lots and stoning deviants. One teacher reads aloud C. S. Lewis's *The Great Divorce,* and its fanciful version of Hell as a place of bleak loneliness sounds so much more believable than the brimstone sermons I hear at church. *Lord of the Flies* tells me all I need to know about depravity without using the word.

My thoughts about race, which have been churning since my experiences at the CDC and at the Patriots' Rally, come to a head when I read the new book *Black Like Me,* by journalist John Howard Griffin. A line on the cover describes the premise: "A white man learns what it is like to live the life of a Negro by becoming one!" Although that stretches the truth, Griffin indeed underwent a regimen of drugs and ultraviolet treatment in order to turn his skin black.

The book recounts his experiences during six weeks of traveling on buses through the Deep South, passing as a Black man. He tells of the "hate stares" that he gets in Mississippi when he asks for directions, applies for a job, or simply tries to buy a bus ticket. In his disguise, basic things I take for granted—a place to eat, somewhere to find a drink of water, a restroom, someplace to wash up—pose a major challenge.

When the pigmentation finally fades and Griffin scrubs his face from brown to pink, everything changes. Once more he's a first-class citizen, with the doors into cafés, restrooms, libraries, movies, concerts, schools, and churches now open to him. "A sense of exultant liberation flooded through me. I crossed over to a restaurant and entered. I took a seat beside white men at the counter and the waitress smiled at me. It was a miracle."

The book has a profound effect on me. At once, I grasp the absurdity of racism based on skin color. John Howard Griffin was the very same man, whether with white skin or temporarily brown skin. Yet sometimes he was treated like a normal human being and sometimes like a dirty animal.

My brain aches after reading his book, as does my conscience. I have mocked Blacks' behavior—their music and dance, dialect, strange food, flashy clothes—without really knowing the persons underneath. Is that so different from the way the folks at the Piedmont Driving Club look on trailer dwellers like me as "white trash," while I look on them as effete snobs? Both of us judge people by externals only.

Unlike John Howard Griffin, I've never been treated—even temporarily—as if I were a Black person. What would that be like? Timidly at first, then greedily, I find books like *Native Son* by Richard Wright, *Invisible Man* by Ralph Ellison, and *The Autobiography of Malcolm X*. The racist stereotypes I have inherited take on a new cast. Maybe Black people "don't keep up their neighborhoods" because they live in dilapidated housing owned by slumlords. Maybe they "have no sense of history" because of what that history represents.

Black people, it dawns on me, don't *want* to have names like ours, use the same grammar and pronunciation, enjoy the same music, wear the same clothes, shake hands the same way, worship the same way. For Blacks, "She thinks she's white" is an insult, not a compliment. Black culture has its own set of gifts.

As I step over the fence to the pony-farm field of the church where we live, I start viewing my own community of white-racist-paranoid-fundamentalism as its own kind of culture. I don't like what I see.

Why, I can smile, and murder whiles I smile,
And cry "Content" to that which grieves my heart,
And wet my cheeks with artificial tears,
And frame my face to all occasions.

—Shakespeare, *Henry VI*

CHAPTER 16

MAKEOVER

I spend my eleventh-grade year moody and confused. I know how to act out an identity: play a character onstage, give a soul-stirring testimony at church or camp, stand at a debate podium and argue convincingly for a point of view or its opposite. All the while, I feel vacant at my core. Who am *I*?

Then my bones start breaking. The first one occurs at a church softball game. I slide awkwardly into home plate, landing on my right arm, which snaps like a dry twig. At the emergency room, I experience a new level of pain as the doctor inserts a horse-sized hypodermic needle and runs the point along the bone until he finds the exact site of the break before injecting anesthetic and setting the fracture.

A month later, still wearing a cast, I trip while playing basketball and twist left to protect the broken arm as I fall. I land on my left elbow, causing another fracture.

My mother, normally sympathetic at such times, runs out of patience. "What were you thinking, playing ball with a broken arm?"

she demands. "Don't you have any common sense? From now on you're paying the doctor bills out of your own money!"

Having both arms in casts complicates life. To get dressed, I hold my undershorts out in front of me with both plastered arms, aiming my feet through the holes and jumping off the upper bunk. Against all odds, I avoid further breaks—for a while.

After a few weeks, the doctor cuts apart the scribbled-upon cast on my right arm with a menacing saw that, he assures me, will stop spinning the second it touches soft skin. He pries apart the split cast and uncovers my quivering, atrophied arm, speckled with black sweat beads. The room fills with a rancid smell.

In the span of just over a year, I have six arm fractures, mostly from basketball and touch football. "You need to be more careful, son," the doctor says, every time. Mother has sterner words. Meanwhile, I have taken on a paper route to pay the medical bills.

In addition to the broken arms, I suffer one more injury when my church friend David pays me a visit. We walk together to a public swimming pool, pay the thirty-five-cent fee, and change into our swimsuits. I make the mistake of telling David that I don't know how to do a flip off the diving board. "I can do a straightforward head-first dive, but flips scare me."

"There's nothing to it," he scoffs. "You're probably thinking too much about ducking your head down toward the water. Focus on getting your knees up to your chin as fast as you can. When you do that, you'll automatically roll forward in a somersault."

Before even taking a dip in the water, I climb the ten steps to the diving board, walk to the very end, and give it a few tentative bounces. *Knees to the chin, knees to the chin,* I tell myself. Then I retrace my steps, make a running start, and bounce high off the board, bringing my knees to my chin as fast as I can.

The next thing I know, I'm underwater, dazed, with blood spilling out the side of my mouth and a searing sensation in my jaw. I must have slammed my right knee into my chin, in the process badly biting my cheek. I kick to the surface and paddle over to David. "Something's wrong," I sputter. "I think I'm hurt."

David has little sympathy. "There's no way we're going to leave now, after just paying for admission," he says. I float around on my back for half an hour, and the pain doesn't subside. Eventually I talk him into walking back home. When I eat a Krispy Kreme doughnut, my face feels like it has caught fire.

Back at the doctor's office, I learn the reason. After X-raying my jaw, the doctor says, "You're a lucky young man. Your jawbone is split in two, with a jagged edge just beneath the surface of your right cheek. If you had eaten anything more solid than a doughnut, the bone probably would have popped right out through the skin." I wince, and the pain shoots across my face.

He presents two options. I can go to the hospital and have the jaw wired shut for six weeks—"in which case you may lose your teeth since you can't brush them very well," he says—or I can let the jaw heal on its own, "but only if you swear on a stack of Bibles that you'll not touch any solid food for six weeks." I swear, and my fast begins.

The liquid diet gives me an excuse to drink a milkshake every day. In time I graduate to mashed potatoes and then master the art of swallowing peas and butterbeans whole. Sleeping poses the real challenge. If I lie on my back, my lower jaw slides downward, pressing the jagged end against my cheek. Sleeping on either side puts intolerable pressure on the fracture site. So I resort to sleeping on my stomach. I make a rectangle out of pillows and towels and rest my forehead on the top border, with my face hanging down in the empty space in the center. Although I get little sleep that summer, at least I escape having my jaw wired shut.

By now Mother has grown concerned. She's been blaming me for the injuries, but what if there's something medically amiss? We visit a specialist, who recommends a bone biopsy.

Before we can schedule the procedure, I contract mononucleosis, or glandular fever, and spend a month in bed. Every Saturday I go to a hospital for a blood test, as my high white-blood-cell count has raised the possibility of leukemia.

In self-pitying moments I fantasize about leukemia. Would anyone care if I died? I mentally compose farewell letters. One to my brother, willing him all my goods. One to Mother, asking her to take it easy on Marshall. Another to my pastor, telling him all the things I resented about his church and camp.

Death seems almost a comfort, a way to get postmortem revenge on anyone who has wronged me.

MOTHER LOCATES A specialist in adolescent diseases, a gruff, elderly man who has a fleshy double chin and tired-looking eyes. He thumbs through my medical charts and X-rays as Mother describes my string of childhood illnesses and recent injuries. He peppers me with questions. Then he sits on his stool for a while, glancing up at me as I perch in my undershorts on the edge of the examining table. His mouth opens and closes a few times, as if he has something to say.

I wait for some exotic diagnosis that will explain everything. At last he says in a weary voice, "Son, I don't think there's a thing wrong with you. I think you're weak. You have bad posture. Maybe you like being sick or hurt. It's up to you to be well, to get strong. There's nothing I can do for you."

His words lodge, like a splinter under the skin. Over the next few weeks, as I reflect on my life, I realize he may be right. At home, I usually get Mother's kind attention when I'm recovering from something. Marshall is the strong son, and they fight all the time.

A disturbing thought edges in: *Do I somehow* need *physical suffering?* I have heard of kids who inflict harm on purpose, by cutting, scratching, or burning themselves. Could I be one of them? I haven't *planned* all those broken bones, yet neither have I made any effort to avoid them.

Marshall has confided in me that masturbation is the only thing in his life that feels authentic, his surest emotional connection to reality. Maybe for me pain is the link. It assures me I am alive, and gives me a reason to keep going: I can bear it; I can survive. It also provides a twisted kind of identity. When I show up with both arms in casts, teachers cut me slack. Classmates take notice of me and write messages on the plaster. I am somebody.

Maybe I am sicker than I know. Or, as the doctor said, maybe not sick at all.

I DECIDE I should work at becoming more normal, whatever that means. For starters, I need to learn how to relate to adults.

Adults, I notice, tend to ask the same questions. *What grade are you in? What's your favorite subject? What do you want to be when you grow up?* I practice some stock answers that satisfy the questioners. Women, especially, seem to have an allergic reaction to silence. If I remain quiet, they talk all the more. I merely have to nod and feign interest.

One of the books we study in literature class, *The Heart Is a Lonely Hunter,* describes a mute man who develops friendships simply by listening to others talk. People pour out their stories to him because they know he won't repeat them. The book gives me an idea: I can act interested in what other people say, even when I'm not.

I practice asking some basic questions, such as "Do you have any kids?" and "Where did you go to high school?" A "second me" rides on my shoulders, evaluating my performance and taking mental notes for future reference. I am trying to become an authentic person—artificially.

I put my self-improvement program to the test on my paper route, my main source of income. Whenever a new resident moves in, I introduce myself and offer two weeks of free delivery. "It's a great way to find out what's going on in your new neighborhood," I tell them. Sometimes they ask about the best grocery store nearby or a good place to take a walk, and I get caught up in a real conversation.

Behind those lighted windows, I find, live hermits and businessmen, good-looking housewives in bathrobes and crabby old ladies, along with lots of squabbling children. One old man, who lives alone in a house full of books, always invites me in and talks to me about what he's been reading. I enjoy the paper route, mainly because it keeps me away from the trailer and the tensions at home.

Of all unlikely people, Eugene Crowe's blue-collar father gives me new life. I'm helping Eugene with his homework one evening, and his father overhears us from the next room. As I'm leaving, he says, between puffs on a cigarette: "You know, if I was runnin' a construction site and needed to get some stuff moved with a wheelbarrow, I'd sooner hire you than some big strapping kid. You'd figger out how to do it better, in less time."

A compliment from an adult! Walking home, I realize that must be his way of thanking me for helping his son. I tuck away what he says, deep inside, where I have learned to keep the most important things.

FROM MARSHALL, who has read some psychology, I learn about the onion theory of personality. "It's like this," he says. "Most people see the outer layers of the onion, the self you present to the world. When people get closer and you trust them, then you peel away some more layers. Deepest of all you find the inner self, your true core."

I think long and hard about the onion theory. It makes sense, but I've learned it's best not to peel back any layers—that's when I get hurt. I feel safest when no one knows what's going on inside me. And when I probe that inner core, I come up with a blank. Maybe I should just concentrate on the outer layers.

I ask myself, *What kind of personality do I want?* I know already that I will never excel at sports or win a popularity contest. I settle instead on a reserved, serious personality. To my surprise, at the beginning of my junior year I receive an invitation to join the Key Club, a high school branch of Kiwanis International that takes on service projects such as cleaning up parks and public areas. The club needs a secretary, and I assume they picked me because I seem the studious type who won't mind taking notes.

Encouraged, I begin a makeover project. First, I tackle my accent, vowel by vowel, trying to erase traits of the Deep South. I work on words like *ten* and *y'all* that Philadelphians have made fun of. Since the rest of the nation judges Southerners as backward, ignorant, and racist, I want to disassociate myself from my region.

Next, I reconfigure my handwriting. Mine seems fussy and frilly, too much like a girl's. I practice forming each letter in a more modern, streamlined style.

According to a book on adolescence that Mother gave me, I am supposed to be caught in a roller coaster of emotions, laughing one minute and crying the next. Quite the contrary, I don't know what my feelings are supposed to be or even what they actually are. Perhaps the safest path is to squelch all emotions. Too many times I've listened to Marshall and Mother scream at each other—as if rage has collected behind a steel door that suddenly bursts open to let the heat gush out.

To me, emotions seem a waste of energy. You let anger build up and explode at someone, then grovel back and try to make peace. You sense fear and flee in terror from a harmless mouse or spider. You feel happy one evening and the next day wake up depressed or hungover. Wouldn't it be simpler to skip the emotions and just get to the end state?

In my speech class the teacher reads aloud selections from *Siddhartha,* a novel about a young disciple in the time of Gautama Buddha. I know nothing about Buddhism, but as she reads the story I identify with Siddhartha's search for a cure to his sickness with life. He disciplines himself to overcome desire and achieve the "ecstasy of indifference." I adopt that phrase, and long for what it expresses. I practice an impassive facial expression and a fake smile, a quick upturn twitch of the lips.

I begin reading novels by Sartre and Camus, some of which are just making their way across the Atlantic. "It makes little difference whether one dies at the age of thirty or threescore and ten," says a character in Camus's *The Stranger,* "since in either case, other men and women will continue living, the world will go on as before."

The words leap from the page. *That's me!* I think as I read. I like the flat, fatalistic tone of these novels, so different from the hyped-up emotions of church and revival services.

The ideas in these books set my heart racing. They contradict everything I have heard at church, where I'm taught that every action or thought has eternal consequences. Then, in the philosopher Søren Kierkegaard—a *Christian*!—I find the same spirit of indifference: "Marry, and you will regret it. Do not marry, and you will also regret it. . . . Laugh at the stupidities of the world or weep over them, you will regret it either way. . . . Hang yourself, and you will regret it. Do not hang yourself, and you will also regret it."

I think of the times I have attended the funeral of a distant relative and stood unaffected on the sidelines as friends and relatives threw their arms over the casket and wept. That is how I feel about all of life during these shut-down years.

I begin looking at high school through jaded eyes. I loathe the football games, where oversized gladiators gain their classmates' adulation by chasing a leather ball back and forth across the field. On the sidelines, milky-legged cheerleaders in short skirts jump up and down clapping their hands to nursery-rhyme cheers. I watch the "drill team" toss shiny batons in the air like circus-clown jugglers, and the "homecoming court" with its absurd mimicry of medieval kings and queens. It all seems a stupid, meaningless charade.

MY INNER CORE, the center of the onion, is hardening so that no one can reach it.

One day I say something Mother thinks impudent, and she slaps me full in the face, so hard that it leaves the red imprint of her fingers on my cheek. I read on her face a flicker of fright at what she has done. We both remember last summer's broken jaw, and stare at each other for a few silent seconds. Then I give her my one-second fake smile and turn away. She has lost the power to physically hurt me.

Around that time, I encounter Friedrich Nietzsche. Long ago, this famous German philosopher described the path to self-control that I have been stumbling toward. "It's up to you to be well, to get strong," the doctor told me. Nietzsche trained for self-mastery, living on a strict diet and forcing himself to go to bed at two in the morning and rise at six. I think of adventure stories I read as a kid: Ernest Shackleton sailing in a lifeboat through iceberg-choked waters and hurricane-force winds in order to summon help for his stranded men in Antarctica; the undersized scholar T. E. Lawrence depriving himself of food and water for days as he walked a thousand miles across the Arabian Desert.

How can I put these lofty principles into practice? The Buddhist books speak of "refusing to prefer." Heat/cold, bad smell/good smell, harmony/dissonance, pain/pleasure—these are arbitrary categories that can be overcome.

The summer before my senior year, I take an undesirable job working for the county on a garbage truck. On my first day, I notice that people don't even look at a garbageman; they avert their eyes. The career garbagemen are all muscular Black guys who hoist heavy metal barrels on their shoulders and dump them in the growling maw of the truck. One of them sizes me up. "Hey, white boy, you're too skinny for them barrels," he says. "We'll put you in charge of the grass piles and bags of leaves."

I don't mind the sweetly rotten smell of moldering grass. But will I ever get used to the smell of putrefying garbage? To my surprise, after a few days I barely notice the odor. Marshall and Mother certainly do: I come home a sweaty mess, with dirt tracks on my arms and my T-shirts stained foul with scraps of fermented food.

Working outdoors in an Atlanta summer also cures my aversion to heat. Soon the Black workers let me leave my seat in the cab with the white driver and ride with them on the back. After our last pickup I stand on the running board and hang out sideways to catch the breeze as the truck races to the dump. It's the only time all day when I feel less than sweltering—and I don't care.

As the school year begins and the weather chills, I deliberately go coatless, even on rainy days. I am trying to flatten the extremes of heat and cold, to keep them from affecting me. I remind myself of what Shackleton endured on his voyage from Antarctica.

I come across a phrase used by boot-camp sergeants in the French

Foreign Legion: "Pain is weakness leaving the body." Run five miles, and your feet respond with aches and blisters. But keep it up day after day and the pain will disappear as blisters thicken into calluses. This, too, becomes a goal: to absorb pain without succumbing to it or dishing it out in return.

My sixth and final broken arm occurs that year. At church one Sunday, I accidentally smack my right elbow against the sharp corner of a pew. It swells and turns red, though I can tell the bone hasn't broken. I decide to test my self-control. I go to the bedroom and whack it once, twice against the iron frame of the top bunk bed. Immediately, I feel a familiar sensation, the hot stab of a fracture. Yet the pain barely registers. Weakness has left my body.

ABOVE ALL ELSE, I seek self-control. Nietzsche drew a contrast between masters and victims: a master controls his own life, authorizes himself rather than letting others write the script.

I've heard people make comments like *That's just not my personality. I could never do that. I'm not that way.* I resist all such thoughts. Camp and church have taught me that much of life consists of acting. Pray from the pulpit or give a tear-jerking testimony at camp, and suddenly you're a spiritual giant. Do the opposite, and you're a renegade. People judge by the outside—as long as you keep the inside well hidden.

At school, I observe other students like a waiter eavesdropping at a restaurant table. Who do people admire? I notice that wit has the same effect in a high school group as spiritual behavior does at church. I collect a few one-liners and jokes. Before long, friends appear. I listen intently to people's stories, nodding sympathetically with apparent interest. I feel two-faced, but it gets results. For the first time, classmates seem to enjoy being around me.

I practice conversing about a topic in which I have no interest, and then engage a classmate: "I hear Richard Petty's car got banned from NASCAR because of the hemi-head engine." Although I couldn't tell a hemi-head engine from a toaster oven, and have barely heard of Richard Petty, just tossing out that comment energizes kids at lunch for ten minutes. I drop the same sentence at another lunch table two days later, and it produces the same result.

While my classmates are heatedly discussing the new NASCAR rules, I search my brain for another conversation starter: "Did you hear the Beatles are coming to Atlanta?"

I volunteer for the school newspaper, literary magazine, and yearbook. Interviewing other students gives me a way to get inside their heads, to leech off their lives. When I write someone else's story, I can stop being Philip for a time and view the world through a different set of eyes. I attend meetings every afternoon and evening, which has the supreme advantage of keeping me away from home.

Returning to the trailer at the end of the day, I shed my new personality and hang it up like a jacket, receding into my introverted life of books. Mother can sense that she is losing her sons: Marshall will soon depart for college, and I'm spending as little time at home as possible. The divide between school and home widens.

ONE INCIDENT FROM my senior year, more than any other, tests what I have learned from Nietzsche. As the school year starts, a classmate named Hal, a political fanatic, gets the harebrained idea of organizing student government in a way that mimics national politics. Hal draws up a program whereby each homeroom will elect one student to the "House of Representatives," and each grade will elect two senators to the upper chamber. Underclassmen love the idea, because by sheer numbers their three grades will control the House. Hal's American Party signs up a thousand members. Most juniors and seniors, focused on graduation, pay no attention to the scheme.

For a reason I still don't understand, I determine to quash the whole project. Hal is a classic nerd: overweight, unstylish, academic. Perhaps his idealism grates against my cynicism.

To counter Hal, I form the Student Rights Party with a grand total of eight members, my equally cynical friends. The ex-football-coach principal calls me in and grills me. "Exactly what student rights do you have in mind?" he asks with a scowl. I mention a few issues: undercover photos of rats found in the lunchroom cafeteria, censorship of the school newspaper, an overcrowded parking lot. He bristles, but lets me go. I doubt he sees the SRP as any kind of threat.

Since there are five grades at Gordon, eighth through twelfth, the SRP calculates that we only need to win six positions in the student senate to give us veto power over anything the mickey-mouse House of Representatives might pass. We identify two of the most popular sophomores, juniors, and seniors, respectively, and I cajole them into running as senatorial candidates. Two well-liked seniors, a beauty and a jock, I persuade to run for president and vice president.

Hal mobilizes his army with a newspaper, a written platform, and a full slate of American Party candidates for every homeroom, senate, and student-body position. If elected, they promise to propose a Supreme Court to judge student infractions. The Student Rights Party fields eight candidates. In our platform we propose abolishing the House of Representatives. We stay up late creating slogans and making posters that prominently feature the photos of our candidates.

In the end, it's no contest. Hal has recruited a platoon of eager vote-counters from the lower classes. In a large room, supervised by faculty members, they sit at a long table recording the ballots on adding machines. I don't need a calculator to project the winners; I can read the results on their crestfallen young faces. Within an hour, the trend becomes clear. All our candidates are going to win. Hal departs the room in tears, his dream shattered.

For the rest of that school year, Hal and I do not speak, even though we share several classes. Finally, on a debate trip, I see him sitting alone at breakfast and, gritting my teeth, I ask if I can join him. We talk about the next day's tournament schedule until an awkward silence sets in. For a couple of debaters, we are rather inarticulate. I swallow hard, and after a few false starts mumble a kind of apology.

Hal nods thanks and looks away. As he does so, I can see all the pain of the humiliating defeat on his downcast face.

LATER THE SAME year, I have a different, but equally disturbing conversation in my school lunchroom. On a day when I have no energy to fake conversation with my usual crowd, I sit next to a shy, skinny girl who never looks anyone in the eye. Though I recognize her from at least three classes, I don't know her name.

I ask her a few questions about her life, and unexpectedly she lowers her guard. She tells me that when her father gets drunk, he beats both her and her mother. After school, she says, she tries to creep to her bedroom without being seen. She doesn't know what to do. If she leaves the house, her father will meet her with a belt when she returns. If she stays, he might slip into her bedroom unannounced.

Listening, I begin to understand why she jumps nervously when teachers call on her; why she walks to the side of the hall, brushing against the lockers, her head facing the floor.

I say a few encouraging comments and compliment her on a recent report she gave in class. But soon I run out of words. Nothing in my stock of rehearsed conversations applies to someone like her. For the last two years, I have worked on ways to advance myself, not to lift others.

That evening, a flutter of doubt hits me as I'm walking across the meadow to our lighted trailer. For all its faults, my home is nothing like hers. We both feel ourselves to be victims—slaves, to use Nietzsche's word. Yet who is better, the one who goes through life with her head down or the one who finds ways to climb on the backs of others, as I did to Hal?

Abruptly, I see my makeover project in a different light. It occurs to me that deconstructing a person is easier than constructing one.

Families teach us how love exists in a realm
beyond liking or disliking, coexisting with indifference,
rivalry, and even antipathy.

—John Updike, "Brother Grasshopper"

CHAPTER 17
CRESCENDO

In one of my science books, a naturalist stumbles upon a bird and serpent entwined in a dance of death. A large blacksnake has looped itself around the body of a hen pheasant, pinioning her wings so that she cannot fly away. The bird makes a series of leaps several feet in the air, and with each crashing descent she pounds the snake's body against the stony desert ground. Hissing in fury, the snake does not let go, but uses each leap to tighten its grip around the hen.

As I read that passage, I picture not a bird and a snake but my brother and mother, locked in a deadly embrace. During my high school years, as I retreated into a defensive shell at home, Marshall confronted God and Mother head-on.

Two scenes from Marshall's senior year are etched in my memory. In the first, she grabs the belt on his pants and starts to unbuckle it, planning to use it on him. Marshall, now eighteen years old and six feet tall, thinks she is trying to pull down his pants to beat his bare bottom. He wraps his fingers around the belt buckle and pushes her away.

Her eyes burn with rage. The trailer shakes as she runs into our bedroom in search of a weapon. She reappears with a tennis racket and, holding it head-high, charges toward us. Marshall steps forward, catches hold of her wrist, and seizes the racket.

In those few seconds I see the end of my brother's childhood. Already he has outsmarted her; now he can overpower her. Their glares show that both realize something has ruptured between them, perhaps forever.

The second scene takes place with Marshall sitting at our Sunday School–castoff piano, lime green and still plastered with cartoon decals. When Mother starts badgering him about something, Marshall often plays the piano, shouting his retorts over the notes. Words fly back and forth at the speed of thought, and as they escalate in strength and volume, he shifts from Mozart and Chopin to pound out Tchaikovsky and Rachmaninoff. I retreat to the bedroom, hearing every word over Marshall's playing.

"You don't know the first thing about love," she rails. "I'll tell you what love is. Who does your laundry and cooks your meals, huh? I slave for you, pay for your music lessons, and this is how you act. You think the world owes you a living? You're a pig, nothing but a lazy, sloppy pig! When are you going to get that through your thick skull?"

"You're right!" he shouts back over a series of crashing chords. "I *don't* know the first thing about love. And if you call that love, I can do without it."

Suddenly the telephone rings, interrupting both the music and the quarrel. Mother picks up the receiver, cradles it between her jawbone and shoulder, and makes *mm-hmm* noises as the person on the other end talks. I can tell who it is. One of her Bible club hostesses has been calling regularly, distraught over a sick child and a failing marriage. Mother counsels the woman in calm, soothing tones, quoting Bible passages and praying with her over the phone.

The conversation continues for at least twenty minutes, with Marshall still sitting at the piano, waiting. In the quiet I hear rain pattering on the trailer roof. The instant Mother hangs up the phone, Marshall lets loose with an arpeggio and she resumes her tirade in mid-sentence. "And if I ever catch you again with that snide look on your face . . ."

BOTH MARSHALL AND I have kept the scratched-up photo of ourselves that had been clipped to the iron lung at Grady Hospital. On the back of Marshall's, Mother wrote our father's final words to his three-year-old son: "Love your mommy, take care of your brother, and live for Jesus."

Ever after, Marshall bore weighty burdens: his father's name and reputation, a solemn deathbed charge, Mother's Hannah-like vow. All through elementary and high school he valiantly tried. He was the pious son, lecturing other kids on why they shouldn't dance or frequent movie theaters. He resigned from the marching band because they played jazzy music and the girls wore short skirts.

Like most big brothers, mine dominated, excelling in intelligence, musical talent, and athleticism—not to mention spirituality—and I meekly accepted my underdog status. Yet nothing quite worked out for Marshall. When I skipped the second grade, he resented it because he knew he should have been the one. Teachers complained to Mother that although he was their brightest student, he didn't apply himself. Marshall brushed aside their complaints: "Einstein flunked the third grade. President Kennedy had lousy report cards."

But Mother accepted no excuses. "You're plain irresponsible," she told him again and again. "Your problem is, you don't think! You have no common sense."

She had good supporting evidence. One day when she knew she'd be working late, she wrote out instructions for dinner. "Take potpies out of box. Slit the crust. Place on cookie sheet. Heat oven to 400 degrees. Cook for 35 minutes." When she arrived home the trailer was broiling, with the oven door yawning open like a dragon's mouth. "You didn't tell me to close the oven door," Marshall protested.

For much of our upbringing, Marshall and I had an uneasy alliance. We argued, we competed, we sometimes snitched on each other. Everything changed after the incident with Mother and the tennis racket. From then on, we banded together as comrades and confidants.

THE SAME HIGH school that opens new worlds for me fosters an eccentric streak in Marshall. He chooses odd friends, such as Billy Picklesimar, who gets ridiculed for his name, and Malcolm, the tough little guy who eats live grasshoppers and has a KKK uncle. Marshall will try anything. He drinks sixty-three glasses of water in one day just to see what will happen. He perfects the art of catching flies with his bare hand, and kills hundreds of them in the church building across from our trailer. He develops a fascination with bats, possibly because of their fly-catching prowess.

Although he cuts a handsome figure—tall and with dark, curly hair—Marshall cares nothing about appearance. He wears loud, mismatched clothes, most of which he gets from the Philadelphia church's missionary barrel. For some reason, he has an aversion to brushing his teeth. As a child he would hold his toothbrush under running water to pretend he was brushing. He pays dearly as a junior in high school when our quack dentist pulls all twelve of his remaining upper teeth, without Novocain.

"He's no dummy, he knows what he's doing," Mother argues that night, as Marshall nurses his sore jaw and grumbles about having to wear false teeth. "Besides, now you won't have any more cavities." The false teeth make a definite improvement—he no longer has to hold his hand over his mouth to cover the cavities and blank spaces—though the dentures are so poorly made, a dental student later will ask him to donate them to the Emory Medical Museum. The dentures also force him to abandon the trumpet in favor of the piano.

As I pour myself into high school activities, Marshall channels his energy into spirituality. He reads Mother's books about the Victorious Christian Life and earnestly strives to attain the elusive "life on the highest plane." Unlike me, he feels no embarrassment over the school's YFC club, and in fact volunteers to serve as its president. Far more diligent than I, he carries the big red YFC Bible on top of his schoolbooks as a visual witness. Whenever someone compliments him on his piano playing, he responds, "It's not me, it's the Lord."

Marshall gives up baseball cards and Monopoly for being too worldly, though he continues to go bowling. His senior year, he regales me with stories about his new girlfriend, who has transferred to Gordon High from a private boarding school in Virginia. Natalie is sophisticated and sarcastic, and Marshall's spiritual intensity attracts her. He persuades her to give up makeup and roller-skating, but feels guilty every time they hold hands or kiss. When he suggests they avoid all physical contact, she balks. A few days later he gets a card in the mail that reads, "You take the worry out of getting close." Natalie has put a quick and painful end to my brother's first true romance.

High school presents little intellectual challenge for Marshall. Friends call him "the Walking Encyclopedia" because he remembers most of what he has read in the Britannica volumes. The various steps in solving algebra and math problems seem to him a waste of time; he goes right to the bottom-line answer. He spends class periods playing chess on note cards passed furtively across the aisles. In Latin, he translates passages in advance and then pretends to read, haltingly, to make it sound spontaneous.

Some of the faculty try to engage Marshall. His Latin teacher prods him to apply for a scholarship to the University of Georgia. One evening Mr. Pickens, his favorite, drives him to hear the famous conservative thinker Russell Kirk. Marshall comes home excited and wakes me up to announce, "I've just realized that until tonight I've never had an independent thought!" I tell him to turn out the light and go to bed, and never do hear about that first independent thought.

BORED BY HIGH school, Marshall starts taking music more seriously. One day he tries explaining to me the different moods of key signatures, as if they have emotions. "Listen to this in G major—don't you think of sunlight and summer? Compare that to a passage in F minor. It sounds gloomy, like a storm." I nod, humoring him.

The green piano in our trailer has only sixty-four keys, missing twelve on each end, which suits our crowded living room. For more demanding pieces, Marshall retreats to the concrete-block Sunday School building next door, where at least he can practice on a full keyboard. On those two shabby instruments, the perennial underachiever begins to display the talent of a prodigy.

One day I am sitting at the piano in our trailer, muddling through my Czerny exercises, when Marshall stops me. "Play a note, any note," he says.

I plop my finger on a random key. "F-sharp?" he asks.

"How'd you know that!? Were you looking?"

"No, no, try it again."

Making sure to block his view with my body, I plunk down another key, and another. He identifies the notes correctly every time. When I put my fingers down on any ten discordant notes, he rattles them off in sequence.

We make a game of it. "What's the dial tone on a telephone?" I ask. He picks up our rotary-dial phone and guesses a combination of F and A above middle C. Only one person in ten thousand has absolute pitch, and my brother somehow got the gift. He practices identifying car horns and sirens, and tracks the Doppler effect of train whistles.

Marshall also possesses a near-perfect memory. He can hear a complex piece of music on the radio and later sit down and reproduce it. Watching these feats, I gain a new level of respect for my brother. His talent seems to me Mozartean, the kind before which you bow. I have read of Beethoven's slovenliness and of Liszt's eccentricity—could my "irresponsible" brother actually be a genius?

His junior year in high school, Marshall enters a piano contest at a YFC conference in Jacksonville, Florida, and is overwhelmed by the quality of the competition. Inspired, he directs all his energy toward a singular goal—mastering the piano—and signs on with a new, advanced teacher. Day after day Marshall practices after school, rocking our trailer or the Sunday School room with his scales and lightning-fast chords.

For the following year's competition he chooses variations on the hymn "Come Thou Fount of Every Blessing." His composition begins in the upper registers, a simple statement of the melody played with two fingers. Then it flows into a grand exposition that has his fingers running up and down the keyboard before concluding with a series of stately chords. I can hardly believe my brother composed such a work.

How many times do I hear that rendition of the hymn as he practices?

> Come, thou Fount of every blessing,
> tune my heart to sing thy grace;
> streams of mercy, never ceasing,
> call for songs of loudest praise.
> Teach me some melodious sonnet,
> sung by flaming tongues above.

In Jacksonville, Marshall places but does not win, so he redoubles his efforts. At the end of that summer, he is asked to perform during the offertory at Maranatha Tabernacle in Philadelphia. I sit in the pew, nervous and proud, as my brother plays the simple part in the first movement, knowing the forte passages that will follow.

Without warning, the pastor stands up and says, "Thank you, Marshall," assuming he has finished the piece. My brother slouches back to his seat, humiliated.

To the dismay of his teachers, Marshall doesn't apply to any universities or music schools, instead yielding to Mother's mandate that he attend a Bible college in the adjacent state of South Carolina. "It's not worth fighting her," he tells me. "It'll get me out of here, and then I'll probably transfer someplace else."

In September, Mother and I drive him to the campus. I help him carry boxes of clothes and books up the stairs to his room in the men's dorm. "I hope you like it," I say, and give him an awkward hug. I feel suddenly alone. "Don't forget about me back at home."

"You'll do fine," he says. "You spend so much time at school, you're not home much anyway."

Mother says little on the four-hour drive back to Atlanta, but I notice she's driving very slowly. "I think there's a minimum speed on interstate highways," I say. "Maybe that's why those cars are flashing their lights and honking."

"Since when did you become an expert on driving?" she fires back. "You're not even old enough to have a license." I keep quiet on the rest of the trip.

That very month, Mother decides we have to move. There's some kind of power struggle going on at Faith Baptist Church, and she's on a different side than the pastor's. "I just can't stay here with all that tension," she says. The church is splitting, and most of her friends are leaving.

One of those friends makes available a rental property at minimal cost, and we move into a house, a real suburban home with wood floors and a carport and a fenced-in backyard. The trailer stays behind. In my senior year of high school, no longer do I have to use Eugene Crowe's house as a decoy to conceal where I live.

In a new place, with Marshall gone, I have hope that family life will finally change. It does, though not in the way I expect. Mother's moods prove as fickle as the weather. Sometimes she is cheerful and happy, other times petulant and angry. *Who are you angry at, Mother?* I wonder. *Your husband, who abandoned you? God, who double-crossed you? Your sons, who can never please you?*

Often the old silence descends, and I don't even have Marshall to talk to. He means more to me now that he lives two hundred miles away than he did when we shared a bedroom.

I am deep into my let-nothing-affect-me project, and home puts it to a daily test. Often, as I lie sleepless in bed late at night, I hear from down the hall the muted sound of Mother weeping. I lie there helpless, not knowing what to do. I feel a tug of pity, remembering her hard life: my father's death and, before that, the years in a row house with my stern grandmother.

The next morning I try to be nice, only to find that she has hardened overnight. She sniffles as she stirs the oatmeal on the stove, the metal spoon clanking loudly against the pot.

"What's wrong, Mother?"

"What's wrong? I'm dead, child! My brain's not working! I teach all week, then drive a nursery school bus. You couldn't possibly understand—women have these moods. The pressures I'm under—bills, the church mess, your brother . . . I'm dead! Nobody knows what I put up with. You two are driving me to a nervous breakdown."

The rest of that day, whatever I say makes things worse. If I mention a debate meet coming up or a practice session for a play: "You're never around! You're always gone!" If I suggest a shorter route to school: "I don't care what the map says, son, I know the best way to get there. When are you going to learn to listen?" I feel like a Russian political prisoner called before a judge, knowing in advance that I will be condemned but with no idea what I've done wrong.

In Marshall's absence, I have become the sole target, the outlet for her stormy emotions. I feel trapped, like one of my beetles that can't escape the specimen jar. Unlike Marshall, I don't even try to fight. I fall back on my habit of hunkering down, masking, blocking emotions before I feel them.

IT'S OUR FAULT, mine and Marshall's, that Mother didn't remarry. She made that clear when we were young: "I knew you boys would never accept a different daddy. I wouldn't do that to you." Now she has to slave from morning till night, to keep the household running. And how do we repay her? By slacking off on household chores. By playing tennis instead of practicing our music lessons. By doing stupid things like playing touch football with a broken arm. We leave lights on and the toilet seat up.

The memories sting like paper cuts. I resolve to work harder around the house, and take on Marshall's chores now that he's away. Nothing helps. I go away for a debate tournament, missing the weekly lawn care, and return to find Mother in the front yard on her knees, cutting the grass with a pair of scissors.

Sometimes at night she stands outside my closed door, sniffling again, though with a different tone. "I know I'm not the greatest mother in the world, but I've tried my best, son, really I have. You hear? Maybe I'll just move back to Philadelphia and take care of your uncle Jimmy. Or find some old folks' home. Maybe one day you'll come home and I won't be here. Then you'll know how hard things are. You'll be sorry, when it's too late."

I lie in the darkness, holding my arms across my chest, squeezing tight. *I can't let myself feel. I have to not-feel.*

I want to get away, like Marshall. Only, I want to go to a real college, as the school counselor keeps urging me, not some rinky-dink Bible college. When I won the fellowship at the CDC, Mother acted like I had committed a sin. "You're not ready for a job like that. I should never have let you skip that grade." At the beginning of my senior year, an English teacher confides to me that I have a chance to be the class valedictorian. When I tell Mother, she doesn't even react.

Slowly it sinks in that nothing that Marshall or I do will please Mother, that our lives are a stabbing reminder of her own failed dreams and especially *the* dream—the vow—she had for us. It dawns on me, *that's* why she's so insistent about the Bible college. She can feel us slipping away.

We tiptoe around everything except the truth: that one of her sons has left and the other is counting the days, that she has lost control, and that we will never replace her husband and are incapable of meeting her needs.

I sometimes see in her face a look of fear and loss. I try to think like her—a disillusioned widow and parent. I soon give up. I can only think like me.

One thing becomes clear, though. If this is the Victorious Christian Life—if this is what a person who hasn't sinned in decades looks like—then I want no part of it.

EVERY FEW WEEKS I get a letter from Marshall, written with a fountain pen in his trademark turquoise ink. He seems genuinely happy.

At the Bible college, his gifts were recognized at once. He took a music test required of all freshmen, and the professor announced the results: "One student got 199 of the 200 questions correct. He only missed one question about popular music." Regardless, Marshall still has to enroll in the basic music-appreciation class; this college runs by rules.

Immediately, Marshall falls in love with the glorious nine-foot Steinway in the school chapel, which has a sound and touch like no piano he has played. Other students wander in and sit in the back rows just to hear him practice. To earn money, he signs on to accompany voice students, who are taught by a barrel-chested tenor in a run-down building at the bottom of a steep hill. The voice teacher finds to his delight that his new accompanist can play anything, in any key, with or without music.

One Sunday, Marshall volunteers to fill in as the pianist for a church service. "Brothers and sisters," the host pastor announces, "I want you to choose a hymn, and our guest pianist will on the spot compose a special arrangement of it." Word gets around, and soon my brother's booked every weekend.

Marshall becomes the main pianist for the school's traveling choir. He and Larry, the choir organist, work up dueling keyboard arrangements for the offertories. One night at a church in Ohio, Marshall discovers that the piano, dragged into the sanctuary from a Sunday School room, is tuned to a pitch one half-note lower than the organ's. "It's the most challenging thing I've ever done," he tells me over Christmas vacation. "I had to transpose everything into a different key one half-note higher, on the fly. It drove me crazy to play the A key, which should be an absolute 440 cycles per second, and hear an A-flat. I had to force myself not to *hear* the music, rather to play it as an exercise in pure mathematics." At last, my brother is a hero.

He plunges into class work with enthusiasm, spurred on by a group of upperclassmen who take pride in their reputation as Hyper-Calvinists—hardcore believers in a sovereign, all-controlling God. That same Christmas he talks up the virtues of Jonathan Edwards's sermon "Sinners in the Hands of an Angry God," which I studied without pleasure in my high school English class. By the end of his freshman year, Marshall has read all two thousand pages of John Calvin's *Institutes of the Christian Religion.*

Even on vacation he studies a set of flash cards to learn Greek and Hebrew vocabulary. "The classes are easy," he says. "When I found out that the school charges a flat tuition rate, I signed up for twenty-seven weekly hours of class time"—almost double the normal load of fifteen hours. It appears, for the moment, that my brother has found his stride.

It is better to ask some of the questions
than to know all the answers.

—James Thurber, "The Scotty Who Knew Too Much"

CHAPTER 18

COLLEGE

During my senior year, I apply to the same Bible college my brother is attending in South Carolina. "Are you sure about this decision?" the high school counselor asks. "With your record here, you could probably get a scholarship to a place like Duke or Davidson."

Her words sorely tempt me. But I've witnessed so many clashes between Marshall and our mother over acceptable colleges that I decide not to fight the inevitable. I figure I can tolerate a Bible college for a couple of years, treating it much like a junior college, and then transfer somewhere else—following in Marshall's footsteps once again. It will give us time together my first year away from home. Besides, a year at this school in 1966 costs less than two thousand dollars, including room and board.

On the four-hour drive to the college for freshman orientation, Mother retreats into one of her dark moods, and we barely speak. All week the scowl on her face has warned me not to act too excited about leaving home. When we arrive on campus, I collect my dorm keys and she stands by the car under a hazy September sky as I move the sum total of my earthly belongings—two suitcases full of clothes, a box of books, and a reel-to-reel tape recorder—into my new home. "Take care, y'hear?" are her last words to me.

From the second-floor window I watch, puzzled, as her car circles the campus three times before disappearing. Years later, I learn that she cried all the way to the Georgia border after dropping me off. At the time I have no way of seeing behind her stern mask.

Not the strained farewell or even the oppressive South Carolina heat can dampen my spirits, however. I feel as if a cage door has swung open. I'm on my own now, free at last.

ON DEBATE TRIPS I've visited colleges where the elevators smell like urine and graffiti covers the walls. Not here. The dorm is spotless and smells like Lysol. To control costs, the college requires all students to accept a work detail. I sign up to clean bathrooms—not a prime assignment, but one that doesn't bother me after my summer job on a garbage truck.

Soon I meet my roommate, Bob, a graduate of a boarding school in Asheville, who has two main interests in life, girls and soccer. As he changes clothes after a workout, he catches me staring at his socks. "Yeah, I wear garters," he explains. "It's the only way I've found to hold up my socks. You can see how soccer practice has thickened my calves." I nod, as if all my friends wear garters.

That first night, many of the guys in our freshman class gather on an outdoor patio to get acquainted. One by one they speak, introducing themselves. An older student tells us about his life of sin in the navy, when he had a woman in every port. "I'm thrilled to enter a college where we're sharing our faith in Christ together rather than having a beer party," he says. "I've tasted that life, and it leads nowhere." Another freshman thanks God for a wealthy Christian businessman in Florida, who found him living in a rat-infested shack in an orange grove and offered to pay his way to the Bible college.

I stand at the edge of the group, wondering if I should jump in.

Surrounded by eager Christians, I have that old feeling of splitness. Part of me wants to belong and part of me wants to flee this place. But the best way to fit into a Christian college, I decide, is to act like a Christian—a routine I know well. After swallowing a couple of times, I, too, give a testimony. "Unlike some of you, I've been a Christian almost all my life," I begin. "But I've strayed from the Lord these last few years." I continue along that line, repeating phrases I have perfected in similar gatherings at summer camp.

When I finish, a stranger standing next to me slips his arm around my shoulders and says, "Bless you, brother. I believe God's going to use you mightily." I feel a wave of approval, quickly followed by an undertow of self-disgust. There I go again, doing whatever it takes to climb the ladder.

Even during orientation week I have the sinking feeling that I don't belong here. The students' smiles seem glued on, their music saccharine, their words predictable. I've heard this spiritualese before. "God provided a car for me" really means *My parents gave me a cool high school graduation gift.* "God closed the door for me to attend a state university" means *I didn't get accepted.* "I missed the bus today . . . Well, the Lord must have a reason for it." *Maybe you should set your alarm next time instead of blaming God.*

When my brother arrives a few days later, he introduces me to a few of his upperclassmen friends, who laugh when I confess my skeptical attitude. "Think of life on campus as a kind of game," they say. "It has its own language and its own rules. If you want to fit in here, you have to play it. Just go along, don't make too many ripples, and try to survive. There's life after this school. We're just hanging on."

Sometimes I have the unsettling sense that everyone possesses a spiritual secret but me. Other students speak of God as an intimate friend. They seem perfectly content studying the Bible all day, and unquestioningly accept whatever the professors say. More often, I conclude there is no secret, just a learned pattern of conformity, of mimicking others' behavior and parroting the right words.

I begin to find a perverse pleasure in acting as a renegade. I prepare for class by researching questions that might stump the teachers. I stare silently at other students until their faces flush and they turn away. I sit by a girl in the cafeteria and ask, "Do you think you're pretty?" or "Have you ever had sex?" or "What's the worst thing you've ever done?" just to watch the response.

EVERY STUDENT GETS a copy of the college's rule book, which we must read and sign. Its sixty-six pages make for a perfect setup: "Hey, we get a page of rules for each of the books in the Bible!" The college sees itself as a substitute parent for its students and a strict parent at that. Forbidden activities include bowling, dancing, playing cards, billiards, skating at public rinks, movies, boxing, wrestling, and "the presentation of opera and musical programs which include ballet, dancing, and suggestive songs."

In a series of required meetings, the dean of men reinforces the code. "We take these rules very seriously," he says. "Each of them is based on a biblical principle, and all of you have signed your willingness to abide by them while you're on campus." The prohibition of facial hair and restrictions on men's hair length seem odd to me, since our textbooks depict Jesus, the apostles, and most male saints with flowing hair and beards.

The sixties sexual revolution has swept the culture elsewhere without penetrating this school's airtight environment. "Students must absolutely avoid holding hands, embracing, kissing, and other physical contacts," reads the rule book. To limit temptation, underclassmen are allotted two dates a week—double dates, of course—and one of these must be to a church service. Apart from that, even students engaged to be married can "socialize" just once per day, during the evening meal in the cafeteria. Otherwise, no casual conversation between couples is allowed. No phone contact either.

Female students have even stricter standards. The rules forbid slacks on women, except for certain activities when slacks are permitted if worn *under a skirt*. My freshman year, coeds' skirts must extend below the knee. Staff members stand in the lobby of the women's dorm to scout for scofflaws, making suspects kneel on the floor for a more accurate check.

The school treats sex as something radioactive. As Valentine's Day approaches, a classmate who works in the school office tells me about a bizarre scene she has just witnessed: the dean of women in white gloves individually censoring the tiny heart-shaped candies to be used as decorations for a party. *You're mine, Friends forever, Be my Valentine* pass muster; *Cutie pie, Hot lips, Love ya* go right into the trash can.

Despite the school's best attempts, American culture is changing too fast for the rule makers to keep pace. Over the next two years— the miniskirt era—the acceptable skirt length for women students creeps up to mid-knee and then to the top of the knee. As for male students, Billy Graham steers some of his long-haired "Jesus people" to the school. To their consternation, these new converts are met by deans who order them to a barbershop and confiscate their record albums.

Students are supposed to avoid any music not "consistent with a Christian testimony," a phrase open to much interpretation. Though I still prefer classical music, I sometimes listen to tapes of Simon and Garfunkel or the Beatles in the privacy of my headphones. Elsewhere, rock 'n' roll is taking over the airwaves, and during my freshman year a visiting speaker, Bob Larson, spends several days on campus lecturing on its dangers.

A musician himself, Larson stands in front of the chapel with a shiny electric guitar and plucks a few loud chords to demonstrate the threat we face. According to him, the vibrations permanently alter the medulla oblongata at the base of the human brain. He quotes the manager of the Beatles, who says about his band, "Only Hitler ever duplicated their power over crowds."

Bob Larson's visit sparks an antirock revival. One night, I come across a bonfire in the center of campus. Scores of students are smashing their records and throwing them into the flames. I plead with one zealous young student to please not throw his classical albums into the fire. "They don't glorify God," he says, tossing Beethoven and Brahms on top of the melting vinyl of Elvis Presley and the Rolling Stones.

After a few months I get accustomed to the cloistered environment of the Bible college. It begins to seem almost normal—until I return home for a vacation break. On the streets of Atlanta I see braless women in miniskirts, angry protests against the Vietnam War, and civil rights marches with students raising their fists in a Black Power salute. I experience an abrupt culture shock, not unlike what an Amish person must feel visiting Times Square.

At my grandparents' house I flip through the photos in *Look* and *Life* magazines and see a civil rights leader's bleeding head, housing projects ablaze, cops beating hippies, and a naked young girl screaming from napalm burns. I wonder why no one talks about these things at the Bible college. The United States has sent thousands of young men to their deaths in a Southeast Asian jungle, has suffered riots in major cities and universities, and has undergone a sexual revolution, all while we Bible-college students have been debating the fine points of Calvinism and measuring hair and skirt lengths.

MARSHALL LIVES IN a different dorm, which limits our contact. I can tell that the glow of his first year at the Bible college has worn off. One indication: he spends more of his spare time playing Ping-Pong than the piano. "Let's take a walk," I suggest one day. "You don't seem happy."

"No kidding," he says, bitterly. "Joyce just broke up with me. She says I'm not spiritual enough."

We stroll down a paved road to a dirt path that leads to woods I've been exploring. Marshall brings up a recent incident in his speech class. "This school practices a form of thought control," he says. "In this class everybody has to deliver two speeches on any topic they choose. In the first one I argued that dancing should be permissible. In the second I discussed the school's position on rock music. As you know, I can't stand listening to rock, but the school's ban makes no sense. You can't find anything in the Bible about immoral music."

When I show interest, he recaps some of the arguments from his speech. "The church has long opposed whatever's new in music. For instance, in medieval times they wouldn't allow a composer to use the interval tritone—you know, three adjacent whole tones. They called it 'the devil in music.' Yet now we hear it all the time in classical music. Before long we'll probably start hearing rock music in churches and this school will look ridiculous."

For the two speeches he received a D- and an F. Marshall knew he got those grades not because of his preparation or delivery but simply because the teacher disagreed with his opinions. He appealed to the faculty dean, who advised him, "Just choose a topic that won't upset the professor."

"What'd you do?" I ask.

"I gave a speech on servanthood and got an A+."

A few weeks later Marshall tells me he's not sure he's a Christian. He invited a woman on a date to hear the pianist Van Cliburn. Afterward he critiqued the performance, and then the conversation turned more personal. "I'm not sure I'm saved," he admitted. His date led him through a series of verses from the book of Romans, reviewed the Sinner's Prayer (which he knew by heart), and then prayed with him. The next day, he felt no different.

"I don't know what *should* be happening, but I certainly feel no calmness or peace, like people around here describe. I've never had the sensation of being caught up in something supernatural, something greater than myself." He stops himself, adding, "Except in music maybe. But you don't need to be a Christian to feel that. How do you know what's fake and what's real?"

I have no answer for him, because I've been struggling with the same question as long as I can remember. I bring up a recent example: "Remember that chapel service when Tim gave the tearjerker story about his fiancée dying in a car accident on the way to visit him? The whole school's crying and praying for him. Next we learn from his sister back in Atlanta that Tim's a repressed homosexual, was never engaged, and made up the whole story."

Marshall and I part, our doubts unresolved. A short time later, during a chapel service, I'm surprised to see my roommate, Bob, mount the steps and ask the school president if he can take the microphone. Between sobs he confesses his high school sins in more detail than the administration probably appreciates. I'm stunned, having no inkling of his lurid past.

"Though I'm the son of missionaries, I'm just now becoming a Christian," Bob says. He speaks with such authenticity and power that several other students come forward and ask him to pray with them.

A few months later Bob admits to me that he fabricated much of what he said that day—"I just started talking, and all sorts of wild stories came out."

Marshall's question comes back to me. *How do you know what's fake and what's real?*

THE SCHOOL REQUIRES every student to select a Christian Service assignment to support local ministry. Marshall naturally opts to play the piano at nearby churches. I study a list of alternatives that includes chapel services at Fort Jackson, a stint at an institution still called "Home for the Retarded," door-to-door evangelism, and visits to prisons or a juvenile delinquents' facility.

A classmate who owns a 1964 Nash Rambler invites me to join him and a friend on the chain-gang route. "What's that?" I ask.

"Just what it sounds like, prisons for guys who are chained together. Basically, we tool around to some convict work camps and conduct a church service on Sundays. I did it last year. We get to stop for breakfast at some great Southern diners. Oh, and don't worry about security—these guys are chained."

He proves right about the breakfasts. I've never eaten such deliciously unhealthy food: grits and red-eye gravy, salted country ham, chicken-fried steak topped with fried eggs. After stuffing ourselves, we drive to the work camp, and a warden escorts us to the makeshift chapel. "Try to knock some sense into these fellas," he says with a friendly pat on my shoulder.

A guard stands at the door with a loaded shotgun. Inside, I am shocked to see forty Black men dressed in zebra-striped uniforms, each with a chain around his ankle attached to what looks like a cannonball. Every time one of the prisoners shifts positions, his chain clanks with a grating sound.

We students have prepared a series on the Ten Commandments, and as I sit on a bench beside the prisoners, I wonder what in the world I, a sheltered Bible-college teenager, will say to men who have broken more of those commandments than I can even name. Our team wins them over, though, with some rousing music. One of my companions plays an accordion, and the congregation comes alive when he asks if they have any special requests. He knows "Amazing Grace" and "When the Roll Is Called Up Yonder" but has to fake his way through "I'll Fly Away" and "On the Wings of a Snow-White Dove."

After the service the warden lets us mingle with the prisoners, and I hear a side of life I have only read about: drunken fathers, knife fights, moonshining, juke joints, honor killings, police brutality. A career burglar gives me a helpful piece of advice: "Lot of folk leave a light on at night thinkin' they fool us. We ain't fooled. Jes' leave on the bathroom light—that way we never sure if somebody ain't really still up."

NEAR THE END of the school year, Marshall's spiritual crisis deepens. Mother must suspect something, because in her letters she keeps asking me about the state of his soul. He hasn't written her in months, so I'm her only source of news.

His roommate pulls me aside one day. "What's going on with your brother?" he asks. "Last week, during the compulsory time for personal devotions, he looked up from the Bible and said, 'I think this is just a human book.'" At a college with *Bible* in its name, that's nothing short of treason.

Marshall's cynicism soon outstrips my own. One of his classmates tells me about a sophomore chapel in which the students took turns mentioning a "life verse" they had chosen from the Bible. "We heard some typical verses from Proverbs, Romans, and Ephesians. Then your brother stands and with a straight face recites this verse very rapidly: 'At Parbar westward, four at the causeway, and two at Parbar.' It's from 1 Chronicles—he gave the reference. Say it fast, and it sounds like you're speaking in tongues.

"Later, he gave another life verse, from Psalm 137: 'O daughter of Babylon . . . Happy shall he be, that taketh and dasheth thy little ones against the stones.' You think your brother's all right?"

The faculty and staff add Marshall to their urgent prayer list. Two music students whom he accompanies on the piano invite him down the hill to the practice rooms. With a propane heater hissing in the background, they try to exorcize a demon from him. They press their hands on his head and in the name of Jesus command the evil spirit to depart. My brother feels nothing.

In private, Marshall reveals to me that he has adopted a new goal, to break every rule in the school's sixty-six-page rule book. He starts out with simple transgressions: holding hands with a girl, skipping devotions one morning, leaving his bed unmade. After a few weeks, he grows bored and decides to attempt the most iniquitous act of all—drinking alcohol.

Neither Marshall nor I have ever met a Christian who drank, and we've heard dozens of sermons decrying "demon rum." Christians led the campaign for Prohibition, which only lasted fourteen years, but even in the 1960s many counties in rural South Carolina still prohibit the sale of alcohol.

Two jaded upperclassmen agree to assist Marshall with his goal. They tell him, "First, we have to find a source. That's not so easy in this state. It's illegal to have a sign on a liquor store, so they identify themselves by polka dots on the side of the building." After locating a polka-dotted store, they buy a bottle of cheap rosé wine, obtain three cups of ice from a nearby McDonald's, and drive down a dirt road to a secluded spot by the Broad River.

That evening in my dorm room, Marshall fills in the details. "I felt like I was standing on the edge of a cliff, not a river," he says. "You know how Mother thinks—one sip will turn you into a lifelong alcoholic. So my friends pour the wine into paper cups, and let it chill over ice for a few minutes. I'm about to drink certain damnation. I swear, my hands are trembling as I lift the cup to my mouth."

"How did it taste?" I ask.

"Awful. I felt a little light-headed, and my heart seemed to beat faster, probably from the excitement. I drank the whole cup, and then we returned to campus. That was it." The whole experience seemed anticlimactic.

A few nights later, a great weight descends on Marshall, a pang of conviction over the grave sin he has committed. He reports to the dean of men, who listens intently to the account of his misdeed. "You did the right thing, Marshall, coming to me and repenting. I'll decide on an appropriate punishment." Marshall breathes a sigh of relief.

But the dean has more to say. "However, surely you know that your repentance is not complete. I can't accept it fully until you tell me the names of the students who participated with you."

Marshall's stomach seizes up. It's May, mere weeks before graduation. If he discloses the names of those students, both seniors, they'll likely be shipped home from college, their scholastic records purged as if they had never attended the school. The dean ups the ante. "You're not just confessing to me, Marshall. The Holy Spirit is awaiting your full repentance."

When Marshall breaks the news to his partners in crime, they pace their dorm room in a frenzy. "You can't do this to us! It was your idea, not ours. We've spent four years in this place, paid out thousands of dollars. No, you can't do it!" My brother hangs his head in bitter shame.

The next day, one of the two seniors comes up with a plan so outlandish that it just may represent their only hope. He has reread the entire rule book overnight and discovered an astounding fact: nowhere does it mention alcohol. The sin is so self-evident and so heinous that, much like murder or sex with animals, no one has thought of specifying a campus rule against it.

"We have only one defense," the distraught senior announces. "We've got to act like we had no idea some Christians believe drinking is sinful. I know it's a stretch, but think about it—I'm Episcopalian, and the churches I come from serve Communion wine every Sunday. It's sacred. And the Bible refers to wine scores of times, often positively. Our only chance is to convince the dean of our ignorance."

Marshall's two friends call me in that night and walk me through the plan. "We need somebody to role-play the dean. We've got to keep this a secret, and we can trust you to not betray your brother."

Over the next couple of days, the two seniors practice their defense. Like a prosecuting attorney, I try to catch them in inconsistencies and contradictions, until they get the story down pat. As we practice, my brother sits on a dorm bed, holding his head in his hands. Drops of sweat drip from his nose to the floor.

Guilt-ridden, defeated, torn asunder, Marshall makes his way to the dean's office and surrenders the two names. "God bless you, Marshall. Your repentance is complete. I'll assign you twenty-five hours of college service, and you can consider yourself forgiven. I know this must be difficult, but you did the right thing."

That same afternoon the two seniors appear before the dean. They stick to their story, though they can tell from his demeanor that the dean doesn't believe a word of it. He refers them to a faculty committee, which in turn consults with board members. The two seniors take their final exams not knowing whether or not they will receive a diploma at graduation.

By definition, legalists follow the rules. The college concludes it cannot punish someone for breaking a rule that has not been stated. The seniors graduate, the rule book undergoes a revision, and my brother starts filling out applications to transfer to another college.

It is a curious thing, do you know, Cranly said dispassionately,
how your mind is supersaturated with the religion
in which you say you disbelieve.

—James Joyce, *A Portrait of the Artist as a Young Man*

CHAPTER 19
MISFITS

As Marshall plans his escape that summer, I find a job driving a food
truck, affectionately known as "the roach coach." I'm amazed that a
company would entrust their vehicle to a seventeen-year-old college
student and turn me loose in the Atlanta suburbs. The only down-
side: work begins at 5:00 A.M. Before sunrise, I stock one side of the
truck with coffee, soup, and hot sandwiches and the other with cold
sandwiches, snacks, and soft drinks packed in ice.

Drivers work entirely on commission, and since the good routes
are already taken, I bring home almost no income for the first few
weeks. Just as I consider searching for another job, I hit a gold mine.
I notice a new subdivision being developed at the end of a highway
still under construction. There I meet a foreman named Jake, who
offers me a deal.

"Tell you what," Jake says. "I truck in these boys from Athens
every day." He motions to his crew, shirtless Black teenagers sitting
on stacks of lumber. "We're so far out here, I ain't got time for 'em

to go someplace for lunch. If you show up every day at noontime, and keep a runnin' tab on what they order, on payday I'll take it out of their pay and give you the cash."

I sell more food and drinks that day than I've sold in a week. Speaking in a country accent I can barely understand, the ravenous workers order two sandwiches apiece, along with a couple of Cokes, maybe a bowl of Brunswick stew, and a MoonPie or slice of cake for dessert. In the afternoon I return with more cold drinks and snacks. I take note of what they like and stock the truck with extra portions the next morning.

At the end of the week, the white foreman calls over the workers one at a time. "Lucius, time to settle up for your lunches." Jake is paying his workers two dollars an hour, above the minimum wage at the time, and he pulls out four twenty-dollar bills.

I add up Lucius's food bill for the week, totaling $52.64, which I subtract from the twenties. When I put the change in Lucius's hand, he stares at the money and looks up at his boss. "Suh, this all I git?" For five full days he has bounced along for an hour in the back of an open pickup for the privilege of hauling lumber and pounding nails. Now he has $27.36 to show for it.

"'Fraid so, Lucius," Jake answers. "Maybe y'all oughta cut down a bit on your lunches."

Lucius and his friends order just as much the next week and the next, all through the summer. I am charging the fixed prices set by the catering company, and at the end of each week I take home more than two hundred dollars.

That summer gives me an insider's view of injustice. I squirm from guilt every Friday night as I tally my profits, knowing they amount to far more than those kids made digging ditches, mixing concrete, and hammering studs together under a white-hot Georgia sun. Each new week, I do it again. I have to, I rationalize, in order to pay my tuition bills—for a Bible college.

MARSHALL, STILL REELING from the wine-drinking incident, spends much of the summer applying to other schools. He sets his sights on

Wheaton College, an elite Christian school near Chicago. "It has a conservatory of music, so that's my first choice," he tells me. "I missed the application deadline, but there's a chance they'll let me in as a hardship case."

He adds a caution, "Whatever you do, don't discuss it with Mother. She'll freak, and it may not work out, anyway."

Then comes one of those pivotal days that begins like any other but alters a life forever.

I return home from my job on the catering truck to find Marshall sitting at the kitchen table going through the day's mail. He looks up, waves an opened envelope, and grins like he's just won the lottery. "You won't believe it!" he crows. "Not only did they accept me, they're offering me a scholarship."

"Hey, congratulations," I say. "You got your number one choice. I hear Wheaton's a great school. And it's Christian—surely Mother won't object."

I could not be more wrong. That evening, the three of us eat dinner around the dining-room table. Marshall says little as I describe my day's adventures on the route. I can tell he's churning inside. Just as we finish eating, Marshall brings up the letter. "So, I got some good news today," he says in a nervous voice. "Wheaton accepted me and gave me financial aid."

Mother reacts quickly, as if she's mentally rehearsed this discussion. She knew he was looking to transfer somewhere, and he'd mentioned Wheaton in passing.

"I'd rather you go to some place like *Harvard*," she says in a low, gruff voice, pronouncing the name with contempt. "There, they don't even pretend to believe in God. Wheaton claims to, but they're liberal. They use the same words we do, but they don't really mean 'em. They're apostate, son. You're as likely to lose your faith there as at any secular university—maybe more likely."

Marshall takes the bait. "Get serious. Wheaton's a Christian college, it's just not as narrow-minded as some others. Didn't Billy Graham attend there?"

Wrong answer. Her voice rises: "Yeah, and look at him. Inviting liberals and Catholics onto his platform, meeting with the pope, talkin' about someday visiting Russia. That's exactly what I mean!"

Sensing a storm, I retreat to a sofa to watch the two of them spar. Mother chews on her thumb, and I can see a tendon working in her jaw, a telltale sign of her anger. "How d'ya plan to pay for it? Money doesn't grow on trees, and I certainly won't help you. And how are you gonna get yourself up there—you don't have a car."

Marshall explains about the scholarship, and about his friend Larry, who has agreed to drive all the way from Boston to Atlanta in order to give him a ride to Wheaton. "Larry and I play duets together. He was the choir organist and I played the piano. Now he's also transferring from Bible college to the Conservatory. Maybe we can be roommates."

Mother's eyes contract, and her face contorts into a fierce, wild look that I have never seen before. She spits out the words. "Let me tell you something, son. Nobody's going to drive you to Wheaton. You're not yet twenty-one, and in this state that makes you a minor. Mrs. Barnes from church works for a federal judge. I'll get him to slap a warrant for kidnapping charges on anybody who carries you across state lines."

She pauses, staring him down. "You think I'm kidding? I'll do it. Just try me."

Marshall does not yield. "Then I'll fly. What's he going to do, issue a warrant against Delta Air Lines?"

Silence descends as Mother contemplates the next threat. Her jaw tendon twitches faster, though her facial expression does not change.

When she speaks, the words come in a burst of fury. "Make fun of me if you want. I'll do whatever it takes to stop you, young man. You listen to me. If you find a way to pull off this plan, I guarantee you one thing. I'll pray every day for the rest of your life that God will break you. Maybe you'll be in a terrible accident and die. That'll teach you. Or, better yet, maybe you'll be paralyzed. Then you'll have to lie on your back and stare at the ceiling and realize what a rebellious thing you've done, going against God's will and everything you've been brought up to believe."

Her words hang in the room like a cloud of poison gas. Once released, it cannot be put back in the canister. Marshall pushes away from the table, scraping his chair so hard it leaves marks on the floor. He heads toward his bedroom, and a few seconds later I hear the slam of a door.

I keep my head down, pretending to read a magazine. My vision blurs, and a quickened pulse throbs in my temples. *Be still, my heart* is the only thought I can form.

In the tense quiet that follows, I picture my father, lying motionless in an iron lung, staring at fluorescent lights overhead. *I'll pray every day that God will break you*—she would pray for *that*?

DOZENS, SCORES OF times in ensuing years, my brother and I have replayed that scene together. We recall the same vivid details: the prominent "W" on the acceptance letter lying atop a pile of junk mail, the cold hard words coming from a face twisted in rage. Yet we always disagree about one crucial point, what our mother actually said after the words *better yet*.

I remember the threat of paralysis, while Marshall remembers a different version: "Or, better yet, maybe you'll lose your mind." Those words embedded in him ever after, like barbed wire pressing into a tree's heartwood. To this day, I believe my brother's subconscious has backfilled his memory of her threat with what actually happened at Wheaton.

THE FAMILY SILENCES grow longer that summer. In order to avoid the tension at home, I find excuses to work late on my catering job. Marshall takes a minimum-wage job as an orderly at Grady Hospital, cleaning bedpans and saving every penny for college. He deliberately asks for the evening shift, and sleeps late, to avoid contact with Mother.

Mother refuses to fill out the financial-assistance forms required of parents, which Wheaton graciously disregards. She also makes good on her promise to block Marshall's friend Larry from transporting him. In the end, our uncle Winston drives my brother to the airport to catch a flight to Chicago. At Marshall's age, he had hitchhiked all the way to California, and thought it would do his nephew good to see more of the country. Plus, as he told Marshall, "You've got a chance to become the first Yancey in our line to graduate from college."

Bereft of my main companion, I return to the Bible college as a sophomore. I hang around Marshall's friends, most of whom seem envious of his transfer. By now I've abandoned any effort to play the Christian game. Perhaps my brother's cynicism has proved contagious.

In high school I knew how to compete: by working hard and using my brain. At this place, intelligence seems like a negative.

Bible classes stir up questions for me. What are we supposed to make of all the violence in the Old Testament: Elisha calling on bears to maul his tormentors, Joshua's genocide against the Canaanites, God's deadly punishment of people who make a simple mistake? And should we believe John's account of the Resurrection or Matthew's—which of the conflicting details can we trust? When I raise such questions in class, other students look on me as a heckler intent on destroying party unity or a germ that has broken through the immune barrier.

More and more, I accept the general opinion of me as a "bad seed." Ostracism I don't mind. I have years of experience in turtling down under a hard shell, resisting pressures to conform. I simply can't swallow some of what goes on at this school.

Take Mr. S., son of a U.S. congressman and a legend on campus. He attended the Bible college in its early days and now is a revered professor. He gazes straight ahead and at the top of his lungs shouts his lectures, which are usually held in the school chapel to accommodate all his students. He seems almost robotic, waving his arms and speaking in a rhythmic cadence, with a Southern accent like the one I've been trying to overcome.

"Some people ask me, 'Frank, what's yo' favrit book in the Bible?' I tell them, mah favrit book in the Bible is the book I'm studyin' rat now. And mah favrit chaptuh in the Bible is the chaptuh I'm studyin' rat now. And my favrit vus in the Bible is the vus I'm studyin' rat now."

Or he starts down the alphabet: "Jesus Christ is the alpha and the omega. That means Jesus Christ is the A, Jesus Christ is the B, Jesus Christ is the C . . ." To my astonishment, he goes through all twenty-six letters.

From taking his Old Testament survey course my freshman year, I know it is impossible to derail Mr. S. unless you sit directly in front of him and wave your arms like a person in distress—which I do, regularly. Only then might he tolerate a question. No professor frustrates me more, because Mr. S. has the most extreme views of anyone on campus. He lambastes Catholics. He opposes the J. B. Phillips version of the Bible because Phillips had a friendship with C. S. Lewis, who drank beer and smoked a pipe. He refuses to read the Sunday or Monday newspapers since producing them obligates employees to work on Sunday.

Like most of the Bible-college staff, Mr. S. seems uptight about sex. Married for twenty-five years, he nevertheless directs his wife to sit as far away from him as possible on the car's bench seat, lest someone who doesn't know they are married draw the wrong conclusion from their physical closeness. He disposes of his stock in a department store chain because it sells swimsuits, which goes against his convictions about "mixed bathing." In a baleful tone of voice, he warns the virginal girls in class, "When you wear lipstick, you are saying to the world, 'Kiss me! Kiss me!'"

Some of his views make the administration nervous, though they tolerate Mr. S. as an icon and alumni favorite. Besides everything else, I oppose his style of teaching. He insists, "Sophistication is the greatest barrier to the Holy Spirit," and perhaps for that reason he gives us inane busywork assignments. Every day we complete fill-in-the-blank questions in a 250-page notebook. Not even my high school would use such antiquated methods.

My freshman year, I worked at least an hour each night on my notebook—more time than anyone I knew. Yet Mr. S. gave me a B. Was he punishing me for asking questions in class? I scheduled an appointment with him and asked, "I'd like to know what criteria you use in grading the notebooks, because I want to improve in the future."

A stack of more than two hundred of the thick black notebooks towered behind his desk. Somehow he'd managed to grade them in a mere three days. Mr. S. smiled and answered, with a tone of utter confidence, "The Holy Spirit tells me what grade each notebook deserves." I couldn't argue with that.

But during my sophomore year, my new roommate sees my copious notebooks and thinks, *Why should I do all this work?* Unbeknownst to me, he changes the identifying sheet at the front and submits my notebook as his own. This time Mr. S. awards a grade of A+. My suspicion is confirmed. I doubt that the Holy Spirit would reward a cheater.

ANOTHER PROFESSOR, MR. S.'s opposite in style and temperament, is the most beloved figure on campus. A shy, painfully introverted man, Mr. H. assumes a different persona when he stands before a classroom. "Look up heah," he begins, moistening his lips with a sideways flick of the tongue, and proceeds to captivate students no matter what he teaches. His classes on child psychology, the Prophets, and biblical hermeneutics, or interpretations, are among the school's most popular.

One day Mr. H. approaches the podium in chapel as the scheduled speaker. He stands there for a moment, looking out over the gathered faculty and students. He clears his throat, moistens his lips, and says, "All week I've been listening for a word from the Lord. I never got one. You're dismissed." Then he sits down, leaving the entire assembly stunned. We file out in silence.

After that, I like Mr. H. very much.

He alludes to deep wounds from childhood, which he never spells out. Whatever their source, those wounds keep him from teaching a formulaic faith. Believing Mr. H. is a person I can trust with my growing frustrations about the school, I ask for a personal appointment in his office.

"I don't think I belong here," I tell him. "People treat me like some kind of deviant, but to tell you the truth, the school itself seems a little sick to me." He shows no sign of surprise, and nods for me to continue.

"I don't see much grace on this campus. Some of us are upset about the way the school handled Dan's death." (The previous year, a junior had drowned in a nearby river when a dam release unexpectedly raised the water level.) "Did you know that students openly said in class that Dan drowned as God's punishment for swimming on Sunday? Teachers didn't contradict them either. And then the administration slapped a work penalty on his companion for breaking the rules—a guy who was traumatized over losing his best friend."

He keeps listening, so I keep talking. "We hear all this stuff about the Victorious Christian Life, but it seems to me it just sets up a kind of self-righteousness competition. Students give fake testimonies to appear more spiritual. Professors dismiss C. S. Lewis because of a silly thing like smoking a pipe. And I think you're aware of what the dean put my brother through last year over drinking a cupful of wine.

"I never hear the administration admit they're wrong about anything, even though you and I both know they've made some bad decisions. Rules get changed every year, but the deans never acknowledge the previous rules were arbitrary—they're couched in all this talk of biblical principles. No one challenges the extreme views of a Bob Larson or Mr. S. And that Bible professor who was reported by female students—he simply disappeared, with no explanation. To me it looks like a cover-up."

Mr. H. removes his glasses and rubs his bald head. He hasn't said a word, not once interrupting me. I wonder if I've gone too far.

"I guess what I'm trying to say is that I don't experience any grace here. There's authority and control and high ideals. But not much room for error and not much place for somebody who thinks out-side the party line."

He rocks his desk chair, waiting a while before speaking. "You're right, we've made some mistakes," he says at last. "We're ordinary people here. We're not perfect." His soft tone of voice helps me relax.

We talk for almost an hour, and I feel relieved just having some-one to vent to. One thing that he says sticks with me: "Perhaps the grace is here, and you don't have the receptors to receive it." From any other professor, I would have resented the suggestion, but not from Mr. H.

Perhaps so, I think, as I walk back to the dorm. What is it that tempts me to see the worst in people? Perhaps I'm as much at fault as the school.

A few days later I am sitting in chapel. The school requires stu-dents to attend services daily, with no absences excused apart from illness. This is one of the most anticipated chapels of the year, a visit by Anthony Rossi, owner of Tropicana. An immigrant from Sicily, Rossi has built Tropicana into the world's largest supplier of fresh orange juice, a company ultimately purchased by PepsiCo. We know him as one of the college's major benefactors, a generous man who sends refrigerated trucks to our school direct from Florida. Every week when the truck pulls up, students dash out to help unload boxes of orange and grapefruit juice, which the cafeteria serves at breakfast in unlimited supply.

Anthony Rossi is a school hero. If he spends his chapel time read-ing from Leviticus in Sicilian, we'll give him a standing ovation. We sit quietly, listening to his message delivered in a thick-tongued accent.

Of all the things he could talk about that day, Rossi chooses his greatest failure. One year when an early freeze damaged the crop, he tells us, he illegally dumped sugar into the orange-juice vats to sweeten it—and got caught. He paid hefty fines, and competitors almost drove him out of business. He was humbled by the ordeal, his Christian reputation ruined for a time. But he says he learned more from that blunder than from any of his successes.

In my time at the Bible college, I'll end up hearing several hundred chapel talks. Only two speakers stand out to me: Mr. H. and Anthony Rossi, the only two to admit failure and weakness.

AFTER A CLASS on the Gospels, I conclude that Marshall and I both represent the stony ground described in one of Jesus's parables. Our soil has been baked hard—overexposure to the sun, maybe—and the seeds of faith that fall on us don't take root.

I'm convinced I'll never become a model Bible-college student, which leaves me two options for my remaining time here: I can fake it as a loyal hypocrite or live authentically as a truthful traitor. I choose the latter.

In a sort of reverse-silent-witness, I sit outdoors and read provocative books, such as Harvey Cox's *The Secular City* and Bertrand Russell's *Why I Am Not a Christian*. I take secret satisfaction in my reputation as the antitype of the ideal student. I don't care what others say or think about me. In fact, a devious part of me enjoys the estrangement.

I keep to the margins, flaunting authority just enough to cause irritation but not enough to prompt serious retribution. I begin reading magazines, *Time* and *Esquire,* during chapel. As speakers exposit the Bible, I brush up on the Tet Offensive, the My Lai massacre, and the Prague Spring in Czechoslovakia. Within a few days one of the attendance takers in the balcony reports me, and I receive a summons to see the dean, the same man who nailed my brother for drinking.

"It's come to my attention that you've been reading magazines during chapel," he begins.

"That's right, sir. I have been." A look of surprise crosses his face at my ready admission. But he doubles down.

"We put a lot of planning into these chapels with the intent that students learn from the wisdom of the speakers," he says.

"I understand, and you should know that I've mastered the ability to listen to the speaker and read magazines at the same time."

Evidently the dean has not heard the multitasking defense before, because he sits back in his chair and strokes his chin for a while before responding. "What about the speaker? Surely he can see you reading magazines as he's talking."

"Good point, sir. If you'd like, I'll gladly explain the situation to the chapel speaker beforehand."

That conversation, unlike some others, ends in a draw. Soon a friendly professor lets me know that my name has landed on a faculty committee's special-prayer list. I now rank among the deviants, just like my brother.

It's time to flee the nest. I fill out an application to transfer to Marshall's new home, Wheaton College. Now I need only survive the rest of this school year.

As I STRUGGLE at the Bible college, Marshall is exulting in his newfound freedom at Wheaton. He has arrived during one of the most contentious times in the school's history. Every few weeks he sends me a copy of the school newspaper, which editorializes against the Vietnam War and reports on student protests against mandatory ROTC training. One dissident student has begun standing on the steps of Edman Chapel with a bullhorn, giving instant rebuttals to objectionable chapel messages.

Marshall proves to be a surprisingly faithful correspondent. Each week I get a turquoise-ink letter written in a tiny spidery script, around five hundred barely legible words to a page. And each epistle records a new intellectual adventure.

In one letter he says that at last he has come to accept a rational basis for Christianity, though he doubts he'll ever experience God's reality at an emotional level. Within a few more weeks, he has read a dozen books by atheistic existentialists and concluded that suicide is the only honest response to a meaningless existence.

The next letter reports that he's attending a High Episcopal church, entranced by the artistry and the liturgy. "Maybe I'll try Catholic," he writes. Then comes an enthusiastic account of his campaigning for presidential candidate Eugene McCarthy in the Polish wards of Milwaukee (this from a former fan of Barry Goldwater).

In a rare phone call, Marshall tells me of a weeklong visit to Wheaton by Francis Schaeffer, a speaker from Switzerland, who dresses in knickers, like an alpine hiker. "He's a bit strange, but he knows a lot about modern culture. He quotes Sartre and Camus and refers to the films of Fellini and Bergman. We're not used to that around here."

Marshall mentions that he had a chance to ask some of his questions in private after one of Schaeffer's talks. "You say the Bible is a living Word, and God speaks to people directly through it?"

"Absolutely," Schaeffer replied.

"Then how can you tell the difference between the Bible and, say, Billy Graham or Norman Vincent Peale?"

Schaeffer's answer—"You just know it"—failed to satisfy him.

Marshall's next letter is the most surprising of all. In the school newspaper he sends me, I've read about an authoritarian, almost cultic church frowned on by the college authorities. Out of curiosity, Marshall arranged a visit. "Praise God!" his letter begins. "It happened—I received the baptism of the Holy Spirit and the gift of tongues. I've never had such a powerful experience. I'm beginning to know God."

I don't know how to respond to these letters, because by the time he gets my reply, he's already moved on to something else. As each week passes, the pace of change accelerates, and I fear my brother is losing his grip. His mind, his very personality seems to be spinning out of control.

It happens. At the end of that first semester, Marshall's brain suddenly shuts down. When he tries to read textbooks, he can no longer put two words together. He meets with the school counselor, who grants him a deferral on his impending philosophy exams and refers him to a psychiatrist.

After giving him a battery of tests, the psychiatrist says, "Marshall, I won't treat you unless you agree to enter a mental institution. Frankly, in your case suicide is a definite risk, and as a professional I can't accept that liability."

Marshall retreats to his dorm. He drops his philosophy courses and devotes himself instead to piano, finding a refuge in music. He meets another piano major, an attractive blonde named Diane, and it calms him to play duets with her.

By the time I see him in Atlanta that summer, he has resumed the role of the cosmopolitan older brother. We stay up night after night discussing his experiences. He recounts his first year's highlights: an epic Chicago blizzard, making out with Diane on the roof of her dorm, canvassing blue-collar voters in Milwaukee, the thrill of smoking cigarettes, the Ouija board that correctly predicted all of Wheaton's football scores.

When I mention his report of the baptism of the Spirit, he brushes it off. "Who knows what's real and what's fake?" he says. "It happened, and that's all I can say."

PART FIVE

GRACED

Who would have thought my shriveled heart
Could have recovered greenness? It was gone
Quite underground . . .

—George Herbert, "The Flower"

CHAPTER 20
TREMORS

Meanwhile, I've been on a different trajectory than Marshall's. My own cynicism has gradually softened over the course of my sophomore year. I found some relief in a new Christian Service assignment: "university work." Instead of preaching to prisoners in chains, four of us male students started visiting a nearby state university every Saturday night with the goal of engaging students in conversations about faith.

On our first visit I am dazzled by the plush dorms and student lounges, so different from the utilitarian buildings at the Bible college. Entranced, I study the bulletin boards covered with splashy posters announcing concerts, plays, and other student activities. I want to *be* one of these people more than I want to convert them. I long for a brighter, more invigorating world—perhaps how a North Korean feels when staring across the border at the gleaming lights to the south.

I expect to find the decadence of drug parties, panty raids, and binge drinking. Either that culture hasn't yet hit South Carolina or it stays hidden, because instead I see ordinary college students doing their homework in coffee shops and playing Frisbee on the lawn. Their casual dress, mostly Levi's and T-shirts, stands out. But anything would look casual compared to the Bible college, where we wear sports coats and ties to dinner each evening and blue jeans are banned.

Strolling through the campus, I notice a group of athletes sitting on a patio. "Where are you guys from?" I ask.

"We're with the Yale baseball team. How about you?"

"Um, I attend a Bible college down the road, and we came over here to see if anyone wants to talk about spiritual things." They exchange smirks. I continue, "You see, in God's economy . . ."

"That's funny," one of the athletes interrupts. "I didn't know God had an economy." His teammates laugh, and blood rushes to my face. I head toward the student center to watch TV.

"Don't worry, Philip," my fellow students reassure me when I report on my botched attempt at witnessing. "At least you sowed the seed. God's Word doesn't return void."

After that first attempt I spend nearly every Saturday night in the student center, catching up on sports and the news. I engage in just enough conversation to collect a few tidbits for our required evangelism reports. The rest, I embellish.

CLASS ASSIGNMENTS FORCE me to keep studying the Bible, which unexpectedly captures my interest. I read Ecclesiastes and recognize my own dreary cynicism: "I have seen all the works that are done under the sun; and, behold, all is vanity and vexation of spirit." I read Psalms and Job and marvel that these sacred books would include such angry accusations against God. "How long, LORD? Will you hide yourself forever? . . . For what futility you have created all humanity!" Such biblical outbursts are common, though the professors usually skip over them.

I realize I don't know much about Jesus, apart from the stories I learned in Sunday School. Churches in my childhood focused mostly on the Epistles and the Old Testament. As I study the four Gospels, I encounter more surprises. "You shall know the truth and the truth shall make you free," Jesus promises, which strikes me as ironic on a campus that stifles freedom. I'm beginning to like this guy. When someone asks him a question, he never uses circular reasoning such as "God always answers prayer, but sometimes the answer is no." He's enigmatic, elusive, impossible to pin down. Most times, he tosses the question back to the person who asked it.

If Jesus showed up on campus, I wonder, what would the administration do with him? Would he, too, get shot down for questioning his teachers?

Marshall has encouraged me to read books by C. S. Lewis, which I eagerly do since he's persona non grata on campus. Reading him, I feel a gentle pull toward belief. The book that hooks me most deeply was published the year I entered high school: *A Grief Observed,* a journal of anguish over his wife's losing battle with cancer. I read about Lewis's struggle to survive the "mad midnight moments," then I lift my head and confront the happy-faced students around me, and the oyster shell snaps shut.

Shockingly, the college has hired a sociologist with a degree from Harvard. I sign up for his classes, which soon help me step outside the bubble of the Bible college and better understand my environment.

The professor assigns Erving Goffman's book *Asylums,* a landmark study of what the author calls "total institutions." Goffman suggests that institutions such as prisons, military academies, convents, insane asylums—*and Bible colleges?*—progressively condition their subjects so that in time the insiders habituate to their controlled setting. The ability to make a bed so tight that coins bounce off, or to polish shoes so bright that they reflect the sergeant's face, doesn't help a recruit on the battlefield. It does, however, reinforce a military command structure: "I am in charge, and you must do what I say."

Our school, I realize, is using tried-and-true methods of social control. As if to confirm my suspicions, in one of our private meetings the dean of men admits to me that he retains some petty rules simply to teach students to obey. Which gives me an idea for my sociology project.

I distribute a printed survey form to every male freshman and senior, asking such unscientific questions as "Which rule bothered you most on entering this school?" and "Has your attitude of rebellion against the school declined since you enrolled?" True to my hunch, the seniors accept, and even defend, rules and policies that freshmen think ridiculous.

When the dean finds a copy of my mimeographed survey in a trash can, once again I land on the faculty's watch list. "This is an insurrection!" says the college president, who grills my professor about my project. "He can't survey freshmen. They don't know us!"—which was my point, exactly.

The project helps me separate the school's subculture from the body of faith it so jealously guards. Perhaps, the thought crosses my mind, I am resisting not God but people who speak for God. I've already learned to distrust my childhood churches' views on race and politics. What else should I reject? A much harder question: What should I keep?

At this same time, eight hundred miles away, my brother has begun his manic spiral at Wheaton, accelerating ever faster from aestheticism to atheistic despair to Pentecostalism to mental collapse. I rush to the campus mailbox every day and look for the latest report. My fellow survivor, my pioneer and guide, is failing me. I feel alone, desperate for a solid plank to hold on to, some way to keep afloat.

One scene from the Gospels, in John 6, grabs me. I've pictured Jesus as the crucified Messiah, rejected by his own people. But John's account gives a glimpse of his early popularity. Huge crowds follow him around, dazzled by his miracles and hanging on his every word, eager to crown him as their king. How does Jesus respond? By retreating to a mountain, a place of solitude. Undeterred, the crowds pursue him. The next day, Jesus gives some of his harshest teaching, so alienating the crowd that all but his closest followers abandon him. When Jesus asks his twelve core disciples if they, too, want to leave, they answer, "Lord, to whom shall we go?"

I have always thought of God as an arm-twister, a cosmic bully who schemes to break anyone who dares resist. In this account, Jesus appears wistful, even forlorn, showing no interest in compelling belief. Jesus clearly did not use the techniques of Goffman's total institutions.

Like Marshall, I fully expect God to crush me someday—the threat Mother has held over us. Yet from the Bible I am learning about a God who has a soft spot for rebels, who empowers such people as the adulterer David, the cheater Jacob, the whiner Jeremiah, the traitor Peter, and the human-rights abuser Saul of Tarsus. A God whose Son makes prodigals the heroes of his stories.

Could that God find a place for a cynical sneak like me?

ONE SATURDAY EVENING I return to the Bible college from my ministry assignment at the state university. The contrast between the two campuses puts me in a reflective mood: a noisy, thriving cultural community set in the midst of a city compared to a quiet enclave surrounded by forests and farmland.

I think back to my high school years, living in a trailer on the grounds of a fundamentalist church that prided itself on separation from "the world." We avoided so many pleasurable activities. No artwork adorned the walls of the church. We had music, yes, but much of it expressed a longing for a future life. The goal seemed to be enduring life on earth in hopes of making it to Heaven someday. "This world is not my home, I'm just a passin' through," we sang.

A basic question occurs to me: Why would anyone anticipate a better life without experiencing at least hints of it here?

In my reading I have discovered Augustine, a connoisseur of women, art, food, and philosophy, who celebrates the goodness of created things. He says of his preconversion years, "I had my back toward the light, and my face toward the things on which the light falls." The Latin phrase *dona bona,* or "good gifts," appears throughout his writings. "The world is a smiling place," he writes, and God its *largitor,* or "lavisher of gifts."

A smiling place—not once have I thought of the world like that. Perhaps I lack certain receptors for goodness, as Mr. H. suggested. How can I find the *dona bona*?

SOMETIMES AT NIGHT, after curfew, I steal out of the dormitory and make my way to the chapel and its Steinway grand piano. Living in the shadow of my preternaturally gifted brother, I have never played in public, not since the sixth-grade debacle with Mrs. Wiggins. But I can passably sight-read Mozart, Chopin, Beethoven, and Schubert, as long as I slow the tempo and keep a heavy foot on the sustaining pedal. I spend many hours in that chapel, the room completely dark save for a small light above the keyboard.

I have always faltered at polyrhythm, which calls for, say, the right hand to play a sequence of three notes while the left hand plays two. I start simply, counting out six, with the two hands coming in at different beats. Three notes against four proves much more daunting. Then one day I can do it without counting, and I realize that for the first time my hands are operating independently of each other.

During those nightly interludes, my fingers press some tactile order into my disordered world. In great music, only one right note or chord can come next; miss it, and the mistake jars the ears. The better I play, the more true, even sublime, the music sounds as it echoes through the empty sanctuary. And because classical pieces end with a sure resolution, that satisfying finish gives me a sense of an ending, which the rest of my life sorely lacks.

I am creating something of soul-calming beauty. Doubts, social snubs, buried wounds, hypocrisies, insecurities—they all vanish, displaced by the music. In a way that I feel in my gut but cannot articulate, I leave the chapel more hopeful that all shall be well. For a moment the world is a smiling place.

One night I try Debussy, so unpredictable after Mozart and Beethoven, his melodies light as a cloud. I feel daring, experimental, and my heart flutters in response. Then I attempt Mussorgsky's *Pictures at an Exhibition* and piano transcriptions of Tchaikovsky's symphonies. The music draws out of me emotions I have no words for.

Lenin once said that he refused to listen to Beethoven because the music made him want to pat children on the head. There are no small children on the college campus, but now I understand what he means.

I leave the chapel and step out into the cool night air with its canopy of stars above, feeling refreshed and transported, *humming*—until I climb back to reality through an open dorm window, hoping I won't get caught breaking curfew.

OCCASIONALLY BEFORE TURNING in at night, I jog out beyond the lights of the campus, along a road lit only by the moon and stars. On one such night, a childhood memory comes to mind: a church-sponsored field trip to Philadelphia's Franklin Institute. We kids dashed from exhibit to exhibit, and only one time did we sit still: in the planetarium. The room went completely dark and then one by one the planets and stars shone out. Soon the entire ceiling was sparkling with lights.

Finally, the earth came into view, blue and beautiful, a small dot suspended in space. For a second, a mere second, we saw ourselves for what we were, a tiny group of kids on a tiny planet in an ocean of immensity. As I stared in wonder at the gleaming lights on the dome, I had a sensation strangely new. Only now, while jogging in the dark, do I recognize it as a profoundly fitting sense of creatureliness.

In search of more solitude, I begin taking daytime hikes in the forest surrounding the four-hundred-acre campus. Following railroad ties until I tire of the smell of creosote, I then detour into the deep woods, where the scent of honeysuckle hangs in the air like a woman's perfume. The South Carolina landscape brings back memories of my boyhood explorations with a loyal dog at my side.

One day, a glimmer of beauty catches my eye: a gold-studded chrysalis nestled among fallen leaves, cast aside for the birth of something even more resplendent. I reach down and hold the split cylinder in my hand. It seems art of the highest order, but for whom—and by whom?

I come across a pond and sit there in stillness until the animals forget my presence. After ten minutes a snapping turtle crawls out to sun on a half-submerged log. A muskrat's nose cuts *v*-shaped ripples in the pond's glassy surface. I watch a spotted fawn approach the water, eyes and ears alert, and warily lower its head for a drink. A gangly blue heron, taller than a child, lands gently by the pond's edge and wades in on stilt legs to stand at stiff attention.

Just then I hear a deep bass croak and look up to see a fat green bullfrog, big as a catcher's mitt, closing his wide-grin mouth. He jumps in the water with a loud splash; I flinch; and all the creatures disappear.

They take my breath away, these brushstrokes of nature that happen whether or not any human is there to observe. "I have learnt to love you late, beauty at once so ancient and so new!" Augustine confessed, regretting how long it took him to turn to God. Yet, "in my unlovely state I plunged into those lovely created things which you made."

Classes at the school focus so intently on the invisible world—on concepts such as omniscience, omnipotence, and sovereignty—but here in the visible world, at the margins of belief, I feel the first uninvited stirrings of desire to know the source of such beauty. As G. K. Chesterton put it, "The worst moment for the atheist is when he is really thankful and has nobody to thank."

Nature teaches me nothing about Incarnation or the Victorious Christian Life. It does, though, awaken my desire to meet whoever is responsible for the monarch butterfly.

"AND THE LORD God said, 'It is not good that the man should be alone . . .'"

My freshman year at the Bible college, I asked various female students to join me for dinner in the allotted eighty-minute period of "socializing." These were clumsy affairs in which overdressed male students marched across the sidewalk to the women's dorm to collect their "dates" for a closely monitored time of touch-free conversation. Because of my reputation as a renegade, some women turned me down flat. Others made sure we had a miserable enough time that I would not ask them again.

In my sophomore year, romance does not really interest me. I'm not even sure romantic love exists. Most of the world gets along fine with arranged marriages, often loveless, and I've read that our Western concept of love is an invention of twelfth-century Italian troubadours. From what I can see, romance nearly always leads to misunderstandings and hurt feelings.

To help with tuition bills, I sign up for one of the nastiest jobs on campus, working in the hot and crowded dish pit, where students deposit their cafeteria trays after eating. We workers scrape excess food off the plates, separate glasses and silverware, spray them all down, and run them through a hissing, steaming conveyor-belt dishwasher. In a stainless-steel sink, we scrub bits of meat, pasta, and grease off the large cooking pots. It's smelly, dirty work, reminiscent of working on a garbage truck.

The dish pit is where I meet Janet, a new student who has just transferred in. I notice her slender figure and flip hairdo as she nears the counter, sharing a laugh with her older sister. She makes some lightly sarcastic comment as she hands over her tray, and my eyes follow her as she walks away and out the door. She is wearing a summery cotton dress that tests the mid-knee rule. I am wearing a white T-shirt stained with food and sweat and brownish dishwater.

I talk a friend into letting us join him and his girlfriend on a double date to town the following weekend, and Janet accepts my invitation. The evening gets off to an unpromising start. That afternoon, rushing back to the dorm from broadcasting a soccer game, I hit a rock that sends my borrowed motorcycle airborne. It lands on my leg, breaking it.

The three pick me up at the hospital, where I'm practicing with a pair of crutches. Janet's first words to me—"Some people will do anything to get a little attention"—get *my* attention. She is lippy in a playful kind of way, unlike what I've come to expect from prim and proper Bible-college coeds.

We settle on a pizza place where Janet and I can sit while the other couple roams the downtown streets. "I've always wanted to try pizza," Janet says, and for a minute I assume she comes from a background as sheltered as mine. Quite the opposite. She grew up in Colombia and Peru, the daughter of missionaries. While I was shuffling between suburban elementary schools, she was catching piranhas in a tributary of the Amazon River and looking after her pets: a parrot, an ocelot kitten, and a three-toed sloth.

I am seventeen and she all of twenty, but to me she seems worldwise beyond her years. She has an encyclopedic memory of the lyrics to pop songs from the fifties and sixties. She spent a year at a private college in Mississippi, and another at a community college in Florida. In Mississippi she tried smoking to stay awake while studying and developed a fondness for rum-and-Cokes. "So how'd I end up here? you're wondering. Simple. I ran out of money, and my father promised to pay my tuition if I transferred to his alma mater."

I soon learn that Janet is the only student whose dissatisfaction with the Bible college matches my own. We spend the evening grousing about the rules, the underqualified teachers, and the college's cloistered atmosphere. She seems unthreatened by my smart-alecky attitude and parries each sardonic comment with one of her own. She has opinions about everything and defends them fiercely. When we return to campus, I hop back to the dorm on my crutches as if I have been in a jousting contest—and lost.

I lie in bed mulling over the evening that began with pain and ended with pleasure. I cannot get Janet out of my mind, nor do I want to. She has the quaint idea that emotions are meant to be expressed, not repressed. If she doesn't like something, she gets angry, and lets everyone know it. Her joy is equally infectious. "I wear my heart on my sleeve," she explains, the first time I have heard that odd phrase.

We meet again over dinner the next night, and the next. Janet is impulsive, spontaneous, and fully engaged with anyone she meets—

exactly the opposite of my flatlining, standoffish demeanor. Unlike me, she believes life is meant to be lived, not observed or analyzed. When I catch her in an inconsistency, she shrugs it off with a line from Walt Whitman, "Do I contradict myself? Very well then I contradict myself . . . I contain multitudes." And she does.

That winter the campus receives a rare snowfall. Janet, reared in the Amazon jungle and south Florida, has never seen snow. She rushes out of the dorm in her bathrobe—no doubt breaking a rule—and her roommate snaps a photo that catches her in unposed ecstasy: both palms upward, head lifted to the sky, eyes shining, mouth wide open, with her tongue extended to catch the white diamonds falling through the air.

Beauty, joy, softness, unrestraint—I marvel at what she has so quickly summoned up in me. Hesitantly, I bring up stories from my past, stories I have never told anyone: life in a trailer park, my deliberately broken arm, the turtle episode, my racism, Mother's split personality, Marshall's mental breakdown. Each time, I brace myself for rejection and instead she responds with empathy. Usually I say more than I intend; often I reveal more than I know.

My careful program of emotional self-control has disintegrated.

I WRITE A love letter almost every evening, drafting it in a notebook and copying it over on real stationery in my best handwriting. Janet responds on perfumed stationery that I hold to my nose and drink in before reading.

What does a woman see in a man? I don't know what attracted Janet to me, nor do I give it much thought. I only know that I want her in my life and cannot imagine a life without her.

I send her a poem by Yeats:

> I would spread the cloths under your feet:
> But I, being poor, have only my dreams;
> I have spread my dreams under your feet;
> Tread softly, because you tread on my dreams.

Tread softly she does. She replies with one of Elizabeth Barrett Browning's sonnets:

> And as a vanquished soldier yields his sword
> To one who lifts him from the bloody earth,
> Even so, Beloved, I at last record
> Here ends my strife . . .
> Make thy love larger to enlarge my worth.

What is happening to me? The simple act of a desirable woman extending her hand has changed everything. Goodness has become believable. I feel inspired to dismantle the shell, rejoin the human race, and stop being a jerk.

Over Christmas break, I visit Florida to meet Janet's family. Compared to my own home, bathed in sullen silence, hers seems a beehive. With six talkative daughters in the house, I hardly speak, and don't need to.

For the first time, we have long hours alone together, on the beach or simply sitting on a swing at a nearby park. I find that the Bible college's ironclad rules against physical contact have the unintended effect of making it more exhilarating when away from school. Today's hookup culture cannot possibly fathom the shivery thrill of sitting close enough to feel another's heat, or the brush of fingers under a blanket, or a kiss that on campus would risk expulsion.

"Here's an idea," I say on a whim. "How about if we finish out this school year, then both transfer to Wheaton College, where my brother is? We'd get a much better education."

Spontaneous as always, Janet quickly agrees. "I've already tried three colleges—why not a fourth?"

A few days later I ride a Greyhound bus across the state, where my mother is visiting relatives. As I stare out the window at the flat, featureless landscape, every mile taking me farther from Janet, a lump rises to ache in my throat. Sensing something in my eye, I blink rapidly a few times, and for the first time in seven years, I feel the moisture of tears on my cheeks.

Back at college I undergo surgery to repair yet another broken bone—this one in my foot, caused by a soccer injury. For five days I lie in the hospital staring at the pale green ceiling. Somehow Janet finds a way to sneak off campus and visit me. She rests her hand on my feverish skin and suddenly she is crying, her tears falling straight down like raindrops on my hospital gown. I tremble, though not from cold.

Her birthday comes a few weeks later. Still on crutches, I clomp down the stairs to the dorm kitchen and manage to bake my very first cake. I don't know to soften the butter, and small chips of yellow fleck the chocolate icing. My roommate carries it across campus as I hobble, and once again her tears flow.

That night we skip dinner and I ask her to follow me into the chapel. "I have a present for you," I say. "You'll be the first person since the sixth grade to hear me perform." I adjust the Steinway bench, and Janet finds a spot on the floor, tucked behind a chair, out of sight from anyone who might walk by. My hands are shaking. For weeks I've been practicing Beethoven's *Sonata Pathétique* and must screw up all my courage to attempt such a piece, even for an audience of one. But it's her birthday present, and the name says it all: the Emotional, or Passionate, Sonata.

Her eyes are glistening as I hit the final chords. "Thank you," she says at last. "I'll remember that always." She blows me a kiss—the only kind allowed—and we leave the chapel separately, lest someone report us for being alone together.

"You write such beautiful letters," she says one night as we sit in a borrowed Volkswagen Beetle in the driveway of her grandmother's house, "but I want to hear you say it. Tell me how you feel."

I freeze. We have discussed our futures together, have spoken even of marriage. Still, I have been unable to utter the words. I have said them to no one since childhood because, simply, I have not loved and have not known myself capable. She waits a minute, another, ten minutes in all—ten heart-pounding, dry-tongued minutes before I am able to form and say the words, "I . . . love . . . you." She has drawn them from my deepest self.

Augustine said, "Show me a man in love; I'll show you a man on the way to God." Many exceptions spring to mind, but for me it proves true. In my dorm room one night, I thumb through the book Janet gave me, Browning's *Sonnets from the Portuguese*. Among them I find one that reads:

> My own, my own,
> Who camest to me when the world was gone,
> And I who looked for only God, found *thee*!

I would soon reverse that last line: "I who looked for only *thee*, found God!"

Had I not seen the Sun
I could have borne the shade
But Light a newer Wilderness
My Wilderness has made—

—Emily Dickinson

CHAPTER 21

CONTACT

Nature, music, and romantic love have formed a ladder of ascent from my emotional and spiritual flatlands. But ascent to where? On my walks in the woods, I have the occasional sensation of being watched, the skin-prickling possibility that something unseen—a bear, a cougar—might be out there, stalking me. While playing the piano in the darkened chapel, now and then I feel a rush of transcendent beauty. With Janet I experience the flutter of romance and my first real taste of joy. Never, though, can I mount that top step on the ladder.

God hangs like a mist over the Bible-college campus—sung to, testified about, studied, feared. Yet for me, whether in family, church, or college, the motions of faith have always proved unreliable. *I* have proved unreliable. Too many times I have adopted the guise of a Christian, only to have the reality vanish like vapor.

I resign myself to an identity as the campus apostate. Bible-college students don't know what to do with someone like me, a sophomore who argues with their beloved professors, reads *Esquire* in chapel, and disdains prayer meetings. Mostly, they avoid me. Janet gets painted with the same brush: she is the only woman in her dorm not assigned a roommate, lest she wrongly influence some impressionable young soul.

There are exceptions. After my surgery, my Portuguese friend, Joe, temporarily switches roommates so he can look after me. He builds a cardboard contraption that lifts the bedclothes off my healing foot and brings me food from the cafeteria. Joe and the two other members of the university team know that I am spending most of my Christian Service assignment watching sports on TV in a university lounge. Yet they don't hassle or report me.

IN LATE FEBRUARY of my sophomore year, Mr. H. gives an assignment to his class on hermeneutics: "Write an essay about a time when God spoke to you through a passage of the Bible."

I have no idea what to write. To my knowledge God has never spoken to me, let alone through the Bible. At times I have parroted the correct answers, and prayed the right words, but always with the sense that I've memorized the part for a performance. I can't distinguish the authentic from the fake.

Mr. H. sets the essay's due date for the following week, and I start reviewing my Sunday School past in order to contrive something acceptable.

A few days later the university team gathers for a prayer meeting, as we do every Wednesday. We follow a consistent pattern: Joe prays, Craig prays, Chris prays, then all three pause politely, waiting for me. I never pray, and after a brief silence we open our eyes and return to our dorm rooms.

With the essay deadline looming, I join the team grudgingly for the requisite meeting. Joe prays, Craig prays, Chris prays, and they wait the usual few seconds. To everyone's surprise—most of all my own—I begin to pray aloud.

"God . . ." I say, and the room crackles with tension. A door slams down the hall, interrupting me.

I start again. "God, here we are, supposed to be concerned about those ten thousand students at the university who are going to Hell. Well, you know that I don't care if they all go to Hell, if there is one. I don't care if *I* go to Hell."

I might as well be invoking witchcraft or offering child sacrifices. Even so, these are my friends, and no one moves. My mouth goes dry. I swallow hard and continue. For some reason I start talking about the parable of the Good Samaritan, which one of my classes has just been studying. "We're supposed to feel the same concern for university students as the Samaritan felt for the bloodied Jew lying in the ditch," I pray. "I feel no such concern. I feel nothing."

And then it happens. In the middle of my prayer, as I am admitting my lack of care for our designated targets of compassion, the parable comes to me in a new light. I have been visualizing the scene as I speak: a swarthy Middle Eastern man, dressed in robes and a turban, bending over a dirty, blood-stained form in a ditch. Without warning, those two figures now morph on the internal screen of my mind. The Samaritan takes on the face of Jesus. The Jew, pitiable victim of a highway robbery, also takes on another face—one I recognize with a start as my own.

In slow motion, I watch Jesus reach down with a moistened rag to clean my wounds and stanch the flow of blood. As he bends toward me, I see myself, the wounded victim of a crime, open my eyes and spit on him, full in the face. Just that. The image unnerves me—the apostate who doesn't believe in visions or in biblical parables. I am rendered speechless. Abruptly, I stop praying, rise, and leave the room.

All that evening I brood over what took place. It wasn't exactly a vision—more like a vivid daydream or an epiphany. Regardless, I can't put the scene out of mind. In a single stroke my cockiness has been shattered. I have always found security in my outsider status, which at a Bible college means an outsider to belief. Now I have caught a new and humbling glimpse of myself. In my arrogance and mocking condescension, maybe I'm the neediest one of all.

A feeling of shame overwhelms me. Shame that my façade of

self-control has been unmasked. And also shame that I might end up as one more cookie-cutter Christian on this campus.

I write a brief note to Janet, telling her cautiously, "I want to wait a few days before talking about this, but I may have had the first authentic religious experience of my life."

ALTHOUGH MR. H. has promised to devote the next class period to students reading their essays on "when God spoke to you," he gets sidetracked and glances at the clock to find only ten minutes remaining before the closing bell. "Oh my, we only have time for a couple of your reports," he says with regret. "Who would like to read?"

One student raises her hand and says she had a hard time choosing because God so often speaks to her through the Word. Her reading takes about six minutes. I am keeping track because I have toyed with the idea of reading my account. I feel pinpricks of perspiration on my forehead as my classmate drones on. Now, to my relief, it seems I will miss that opportunity.

After the student finishes, Mr. H. says, "Thank you. And it looks like we have time for one more." Hands shoot up around the room, and I raise mine no more than halfway. He scans the room and looks directly at me. After our private counseling session, I don't think there's a chance he'll call on me.

"Philip, how about yours?" he says.

As I stand, I can see other students exchanging glances. I clear my throat a few times and begin. "C. S. Lewis once said that God sometimes shows grace by drawing us to himself while we kick and scream and pummel him with our fists. That is my story."

The paper is trembling in my hands, and I work to gain control. There is a hush in the room and no one stirs. I continue: "I groaned when Mr. H. announced this assignment. Until Wednesday night, I had no clue what I might write about. Here it is."

I look up at the clock, then back to the paper.

"I wish all of you would ignore me after this class. Your encouragement comes sincerely, I know, but it makes a great crutch, too.

Around this place a testimony and a few well-placed tears usually earn acceptance into any group.

"I'm not blind to what most of you think of me. I don't smile and I sit alone in class. I don't pray before meals. I read magazines in chapel. I think I'm intellectual and try to reason out everything. Just like my brother. Why should I pray before tests when I could get A's anyway? And why pray for people about whom I couldn't care less?

"Before I continue, let me add one item: those who appear the least lovable usually need the most love."

The bell rings, abnormally loud and shrill. Other classrooms empty out and the hallway fills with chatter. In ours, no one makes a move to collect their books and papers. Mr. H. motions for me to keep reading.

I briefly describe the experience in the dorm room and my impromptu prayer.

"I started to tell God how much I hated people and I really didn't care if the whole blasted university went to Hell. I told God I didn't love him, that I never had, I never knew how—as if God didn't know already.

"Something happened. This time God didn't slam the door in my face. I was asking God to somehow, even though I didn't want him to, give me the love of the Good Samaritan. Who loved irrationally, with no reason. Who loved a repulsive, filthy tramp.

"Then it hit me. I was the tramp and God was trying to help *me*. Every time he leaned over I spit in his face. What's more, I wanted to remain a tramp. An intelligent, sophisticated tramp by choice.

"In the words of Job, 'I had heard of thee by the hearing of the ear. But now mine eye seeth thee: wherefore I abhor myself and repent in dust and ashes.'

"That is how God spoke to me last Wednesday night."

I pick up my books and head toward the door before anyone else in the room has a chance to move, and immediately I'm swallowed up by the noisy crowd in the hallway. Other students honor my request all that day. No one pats my arm and welcomes me to the inner circle. They leave me alone, just as I asked.

Part of me—a rather large part—expects this, too, to pass. How
many times have I gone forward to accept Jesus into my heart, only
later to find him missing? I feel a kind of sheepish horror at regain-
ing faith. But I also feel obliged to admit what has taken me un-
awares, a gift of grace neither sought nor desired.

I DATE MY conversion from the tiny prayer meeting in a sparsely fur-
nished dorm room. Some five decades later, it still stands out as the
singular hinge moment of my life. That Wednesday evening the
sand gave way beneath my feet and I had no clue where the next
wave would sweep me.

Once, I recounted the experience to a skeptical friend, who listened with curiosity. He pointed out that there are, of course, alter-
native explanations for what happened. For years I had been reacting
against a fundamentalist upbringing, and undoubtedly that repres-
sion had created a deep "cognitive dissonance" within me. Since I
had gone so long without praying, should it surprise me that my first
prayer, no matter how untraditional, would release a flood of emotions that might induce a "revelation" like that of the Good Samaritan parable?

I smiled as he talked, because I recognized myself in his words. I
had used similar language to explain away the personal testimonies
of scores of my fellow students. Conversions only make sense from
the inside out, to the fellow-converted. To the uninitiated they seem
a mystery or a delusion.

Years later I received a letter from a Christian philosopher researching conversions. I gave him an abbreviated account of mine,
and he wrote back, surprised that I had not responded with convincing rational arguments. "Are you a *fideist*?" he asked. I had to look up
the word in a dictionary: "One who believes based on faith rather
than scientific reasoning or philosophy."

"I don't know," I replied. "All I know is that the event happened,
the surest event in my life, and one that I had neither planned nor

orchestrated. I cannot possibly erase those moments from my life. I felt *chosen*."

In the end, my resurrection of belief had little to do with logic or effort and everything to do with the unfathomable mystery of God. The apostle Paul bowed before that mystery. Why was he, a self-described "chief of sinners," chosen to proclaim the message he had sworn to eradicate? Why was conniving Jacob chosen and his brother Esau rejected? Paul has no answer other than to quote God's own words: "I will have mercy on whom I have mercy, and I will have compassion on whom I have compassion."

I wince whenever I read those words, for I think of my brother, who pursued God even as I did the opposite. And I think of my father, a man far more devout than I, wholly committed to a life of service to God, who died before his twenty-fourth birthday. Like Paul, like Job, I cannot begin to answer for God. I can only accept the free gift of grace with open hands.

Someone is there, I realized that winter night in a college dorm room. More, Someone is there who loves me. I felt the light touch of God's omnipotence, the mere flick of a divine finger, and it was enough to set my life on a new course.

By then Janet and I have already set in motion our transfers to Wheaton College at the end of the school year. We've been accepted and have filled out applications for financial aid.

"Maybe we should rethink the transfer," I say one evening, as we walk back toward her dorm. "Neither one of us has the money to pay for Wheaton. Besides, we both have so many extra-credit hours here that we can graduate a semester early."

All that semester and into the summer, we talk over our options. A new president has hired some promising new professors at the Bible college, and academic prospects have improved. Finally, we write the school asking if we can rejoin our classmates as juniors. We both sense, a bit reluctantly, that we have more to learn at this place.

Tell me, what is it you plan to do
with your one wild and precious life?

—Mary Oliver, "The Summer Day"

CHAPTER 22
MARSHALL

My life-changing experience at the Bible college does not impress Mother. She's seen me fake my way through camp and church. I'm the sneak, the dissembler. Whatever happened in that dorm room probably won't last. Besides, she has to worry about Marshall, who has been careening down another path like a car with no brakes.

The year is 1968, and like a lot of college students, Marshall has joined the counterculture. When he flew home for the summer after his junior year at Wheaton, Mother met him at the airport. As soon as she saw his long, shaggy hair and mustache, she turned her back and refused to speak. She lets him stay in the house that summer, but she bans him from attending church because it would hurt her reputation for people to see her son looking like a hippie. That rule, he gladly obeys.

All that summer I feel caught in a family tug-of-war. I am gingerly edging back toward faith, searching for some steady ground. I'm also concerned about my brother, and I recoil from Mother's attitude of righteous judgment. I wonder whether she has made good on her threat to pray a "curse" on Marshall, but I dare not bring up that volatile topic.

As my mother and brother restoke their old conflicts, I mostly listen from the sidelines, tiptoeing between two emotional titans. In every discussion that comes up—politics, religion, the Vietnam War—he stands for her polar opposite. "I knew what would happen if you went to Wheaton," she says. "Just look at you. It turned out exactly like I thought it would."

Shaken by his first-semester mental meltdown, Marshall begins seeing a psychiatrist. In a series of weekly sessions, Penny hears his life story, and near the end of the summer, she gives him a diagnosis of "chronic paranoid undifferentiated schizophrenia." When he casually mentions that news, I stare at my brother, my confidant. Do I truly know him? He has wild swings of mood and behavior, yes—but mentally ill?

"Tell me the truth," I ask him, as he packs a suitcase to return to Wheaton for his senior year. "Do you really think you're crazy?"

"I dunno, but Penny saved my neck," he replies. "A few weeks ago I had my physical for the military draft board. I passed the exam with flying colors until I handed the sergeant an envelope from Penny marked 'Highly Confidential.' He took one look at the letter inside and dismissed me. Her diagnosis saved me from the army and probably Vietnam."

During their final session, the psychiatrist gives Marshall one more gift. "You know Penny," he tells me later that evening. "She's got that soft accent that makes you think she's one of those saccharine Southern women. She's not. She leans forward, looks me straight in the eye, and says, 'Marshall, I'll deny ever saying this, but you do know your mother's the crazy one, don't you?'"

His voice cracks when he tries to speak again. "Not once had that possibility entered my mind. I didn't respond, but Penny could tell I was a bit stunned. She waited a few minutes and added, 'And if you don't come to terms with that fact, you'll never get well.'"

I RETURN TO the Bible college, and Marshall resumes his studies at the Wheaton Conservatory of Music. His letters that semester have a newly blissful tone after he reunites with his girlfriend, Diane. They spend every spare minute working on piano duets. "Your brother is the most gentle, sensitive, totally romantic person I've ever known," Diane writes me. "Just listening to a piece of music can make him cry." They start discussing marriage.

Marshall and I are both in Atlanta for Christmas break when the bottom drops out. He writes her letters daily and gets none in return—except for one breakup letter. In it, Diane confesses that she told her parents too much about him. Her parents have absolutely forbidden her to continue seeing "that long-haired agnostic."

My brother is disconsolate. He sits in his bedroom brooding or goes on walks through the neighborhood, smoking cigarettes. Nothing I say or do can penetrate his gloom. Silence again rules the household.

Back at Wheaton, he visits the school psychiatrist, who confirms Penny's diagnosis. Marshall decides to drop out of school—just before his final semester. One day at the campus mailbox, I tear open an envelope and read this cryptic note: "It's raining, it's 32 degrees. Home, defeated, judged crazy." He's heading back to Atlanta.

Penniless and with no place to live, Marshall shows up, bereft of hope, in Mother's driveway. For the next few weeks he lives in a daze.

In a phone call I ask how it's going. He gives a bitter reply. "What do you think? I'm a failure. College dropout, crazy, living with a mother who can't stand me." Through the rest of that school year, I keep up with him through letters and phone calls. We've switched roles, as though he's the younger brother and I'm the protector.

Needing income, Marshall calls his old employer, Grady Hospital, and gets rehired. A tough charge nurse takes him under her wing, thrilled to have an orderly with some education. "Mr. Man," she calls him, as she calls every male in the hospital. "How you feel about dead people, Mr. Man? Most all my other mans are skeered of 'em." On his first shift, he grabs the hand of a dead burn victim to transfer the body to a gurney, and a large patch of charred skin slips off the hand like a glove. It doesn't faze him. From then on, whenever a patient dies the nurse summons Marshall.

In the morgue, he studies the bodies laid out on steel tables. Our own father could have lain in that room, had he not been transferred to a chiropractic center. Marshall tries to imagine the victims' lives before the diseases, gunshots, or knife wounds that led to their demise. "I like the morgue," he reports in one phone call. "For one thing, it's air-conditioned. And nobody bothers you. So I take my lunch breaks there, and read philosophy books."

Another orderly gives him *The Urantia Book,* a rambling, 2,097-page concoction of philosophy and spiritism that has influenced Jimi Hendrix and Jerry Garcia. *Urantia* claims to be dictated by celestial beings, and Marshall finds it totally convincing. Then again, he finds everything convincing, for a time.

Each day when Marshall enters the house after work, Mother grimaces. This is the same son who planned to be a missionary, who was a Youth for Christ club president and a choir pianist. Now she sees a long-haired freak of nature. Once, she refuses to let him in because he shows up wearing round, wire-rim glasses like John Lennon's.

To avoid her, Marshall goes bowling after his hospital shifts, staying out past midnight so that their paths won't cross. On warm nights he sits outside in a lawn chair, nude, and smokes cigarettes until he feels like going to bed. His subscription to *Playboy* gets forwarded to the house, sparking a major explosion.

A few days later, Mother returns home to find Marshall's room vacant. He has moved out, and she has no idea where he is. She won't see him again for a year.

I GET OUT of school in May and track Marshall down. He has switched hospitals. He lives in an informal commune with a conscientious objector and his girlfriend, along with a revolving door of drop-ins who "crash" on the floor in sleeping bags. Marshall invites me over. "Hey guys," he says. "Meet my straightlaced brother from a Bible college."

He shows me around, briefing me on the wonders of the peace-and-love generation. Marshall has painted one room orange and another purple, and fashioned a light fixture out of Styrofoam cups glued together. Colorful strips of batik hang from the ceiling, along with spiderweb sculptures made of yarn. He points out the accessories they've bought secondhand: lava lamps, beanbag chairs, and a black padded toilet seat.

I visit him periodically, much to Mother's chagrin. It strikes me that at last my brother has achieved a state of complete freedom. He has a new set of friends, none of whom monitor his behavior or judge him. He eats whatever he wants, mostly mashed potatoes and macaroni and cheese. Some days he won't talk at all, while other times he holds court, spouting philosophy and recounting stories of growing up fundamentalist. And whenever he sits down at the beat-up piano he's scavenged from somewhere, all conversation ceases.

Soon he moves into an apartment with members of a rock band, who school him in their style of music and life. "Try these," they say, and give him some quaaludes. "You need the right stuff to listen to rock." Neither the music nor the quaaludes have any effect. The next night, though, he tries psychedelic mushrooms, and the universe explodes. As the drug takes effect, he listens, mesmerized, to "In-A-Gadda-Da-Vida" by Iron Butterfly, a heavy-metal jam that goes on for seventeen minutes.

Marshall is hooked. "I'm switching careers," he informs me. "I'm going to become a rock organist." I flash back to the letters he wrote me his first year at Wheaton, when his entire philosophy of life changed every week or so. Once again he is spinning like a roulette wheel.

Instead of rock 'n' roll, Marshall gets hooked on drugs, mainly LSD. Every Sunday afternoon he and a few friends pile into his 1949 Plymouth—a recent inheritance from our grandfather Yancey—and drive to Piedmont Park, where they drop acid, blow bubbles, and fly kites.

Or they simply sit cross-legged on the grass and watch as the world around them morphs. A puffy white cloud in the sky breaks into two and drips toward earth, like a Dalí painting. The sun peels into blood-orange segments. A dog on a leash levitates off the ground and turns into a unicorn. Marshall reaches out with his hand and actually feels the tactile sensation of petting the unicorn.

The world looks and sounds and feels better on acid. Flowers glow with an otherworldly intensity—yellow petals are spun gold, red roses are like rubies nestled in leaves of emerald—and they sometimes talk! Someone strikes a match for a joint: *What radiant light!* A nearby band is playing music, and Marshall can hear every individual note by every instrument.

Marshall becomes an evangelist for LSD. "You ought to try some," he urges me. "Timothy Leary at Harvard says it can help cure schizophrenia, and I think he's right. Acid makes me forget my problems, and it opens up my mind. Maybe it would help you explore the spiritual, or even the supernatural." I politely decline.

I've learned never to say anything that might sound like judgment or even mild disapproval—it triggers mother-memories, and Marshall erupts.

AFTER THAT SUMMER I return to the Bible college for one final semester. Janet and I graduate early, in January 1970, and move back to Atlanta to plan a June wedding. We both land jobs at the Census Bureau and start saving money for a move to Wheaton, where I've been accepted to the grad school.

One cool March evening I am sitting at home alone, with Mother off teaching a Bible class. She hasn't seen Marshall in almost a year, and I've provided very few details of his new lifestyle.

The phone rings. "Is Mrs. Mildred Yancey there?" a man asks when I pick up.

"No, she's not. May I take a message?"

"What about Philip David Yancey?"

"Speaking. May I help you?"

"Yes, this is the DeKalb County Police Department. We have a Marshall Yancey in custody, and he's in pretty bad shape. He says he's on acid—I don't know. You better get over here, and I recommend that you bring along the strongest person you know."

"Could I ask why?"

"Yeah, because he's violent."

"My brother's a pacifist," I protest. "He wouldn't hurt anybody."

The man laughs in a friendly sort of way. "Oh, really? He's already flattened two people, and he had me on the ground in a hammerlock. You'd best not show up alone."

When I hang up, my heart is beating so hard I can feel it against my rib cage. I'm scared, agitated, and unbelieving all at once. I call Penny, Marshall's psychiatrist, and ask her advice. She says I should take him to a safe place—she'll work on lining up someone—and try to get him to eat and drink. "He's hallucinating, so it's important that you stay with him until he comes back down," she says.

Next, I call our dependable uncle Winston and ask him to meet me at the police station in Decatur, an Atlanta suburb.

It's forty degrees outside, and I throw an extra jacket in the car in case Marshall needs it. I force myself to stop at red lights and keep to the speed limit, even though my heart is throbbing like a race-car engine.

The friendly officer, a sergeant, greets me at the station and fills me in. We are meeting in an open office, surrounded by crackling radios and policemen drinking coffee out of Styrofoam cups. "So it's like this," he says. "We got a call from an elderly gentleman. He was out raking leaves when an almost-naked hippie wandered into his yard—that would be your brother. The old man asked your brother if he needed any help and got slugged in the jaw. You're lucky the guy's not pressing charges.

"We showed up and found your brother sitting on the grass in his underpants. I'm the one he wrestled to the ground. It took two of my colleagues to pull him off me—and, as you can see, I ain't a small guy."

Soon my uncle joins us. We talk for a while, giving the sergeant some of Marshall's history. Finally, he says, "Tell you what, I'm willing to give your brother a break. Far as we can tell, he's got no record. Maybe this will teach him a lesson about those drugs. I can release him into your custody. I just have one question to clear up. He's got needle marks all over his arms. When I asked him about it, he said he gives blood. Come on—nobody gives that much blood. Is he on heroin?"

I explain that Marshall has a rare blood type and regularly gives blood plasma to earn extra money. The sergeant seems satisfied, and he leads us to a concrete holding cell. Directly under a bare lightbulb sits my brother on a metal stool. His wrists are handcuffed together behind his back and around a pole, forcing him to hunch over. He's barefoot, still wearing nothing but underpants, shivering. His hair, a mass of unwashed curls, puffs out from his head. His glasses are missing. Slowly he lifts his head and his glazed eyes locate me, though with no sign of recognition.

He keeps staring, and I feel a sudden chill on the back of my neck. Marshall has always been my sophisticated big brother. I have seen him quoting philosophers at university-hosted debate tournaments and performing at classical concerts in a tuxedo. This creature before me resembles a wild animal.

I put my hand against the wall to steady myself. "Marshall, it's me, Philip. And Uncle Winston. We've come to take you home."

The sergeant unlocks Marshall's handcuffs. "Let's go, buddy," he says. "We're lettin' you off this time. Just don't ever do something stupid like this again." My brother rubs his wrists, but gives no reaction.

I hurry to the car to retrieve the extra jacket, and the sergeant scrounges up a pair of dirty sweatpants for Marshall to wear. As we walk out into the cold, I can see my brother's lips moving, and I realize he's talking to himself. I open the passenger door for him, unsure whether he might turn on me. He looks me in the eye for the first time all evening.

"Relax, kid," he says, once again my older brother.

TRUE TO HER word, Penny has found a safe place, the apartment of a trustworthy church employee. We drive to Chloe's, and over the next few hours wait for Marshall to rejoin reality. He sits on an over-stuffed sofa, and every few minutes he looks up and stares at me intently for long stretches of time. His pupils have dilated, crowding out the brown of his irises. I can't hold his gaze. As kids we used to have staring contests, and I always lost.

"Would you like something to eat, Marshall?" Chloe asks. "What about a ham sandwich?" He turns his laser stare on her and gives a barely perceptible nod. "Great! Do you like mayonnaise? Mustard? Cheese? What kind of bread do you prefer?" No response.

I brief Chloe on my brother's food preferences, and she scurries into the kitchen. Both of Marshall's thumbs are working up and down his curled index fingers. He showed me once that he's marked out an imaginary keyboard, an octave on each index finger, to practice the music that is always playing in his head.

When Chloe returns with the sandwich, Marshall takes it in one hand and holds it up to a table lamp. He twists it in all directions, studying it, not taking a bite but not setting it down either. He does drink some iced tea, though—one sip at a time, tentatively, as though it might be poisoned.

"Do you know where you are?" I ask him. He turns in my direction, and again I fail to hold his gaze. I explain about Chloe's apartment that Penny helped line up. "Don't worry, we'll drive you home soon."

Ten minutes later he asks, "Where am I?" and I repeat the explanation.

At last, sometime after midnight, Marshall asks to go home. He seems calmer, more rational, and on the drive he quizzes me on what happened. He can't remember hitting anyone and doesn't know how he got to the place where he was arrested, some five miles from where he lives.

Back at his residence, seven friends are still up and waiting, delighted to see us arrive. Marshall and I get hugs all around, and I give them a short account of the day. They respond enthusiastically: "Far out, man—you beat up a cop, and they let you go? You're the luckiest SOB in the world!" As they laugh and slap his back in congratulation, Marshall visibly relaxes.

Everyone quiets down, and together we try to reconstruct the sequence of events. That afternoon in the living room, Marshall's friends passed around some LSD tablets. "I don't know why," Marshall recalls, "but suddenly I thought you all wanted to kill me." He ran outside, chased by two of them. When his friends grabbed him, he broke loose, swinging his fists wildly, and started running. They last spotted him racing down the middle of Ponce de Leon Avenue, one of Atlanta's busiest streets.

Those details trigger something in Marshall's memory, and he picks up the story. "Sorry, guys. It's just that I saw danger everywhere. Demons wearing grotesque masks were firing machine guns at me from every car. Houses had bunkers with protruding cannons. I felt a pounding sensation in my chest—a demon had seized my body. I knew I had to keep running, or die . . ." He pauses, and no one says anything.

"Finally, I did die. I ended up in Hell before a great tribunal court, the council of evil gods. This didn't feel like a dream. These creatures were real. I could touch them. They demanded that I testify what value my life has been. I had to prove that my life has some worth, some validity, before they'd let me back into reality."

His voice grows softer, and we have to strain to hear him. "So I'm standing naked before the court, and I have nothing to say. I'm a loser. I can't connect with anyone. I'm all alone. Then I see a person right in front of me, and I reach out to him. That's the last thing I remember. Now they tell me that person was an old man who I slugged in the jaw. I guess he's the one who called the cops."

Marshall's friends break into clapping and cheering. It's the best

trip story they've ever heard. LSD is a "Heaven and Hell drug"—my
brother's been to Hell and lived to tell it.

RATTLED BY THE experience, Marshall decides to lay off drugs. But
the memory of that hallucinatory trip depresses more than sobers
him. The judgment of the evil gods has confirmed what an inner
voice has told him all along. He's a failure. He can't come up with a
single valid reason to keep living.

I have never seen Marshall so dejected. Janet and I have scheduled
a wedding in June, after which we'll immediately depart for Wheaton, and it frightens me to think of leaving him in such a state. He
won't commit to attending our wedding, and I have little hope that
he'll show up.

I'm still living at home, and as June approaches Mother sinks into
a mood as dark as Marshall's. I've told her nothing about his communal life or the drugs. But she's seen what happened to one of her
sons at Wheaton and can only imagine what will happen to me.

We plan a simple wedding on the cheap, budgeting a total of $300.
Janet rents her wedding dress, and our reception consists of snack
foods like nuts and mints. We just want to escape my troubled family, get out of town, and start life together. But Mother manages to
hijack our celebration with one last scene.

When I open the door of the church, there stands my brother,
dressed on one of Atlanta's hottest days in a three-piece wool suit he
found in a thrift store. I fight back the tears, aware of what it means
for him to leave his counterculture setting and enter the straight world
of a church ceremony, especially knowing our mother will be present.

Our traditional ceremony proceeds, with organ music, a sermon-
ette, and vows that we've modernized only slightly. All goes well until
the reception in the church basement, when the photographer, a distant relative, gets an idea. "Hey, let's have all the Yanceys together in a
group photo. Come on, everyone whose last name is Yancey."

A commotion breaks out on the other side of the room, and then
I hear Mother's loud voice. "I'll not be in any picture with that so-

called son of mine!" she announces. She stalks out of the reception hall, which grows as quiet as the empty sanctuary upstairs.

Marshall wears an expression somewhere between pain and embarrassment, and I hurry over to apologize for what has just happened. "What'd you expect?" he says. "I never should have come."

THE NEXT DAY Janet and I begin the drive toward Chicago, a poor couple's honeymoon. At first the scene in the church basement hangs over us like a cloud. Janet is understandably bitter. I'm more concerned about my brother's mental state. After a day or so, however, a sense of freedom blows in. We make our leisurely way north, enjoying whatever there is to enjoy between Atlanta and Chicago, and begin planning our new life, far from the family turmoil.

After arriving and settling into our one-room Wheaton apartment, I call Marshall, only to find him more despondent than ever. He dismisses my concern about the wedding and talks instead about committing suicide. "I have to follow what I believe," he says. "My life has no meaning. Camus said suicide is the only truly serious philosophical problem. He's right. But it's only a problem if you don't act on it."

He tells me of his scheme. He'll drive across the country, recording his impressions on a cassette tape, then jump off the Golden Gate Bridge, leaving the cassette recorder behind as his parting gift to me. "Maybe you can find something in it to write about someday."

His somber tone convinces me this is no idle threat. *Keep him talking,* I tell myself, recalling a news story about suicide hotlines. I can't let him sense the panic I feel. So I calmly ask him to choose a route through Chicago, figuring I can get psychiatric help if he still seems intent on killing himself. "Sure," he promises. "I'll stop over to say goodbye."

Over the next few weeks, Marshall signs up for all the free credit-card offers that come in the mail and buys gifts for his friends, including expensive stereo sets. He schedules a final farewell party to thank them for their friendship and to present the gifts he's bought them. A few who know of his plan try their best to dissuade him, to no avail. He is determined to die.

The night of the farewell party, loud music is playing, couples are dancing, drugs and alcohol are flowing freely. One of Marshall's friends sidles up to him: "Hey, man, wanna drop some acid?"

"Nah, I don't do that anymore. I had a really bad trip."

"Ah, come on, just for old times' sake. One pill won't hurt you. I've got this great album called *Tommy*, by The Who. It's a rock opera—they played it at Woodstock—and I think you'll love it."

Marshall demurs, but when he sees all his friends doing drugs, he decides to join them. He swallows the LSD tablet and sits in front of the stereo speakers waiting for it to take effect. As he reads the liner notes and focuses on the music, he sees in *Tommy* a hallucinogenic mirror of his own life. Tommy was a freakish kid, "deaf, dumb, and blind," whose senses were shut down by his brainwashing mother. After a life of abuse, he takes a magic pill from "The Acid Queen," and eventually finds spiritual liberation and recovers his senses.

Once again for Marshall, music and drugs open the gate to another dimension. His soul floats up somewhere above his body. Every few minutes he feels himself about to slip into another reality, and he struggles mightily to will himself back to earth.

The next morning, when my brother wakes up, some part of his brain has chemically rearranged itself. *Suicide?! Why would anyone want to commit suicide? Green grass, blue sky, groovy friends—life is beautiful.* In an instant he abandons the plan he's been working toward for weeks.

He calls me the next day. "I won't be going to California after all," he says. "I've got some big debts to cover. I guess I'd better find a second job."

The past is never dead. It's not even past.

—William Faulkner, *Requiem for a Nun*

CHAPTER 23
THE CURSE

After I leave for Wheaton, my life takes a radically different path from Marshall's. Although we are both recovering from the toxic effects of our childhood, we react in opposite ways. Marshall becomes a proud atheist, shunning all religion. I accept a job with a Christian magazine, *Campus Life*.

Looking back, it seems inevitable that I would find a career in writing. Marks on a page are less overbearing than the shrill voices I heard in church revival meetings and in Bible college. They give me a quiet space in which to make up my own mind, to decide what should be salvaged and what jettisoned.

For almost ten years I collaborate on books with Dr. Paul Brand, a saintly surgeon who devoted his life to some of the lowliest people on the planet, leprosy-afflicted patients in India. Through him I meet other sterling Christians, such as the founder of the modern hospice movement, and the director of Kew Gardens in London.

Such interview subjects help my faith settle on a solid foundation, and the wounds of the past gradually heal.

Finally, I sense the time has come for me to explore my own faith, not just piggyback on someone else's. The titles of my books give a clue to my first tentative steps, beginning with *Where Is God When It Hurts?* and *Disappointment with God.* Years will pass before I tackle more central issues, and even these I usually frame with a question, such as *Prayer: Does It Make Any Difference?* and *Church: Why Bother?*

Whenever I write, my brother sits like a mocking dybbuk upon my shoulder. "Do you really believe that," he asks, "or are you just spouting platitudes and propaganda?" When I'm tempted to cover the church's blemishes with verbal makeup, Marshall keeps me honest. *What is real, and what is fake?* he has asked me more than once, a question I circle around in all my books. I bend over backward to honor the stance of a skeptic, for I remember how I was treated at the Bible college.

While Marshall reinvents himself every few years in an attempt to flee the past, I have found a career in which to excavate it.

I MARVEL THAT two brothers from the same family and same background could have ended up on such divergent paths. As it happened, Marshall's fixation with suicide soon faded away, replaced by a preoccupation with sex.

On my first visit to Atlanta after the wedding, he describes his odyssey to me in lurid detail. He lost his virginity to a nurse at the hospital where he worked and soon was staging orgies with three or four employees. Next, from the book *Group Marriage,* he got the idea to found a commune based on free sex.

"So I chose another nurse, Linda, at the hospital," he says. "She has an attractive face, and she's always been nice to me. The problem is, she's overweight and quite ashamed of it. We used to take breaks together, and she confided that she's never had a date in her life. How criminal is that? Here's this lovely person, but because America has an inane cult of beauty, she's branded a loser. I gave it some thought and then on a whim asked her to move in with me. I explained about the group-marriage idea, and she agreed to give it a try."

We are sitting in their communal home as Marshall tells me this, and I see that Linda has imposed some domestic order on the place. No more empty wine bottles lying around, no more stacks of dirty dishes and piles of clothes, no more nude centerfolds on the walls.

"Who all lives here?" I ask.

"It varies night to night," he says. "Basically, anybody who needs a place to crash. Right now there's a dental student from Emory and his girlfriend, who plays the cello and saxophone. Some nights we burn incense, smoke a few joints, and—you'll like this—we sit up for hours playing hymns. I refuse to play classical music on our clunky piano, and I don't know any popular music."

He steps out of the room for a moment, and Linda comes in from the kitchen. "We all get along," she says. "I must say, though, your brother has a high tolerance for filth, so we're still working on that. One time I made the mistake of calling him a slob, and he went berserk. I must have set off some memory of your mother."

At least he's got some friends and is no longer talking suicide, I think, as I return to Illinois. My brother seems to have calmed down. He has even found a new career, tuning and repairing pianos.

But a year later, when he calls to say he might drop by for a visit on his way to California, I catch my breath. "You . . . you're not planning anything like that again, are you?" I ask.

"No, no, I'm not planning to kill myself this time. I just want to start over. Linda doesn't interest me anymore. I'm bored. I thought I could overlook her fat body, but I was wrong. We've had a couple of years together, and that's enough."

Late one rainy night, with no advance warning to Linda or his piano-shop employer, and certainly not to his mother, Marshall packs his few possessions into the back of his Fiat and strikes out for California.

Over the next few weeks, I field Linda's frantic phone calls. "Yes," I tell her, "he came through here two days after he left you." And,

"No, I don't know how to reach him. I think he was headed to the San Francisco area."

SEVERAL MONTHS LATER, Marshall and I reconnect. Having escaped the Bible Belt, he is thriving in live-and-let-live California. He plays for a local opera company and has bought the practice of a retiring piano tuner. Baldwin, a major piano manufacturer, even hires him for special Bay Area events. "I recently got called to tune the pianos of two famous people," he boasts, "and you'll never guess them in a million years." I try every name I can think of, and miss both answers: Liberace and the pope.

Women are the center of Marshall's life in California. He meets a musician at the opera company and promptly moves in with her. They split up after a year, but he talks her into continuing a purely sexual relationship, which lasts another year. When they part, he goes into a tailspin, talking again of suicide.

Soon, though, he finds another partner and his spirits lift. I schedule a trip out West a few months later, and he excitedly fills me in. At a local club he met Andrea, a waitress of Italian descent, who shared his free-love ideas and proposed a relationship centered on sex. She introduced him to dominance-and-submission, and the two signed a contract spelling out their roles. Marshall agreed to serve as her slave, doing whatever she commanded.

"I can't explain it, but there's something very rewarding in serving someone else," he says with obvious enthusiasm, a tone I haven't heard from him in years. "It's like she's living through me. She makes all the decisions, I just have to carry them out. It's liberating, in an odd sort of way. I've never been happier."

I've learned not to be surprised by any of Marshall's choices, but this is pressing the limits. "Help me understand, Marshall," I say hesitantly. "All your life you've been trying to get away from a domineering mother. Now you're using the same words that appear in the Victorious Christian Life books, only this time you're applying them to a woman, not to God—"

"I know, I know," he interrupts. "Believe me, I've thought about that. I guess something in my personality pushes me to submit to someone. I was brought up to be a complete slave to God, whatever that means. I never managed it, at least not without playacting. Now I have the same opportunity, only with a woman. Somehow it fits my psychological makeup."

Andrea orders him to rise early, brew the coffee, and meet her after her morning shower with a clean towel and a cup of steaming coffee. She determines whether or not he can drink wine each night, when he can go to the bathroom, and when they might—or might not—have sex.

Marshall has always enjoyed shocking his younger brother. He proceeds to describe what else is involved in the submission role. Andrea bends him over her knee and spanks him with a paddle or a whip. She handcuffs him and ties him to the bed. She even orders him to wear a remote-controlled collar around his body parts; if he does or says something that displeases her, she gives him an electric shock on a level of one to ten, depending on the offense.

I bite my tongue, do my best not to react, and change the subject. Marshall, however, can talk about nothing else. As he continues, giving more graphic detail than I want to hear, it occurs to me that my brother is still looking for ways to break every rule in the book.

Andrea lasts a year, until she tires of him. Next he meets Brenda. This time Marshall takes the dominant role, and Brenda goes along with it for a while. Eventually, the kinkiness makes her so uneasy that she joins the group Adults Molested as Children and comes to terms with her sexual abuse as a child. As soon as she sets boundaries, the relationship falls apart.

Each breakup sends Marshall into a downward slide. After Brenda's departure, Marshall and I spend many hours in phone conversations. "I can't understand why breaking up has to end the physical part," he says. "What if I pay her to have sex, just like I pay her to schedule my piano-tuning appointments?" I try in vain to explain why she might object.

The next phase of Marshall's life is the most unexpected of all.

Gradually, after a decade in California, my countercultural brother becomes a full-fledged member of the middle class. He takes up golf
and becomes a wine connoisseur. Above all, he devotes himself to
bridge. His remarkable memory allows him to keep track of all cards
played, and he learns enough strategy to start winning tournaments.

During cocktail hour after bridge one night, he meets Molly, a
mother of three who has recently divorced her second husband.
Molly has a high-paying job, and when they move in together, Marshall lives without financial worries for the first time in his life. They
travel overseas, go on cruises, and gamble in Reno and Las Vegas.

Soon the two have a formal wedding, which I attend. Molly likes
luxury cars, expensive jewelry, and romance novels—a decidedly different style from Marshall's. Somehow, though, they make the marriage work. Compared to Molly's two previous husbands, who had
addiction issues, Marshall looks like a winner.

DURING ALL THIS time, Mother and Marshall have no contact. In
fact, my ongoing relationship with Marshall causes a constant prickly
tension between Mother and me. She believes that any friendly asso-
ciation with him would imply approval. I believe the contrary, that
Marshall needs to feel love for the person he is, not just the person
he should be or could be.

Whenever I bring up the curse she put on him when he went to
Wheaton, Mother defends it as "turning him over to the Lord,"
who will deal with him someday. "After all those people prayed for
him to do the Lord's service, it's only right that God would take
away his mind when he rebelled," she says. "You can't run away
from God."

Long ago, on a mound of dirt in a cemetery, she presented him to
God as a sacred offering. In her view, he sabotaged that transaction
through one deliberate act of rebellion after another.

Occasionally I drop tidbits about him, which she routinely ignores. On one visit to Atlanta, I am driving her on an errand. "Did
I tell you that Marshall got married a few years ago?" I ask, some-

what mischievously. She doesn't respond. I glance over at the passenger seat where she sits, impassive, showing no interest in news about her son.

I reach in my shirt pocket. "Here, I have a picture from the wedding. It was held outdoors, at a garden near San Francisco." To my surprise, she takes the photo and examines it closely, as a doctor might study an X-ray.

Her firstborn—she last saw him as a hirsute hippie dressed in flamboyant, sixties-style clothing. Now she is looking at a mature, well-groomed man dressed in a suit, his arm curled around the waist of a woman in a bridal dress. *What is going through her mind?* I wonder.

A full five minutes pass. At last she speaks: "Did he ever get his bottom teeth fixed?"

Even after disowning him, she can't stop thinking like a mother. But as she hands back the photo, she can't resist a barb: "I wonder how long this marriage will last."

WHEN MARSHALL AND I see each other, we try to gain perspective on our fractured family. On one such visit, we start talking about *The Great Santini*. Based on Pat Conroy's memoir, the movie portrays a family dominated by an abusive father who's an officer in the Marine Corps. Santini calls his kids hogs and makes them march in formation. In a scene difficult to watch, he beats the daylights out of his son, who bested him in a basketball game.

"I cried and raged for three days after seeing that movie," my brother says. "It brought back all those memories of living with Mother."

"The movie got to me, too," I say. "But, Marshall, kids survive family trauma much worse than ours. We weren't sexually abused. No one hit us with a two-by-four or kept us behind barbed wire."

"I know," he says. But the pained look on his face shows me that lacerations of the soul can wound as deeply as those of the body.

I encourage him to write to our mother and unload some of his feelings. "Everything I know about victims indicates that 'getting it out,' and especially confronting the abuser, is an important part of the healing process."

He must have heard me, because he soon composes a one-page letter, his first correspondence with our mother in almost three decades. He mails a copy to her and also to me.

> Perhaps you will recall one of our last conversations in which you told me that every day you will be praying that I will either die or lose my mind. Yes, you did say precisely that. I have yet to find anyone who can believe that a mother would say that to her son. Not one. All because I wasn't going to become the missionary that you had decided I should be.

On Marshall's birthday, *four months later,* Mother sends a letter in reply. She explains away some other misunderstandings but mentions nothing about her notorious prayer.

Marshall regrets initiating the contact. "It irritates me when I'm reminded she's alive," he says.

AFTER TWO DECADES in Chicagoland, Janet and I move to the foothills west of Denver, Colorado. And in August of that year, Marshall pays us a visit.

For a week we drive around, exploring the natural beauty of our new state. On the last night of the trip, Marshall pulls out of his suitcase a bottle of expensive red wine, bubble-wrapped for travel. He drinks a glass, then another, then another, growing more morose with each one. His speech becomes slurred, and without warning he chokes back a sob.

"What's wrong, buddy?" I ask.

"It's just . . . well, being with you and Janet, I see what meaningful lives you have. You travel around the world on book tours. You affect people, and they care about you. If you died, people would miss you. *I* would miss you. I can't imagine living without you."

He pauses, takes another sip of wine, and works to control his voice. The room is warm and very still. "If I died, nobody would care. I've never done anything meaningful. I'm a failure. My life is one screwed-up mess."

Janet and I interrupt, assuring him that we care, that we love him.

"Marshall, you're forty-five years old," I say, trying to lend comfort. "You talk as if your life is ending. My goodness, you're just getting started. What would you like to accomplish? Your life isn't over, not by a long shot."

He leans forward, staring intently at his wine. A tear falls, splashing scarlet drops against the inside of the glass. "You know I can't change. Not as long as *she's* still alive. That's her legacy to me."

"What are you talking about? Marshall, our mother is sixty-eight years old. She has white hair and wrinkles, and sometimes she walks with a cane. You haven't seen her in at least twenty years. You live three thousand miles away from her. Are you telling me you're still letting her dominate your life?"

"It's the curse," he says. "She cursed me. She never believed in me, and if your own mother doesn't believe in you, how can you believe in yourself?

"And then I went to Wheaton. My own mother wished me dead. Or crazy. She prayed for it—still does, for all I know. It's like a witch's curse. I'll never amount to anything as long as she's alive. Even if I felt productive, there's nothing to produce. It's me or her." He sounds more weary than bitter, as if the alcohol has slurred his emotions along with the words.

My brother has never before let me see the depth of his wounded soul—cursed not only by our mother but by God, as if he can't separate the two. We talk late into the night, and nothing I say makes an impression. He sounds utterly, irredeemably lost.

Just before the clock strikes two, I stand up. "Marshall, you've got an early flight, and we all need some sleep. But I promise you one thing. If you believe you've been cursed, then as your brother I promise you that on my next trip to Atlanta I'll confront Mother and ask her to remove that curse."

He exhales with something between a snort and a stifled sob. "Good luck," he says.

JANET AND I have already made plans to spend Christmas in Atlanta, in a condominium I helped Mother buy. We fly down, rent a car, and over the next few days go through the motions of decorating a tree and exchanging presents. My insides are churning as I plan how best to fulfill my pledge to my brother.

The day after Christmas, Janet purposely goes for a long walk, and I ask Mother to join me at the kitchen table. "There's something I need to tell you," I say. She shoots me a look of suspicion, and I notice that already the tendon in her jaw is twitching.

I begin. "Mother, as you know, I've kept in touch with Marshall all these years. I feel caught between you and him because I care for you both. There's no question he's been through some rough times and made lots of bad decisions. But I've got to tell you, Mother, he's come a long way. He's married now, has three stepchildren, and is more stable than he's ever been. He's changed a lot."

She looks at me with fiery eyes, a gaze that would melt a glacier, saying nothing. I would not have believed that a person could look so angry. I take a sip of water, moisten my lips, and describe Marshall's visit to Colorado in August. I repeat what he said that final night, almost verbatim. "So, the bottom line is, he believes he's been cursed by you, and you're the only person who can remove that curse."

I have carefully thought through her potential responses. She might be dismissive: *Well, we all say things in the heat of the moment that we later regret.* Or she might deny the fateful scene when she "cursed" him for transferring to Wheaton College, although she knows I heard the whole conversation. I have envisioned every possible scenario—except one.

She stays silent for at least three minutes. The refrigerator motor kicks on, then off. I hear the growl of a garbage truck outside. The sweat under my arms feels cold. When she finally speaks, she does so with clipped syllables and a disembodied voice, like something out of *The Exorcist*.

"I told your brother I would pray for God to do whatever it took to break him, so he'd come to the end of himself. Even if that meant an accident. He was asking my blessing to go to that school. You think I'm gonna bless my own son to do whatever he wants, to go against everything he's been taught? That's like feeding a kid rat poison."

I feel the heartbeats inside my ear, and in the tips of my fingers against the table. As gently as I can, I say, "Can you see how Marshall has a hard time reconciling that attitude with love?"

She pounces. "You wouldn't understand that kind of love! I wouldn't expect you to."

"You're right, Mother, I don't."

"I saw Brother Paul recently, from the Colonial Hills church. He told me that deep in his heart he thought Marshall knew God. I asked him, 'Brother Paul, knowing the Scriptures as you do, do you really think he should still be alive? There's an unpardonable sin, a sin unto death, you know.'"

I work to control my voice. "Mother, do you *want* Marshall dead?" I ask at last. No answer. A cardinal is singing cheerily outside, as if in mockery. "Tell me, do you wish your own son was dead?"

"He has no right . . ." she mumbles, and leaves the sentence hanging. She mentions a passage from 1 Corinthians, in which Paul hands over a man to Satan "for the destruction of the flesh." She adds, "A few verses later, the apostle says we shouldn't even associate with such immoral people." I feel the jab directed at me, and my mind races to prepare a self-defense.

We both start as the outside door swings open. Janet has returned.

I get up, walk back to our bedroom, and tell her about the conversation. Then I call United Airlines to change our flight to the next day, cutting short our Christmas vacation. I need to flee from the spirit in this place—righteous evil unleashed in the name of God.

On the plane trip back, I think back to how it all started. How could a sacred vow, by a distraught young widow, corrupt to such a degree?

When I report to Marshall on my attempt to lift the curse, he laughs. "What'd you expect?" he says. "At least you get credit for trying."

IN SEPTEMBER 2001, Mother's anger boils over again. I have just published the book *Soul Survivor,* which tells of my racist past and the Southern fundamentalism I grew up under. *The Atlanta Journal and Constitution* has shrewdly assigned an African American reporter to profile one of Atlanta's native sons, now an established Christian author.

The reporter asks me bluntly, "Did you really believe that racist stuff, or were you just going along with what others thought?" I hesitate, and tell him the truth, that I really believed it. I wrote a school paper on the Ku Klux Klan. I sometimes used the *N*-word and told racist jokes. Until high school days, I bought into what my church taught about the Black race being inferior.

He asks me how I would feel if he interviewed my mother and tried to contact my brother. I smile, imagining what he'll hear in those conversations. "I'm a journalist, too, and it's a free country," I reply at last. "If you can locate them, you're welcome to interview them."

A few weeks later the Sunday magazine feature leads with this paragraph:

> Philip Yancey has sold 5 million books, traveled the globe and won the highest awards in Christian publishing. Yet he's been unable to make a fan of one 77-year-old Atlanta woman, despite years of personal effort. His mother, Mildred Yancey, refuses to read any of her son's 15 books, though she shares his Christian faith. Nor will she say why. "He's just like his father. He's a Yancey," Mildred Yancey says when asked about theological differences with her son. "Let's just leave it at that."

I puzzle over what she meant by the comment about my father— some suppressed resentment perhaps?

The article goes on to quote Marshall, who recounts his turn away from any faith. And it reports my answer to the question of how my view of Christianity differs from my mother's: "She's more comfortable with the Old Testament God of judgment and wrath, with having very few people in the world that God loves."

I wait a few days after the article is published. Then I phone my mother for what I know will be a difficult conversation. The date is September 12, 2001, and I talk for a few minutes about the terrible tragedy our country has just experienced in the World Trade Center attacks. She doesn't respond. She maintains silence until I say, "I presume you saw the article on me in the Atlanta paper?"

When she finally speaks, I recognize the same tone of voice from that tense Christmas when I confronted her about removing her curse. "A doctor friend told me that was the worst case of mother-bashing he's ever seen," she says. Then, "Maybe I should have had that abortion after all."

It takes me a minute to grasp that the abortion comment refers to *me*. This from a woman who rates abortion at the top of the sin list.

Several retorts leap to mind, and I forcibly squelch them. The journalistic instinct has kicked in, and I wish for a tape recording that I could later replay to make sure I've heard her right. I try to calm myself by writing down on a pad of paper exactly what she is saying.

"Back when your daddy died, a woman offered to raise you so I could go to the mission field like I'd planned. Maybe I should have taken her up on it. We'd all have been better off."

Abortion, abandonment—she is digging deep for revenge. I keep writing her words, suppressing my own emotions.

The conversation shifts to Marshall. For three decades now he has been a phantom figure to her friends and family, as though he doesn't exist. Now he is being quoted in the local paper. "I tried every mode of Christianity that I could find," he told the reporter. "There's nothing anybody could say or do that could create a change in me."

Mother seethes over that quote. Her own son, a prodigal, a self-confessed heretic. "One of these days, you wait and see, the Lord's going to break him!" she says in a shrill tone.

I interrupt. "Maybe melt, not break him?"

"No, in his case, the Lord's gonna break him!"

"You sound angry," I say.

"I'm not angry, I'm hurt! There's a difference. Anger you can get over. It goes away. Hurt stays inside. It never goes away."

> . . . But wag'd with death a lasting strife,
> supported by despair of life.
>
> —William Cowper, "The Castaway"

CHAPTER 24
BROTHERS

In June 2009, on a safari trip to Tanzania, Marshall had a severe coughing fit. "I barely slept," he tells me when he and Molly return to California. "I thought I was going to cough my guts out. We were in a tent in the middle of nowhere and had no medicine or any way to stop the coughing."

Five days later, while playing golf, he starts seeing double and can't judge where to swing. Over the weekend he tries to sleep off a headache and waves of nausea. By Monday he is feeling so bad that he drives himself to see a doctor, who immediately orders an ambulance.

Molly phones me from the hospital later that day in a panic. "I don't know what's happening to your brother," she says. "He's no longer making sense. He has trouble walking. They suspect a stroke and are giving him blood thinners."

She puts Marshall on the phone, and I ask him a few questions. Each time he replies in utter gibberish, not a single recognizable word. "What are they telling you?" I ask. He manages one intelligible sentence before slipping back into gibberish: "They don't tell me shit!"

Doctors soon diagnose a rare kind of stroke, a dissection of the carotid artery. In Tanzania he coughed so hard that the force crushed the major artery in his neck against his spinal column, tearing the inside of the blood vessel. The torn flap then blocked most blood supply to the brain. For a week, his oxygen-starved brain has been shutting down functions—"much like the pilot of a jet switching off systems to conserve fuel," explains the doctor. Now the blockage is affecting vital processes such as speech and mobility.

The doctor arranges a transfer to nearby Stanford Hospital, where Marshall will be evaluated for possible brain surgery.

I cancel a planned trip to visit our elderly mother in Georgia and instead book a flight to California. Molly meets me at the airport, and we drive straight to Stanford, where my brother is in the intensive-care unit, awaiting surgery. What I find there makes my legs go weak and my skin go cold. Marshall is laid out in a hospital gown with a skein of at least fifteen tubes and wires coiling from his body. Lying on his back, comatose, he stares straight ahead. His dilated eyes register nothing as we approach the bed.

"He's showing no reflexes," the nurse informs us, "none at all." To demonstrate, she claps her hands in front of his face, and he doesn't blink.

I look down at his motionless body. An arterial line hangs from his arm, and the strong right hand that has tuned and rebuilt pianos is now limp, its fingers curling inward. A feeding tube pumps nourishment through his nose and an IV bag drips a cocktail of drugs into a port in his neck. Blood spots mark the gauze wherever needles have entered.

Janet gave me one last bit of advice as I left for the airport: "Be sure to keep talking to him." A hospice chaplain, she knows that comatose patients can hear, even when they show no reaction.

That first day, I bend down to Marshall's ear and whisper a prayer. "Marshall, I know you think God hates you. It's not true. God's not like we heard about growing up. God loves you, and wants you restored. I've sent out emails and have heard back from dozens of people who are praying for you daily."

When I open my eyes, a jolt like an electric shock shoots through me. From Marshall's unblinking left eye, a single glistening tear is making a track down the side of his cheek. My own eyes are stinging. Over the next few days, I see the same phenomenon again and again—every time I pray—the only sign that something of my brother remains inside that still, insensible body.

All that week Molly and I sit in the waiting area outside the ICU, permitted into Marshall's room for only five minutes every two hours. The doctors say his only hope is an extreme surgical procedure called ECIC (extracranial-intracranial), which they must delay because of the blood thinners. Fortunately, Stanford has a neurosurgeon who specializes in the delicate operation. He describes it: "I'll open the skull and dissect out an artery that feeds scalp tissue. Then I'll tunnel that artery deep into the brain. In effect, we'll create a bypass route around the blockage in his carotid, restoring the brain's blood supply."

The surgery lasts almost seven hours, leaving Marshall with a long *s*-shaped scar on the side of his shaved head. When Molly and I are admitted to see him, I notice one change right away. His eyes lock on us at the door and follow us to his bedside. He cannot speak and can barely move one leg, yet when I ask a question, he sometimes squeezes my hand.

I VISIT CALIFORNIA each month for the rest of that year, checking on his progress. The stroke has paralyzed his right side and damaged portions of the brain controlling reasoning and speech. "Is your name Marshall?" the speech therapist asks. *Yes.* "Is your name Frank?" *Yes.* "Complete this sentence for me, Marshall: 'She unlocks a door with a _____.'" He thinks for a moment and answers confidently, *hat.* "Does that sound right, Marshall? She unlocks a door with a hat?" *Yes. Right.*

Over time I watch my brother progressively return to life. First he learns to maneuver a wheelchair with his left hand and foot. Six months after the surgery he calls to report with childish pride, "I stand! I stand!" Molly coaches him in the background, "No, Marshall, tell him you can *walk*. You took two steps with a cane." More than a year passes before he feels brave enough to give up the wheelchair and walk with a cane, swinging wide his stiff right leg in an unnatural gait.

Speech comes hardest. His brain thinks one thing, but often nonsense comes out of his mouth, causing him endless frustration. Before the stroke he would try learning something of the language of a country before visiting it. In preparation for his trips with Molly, he studied basic Spanish, French, Italian, Turkish, Chinese, and Swahili. All that is gone now. He struggles mightily to speak a child's English.

From Colorado I connect to his computer twice a week, and together we go through a series of exercises designed for stroke patients. "Which item does not belong in this list: *hammer, rabbit, dog, horse.*" He thinks for a minute and decides on *horse.* "Why did you choose *horse,* Marshall?" *Big, too big!* "Yes, that's true. But can you think of anything these words—*rabbit, dog, horse*—have in common that's different from a hammer?" After a long pause he says, *No. It's* horse.

At my suggestion, Molly buys him a book of piano music written for the left hand, but he gives up after a few frustrating attempts. The stroke has taken his language, his independence, his ability to form rational thoughts, and now it has robbed him of his greatest love.

WHEN I FIRST heard about Marshall's symptoms, I emailed Mother a quick note, warning her that I might not make it to Georgia after all. Later, I called her with more details. She commented, "Interesting, isn't it—he once wanted to be a missionary to Africa. He finally went there as a tourist, and now this . . ."

The distressing thought crosses my mind that perhaps she views the debilitating stroke as the answer to her prayers. Yet, after the brain surgery, she sends him a card in which she writes words she has never before uttered—"I've always loved you"—and adds a

Bible verse about God being "able to do exceeding abundantly above all that we ask or think." That stops me for a moment. Is she beginning to soften?

Molly wastes no time in phoning me to vent her fury. "What the hell does your mother mean with this card? Did you tell her about his stroke? How can you still relate to that evil woman?"

I try to explain that no matter what has happened, Marshall's mother has a right to know her own son is in mortal danger. "Surely you understand that, as a mother yourself."

"She *has* no rights. Your mother wished my husband dead or mindless. She forfeited every right to be his mother long ago. If she was on fire, I wouldn't walk across the road to spit on her."

Once again I feel caught between two giants, both separated by the chasm of an unresolved past.

I MAKE ONE more attempt to break through to Mother in 2014, the year she turns ninety. She has always loved the ocean, and so I rent a South Carolina beach house, equipped with an elevator that can accommodate her aluminum walker. She enjoys sitting on the balcony, watching the waves and the children playing in the sand.

"You've just turned ninety years old," I say one afternoon as we sit there together. "That's quite an achievement. As you look back on your life, do you have any regrets?" She thinks awhile and finally says, "No."

I press her. "What about with Marshall. Any regrets there?"

She mentions the last time she saw him, back in Atlanta more than four decades ago. She was recovering from minor surgery, shortly after my wedding, when Marshall "and some woman" visited her in the hospital. "Let's put the past behind us and start over," she told him. In her mind, that constituted an apology, and he should have accepted it as such.

I stay silent for a time. Obviously, Marshall didn't receive those few words as an apology, let alone a step toward healing their relationship, because he never saw her again.

"It's sad, Mother, that neither Marshall nor I ever felt we had your approval, your blessing," I say at last.

"Yes, it is," she replies quickly. Nothing more.

"And it's sad, too, that you never felt approval from your own mother." She nods, expressionless.

"Did you ever consider remarriage?"

She sits up in her chair, suddenly energized. "No, Marshall never would have stood for that!"

"Mother, he was only three years old. Millions of people remarry. He could have adapted to a stepfather."

We talk for almost an hour, guardedly, with old wounds and resentments lurking behind every exchange. I express appreciation for all she did for us, while also letting her know she has said some very hurtful things.

"Sometimes your deep anger flares up," I tell her. "Promising to pray that Marshall would die or be paralyzed or lose his mind—think how that must feel to him now, in his disabled state. And creating that scene at my wedding reception. And saying to me, 'Maybe I should have had that abortion after all.'"

She doesn't interrupt, so I plow ahead. "I know that Marshall and I have hurt you—Marshall through his life choices, and I through some things I've written. You made a vow to God over us, and we've disappointed you. I get that. But when you respond, there's a big difference between 'You hurt me,' and 'I wish you were dead'—as you said to Marshall—or 'had never been born,' as you said to me."

Still she doesn't interrupt or even look away. "You know what, Mother? Everyone loses control at times, and we all say things we'd like to take back. That's what grace is all about. That's why Marshall and I both see your perfection theology as a kind of prison cage. If only you could face up to mistakes, acknowledge them, say you're sorry, and move on . . ."

She offers no response, and I give up. I leave that weekend feeling empty, doubting that anything has sunk in.

One month later, on a quick visit to Atlanta, I meet Mother for dinner. She hands me a five-page letter that she has laboriously typed on her computer, despite her deteriorating eyesight. "If I send this to Marshall, he won't read it," she says. "Would you be willing to read it to him the next time you see him?" I assure her that I will.

As it happens, Marshall has been planning his very first plane trip since the stroke. Molly drives him to the airport in California and checks him in. Airport escorts wheel him to the gate to catch the flight to Denver.

I have saved the letter for his visit, and I tell him about it on the drive to our home from the Denver airport. "It's intense. You can decide when you want to hear it—anytime while you're here."

"Tonight!" he says. I'm taken aback by his forceful response.

"Are you sure?" I ask. "It could be a rough way to begin a vacation."

"Yes, yes!" he insists.

After dinner we sit in the living room and I read the letter slowly, stopping after each paragraph to let his damaged mind absorb what she is saying. Mother has written vulnerably and tenderly. She does not deny her threat to pray curses on him, but insists that she never followed through on that threat:

> Never did I pray that way; when you're trying to make a point, you probably say things you do not necessarily mean, in order to let the other person know you are serious. Meanwhile, I am truly truly sorry for the way things turned out. I didn't mean for them to be this way and can only ask for your forgiveness.
>
> I don't guess my asking your forgiveness will do anything for the relationship. But you have it anyway. You are my firstborn and I carried you under my heart for almost nine months. A Mother doesn't forget that. You've had my prayers and best wishes through your life, even if you can't think of me as your Mother. I did give the best years of my life to look after you and would do it all over again if I had a choice to make.

It takes me nearly half an hour to read through the letter. In all that time, Marshall is wiping away tears with his good hand and speaking up when he objects to something she has written. He has two verbal responses. "Bullshit!" he cries each time he disagrees with Mother's version of events.

And, three times, when I read the most touching parts, he shouts, "Too late! Forty-five years too late!"

THE NEXT MONTH, while on a book tour in Asia, I get an email from Molly. She writes that she came home from bridge club to find Marshall passed out unconscious on the floor with a half-empty gallon of whiskey in one hand and a bottle of vermouth nearby.

"I let him have the full fury of my wrath," she writes. "He said he was trying to kill himself. Told him he needed to do a more thorough job such as driving his car off a cliff or shooting himself in the head, that he was worthless and an albatross around my neck— maybe I was too harsh but as I told him, I am this close to divorcing him . . . already divorced one alcoholic, why stay with another one."

My heart sinks. I spend a sleepless night, waiting until the next day to call her because of the difference in time zones. By now she's learned the full story: in addition to the alcohol, Marshall swallowed at least thirty Ambien tablets and thirty Valiums. He had researched on the internet what it would take to kill himself and planned to do just that. The concoction should have been deadly, except that Marshall had built up a tolerance to the drugs, which he had been taking daily for five years, ever since the stroke.

I call the airline to schedule a stopover in San Francisco on my return. My tour lasts another ten days, and I stand before audiences in Korea and Taiwan speaking on the problem of pain and the power of prayer, while my mind is six thousand miles away, wondering what will be left of my brother.

When I finally get to the United States, I find a broken, humbled man. In his halting speech he tells me he had intended to jump overboard while on a cruise with Molly on the St. Lawrence Seaway. Because of his disability, he couldn't manage to climb over the railing. So he decided on the pills and alcohol.

"Never again," he assures me. "Worst hangover ever."

He still seems groggy as he describes the ordeal. He woke up with a pounding headache, shocked to be alive, and then waited six days to visit a doctor. Following protocol after a suicide attempt, the doctor put him on a seventy-two-hour psychiatric hold in the county hospital, a place where paranoid schizophrenics paced the floor, ducking as they passed each window to hide from imagined enemies outside.

"It was hell," Marshall says. "Cuckoo's nest. They took my cane— thought it weapon—so I couldn't walk." They removed his false teeth, which meant he could barely eat. They confiscated his meds, too, leaving him with a roaring headache the entire time. At night they locked him in a room with another patient, a three-hundred-pound bodybuilder covered with tattoos. In the next room, a psychotic screamed obscenities all night. "No sleep," my brother recalls with a shudder. "Zero!"

A short time later, Molly files for divorce. Thus begins the next phase of Marshall's life, which continues to this day. In a flurry of visits, I locate a social worker, a divorce attorney, and a real estate agent. A network of Christian friends help Marshall move into a new apartment.

After all we've been through together—Blair Village, a trailer, broken bones and illnesses, Faith Baptist, Bible college, weddings, the sixties—I have now become my brother's keeper.

THREE YEARS LATER, Marshall makes another trip to Denver. This time I have to make arrangements on both ends of the trip, finding a friend in San Jose who can drive him to the airport and check his baggage. He has managed to live alone, with the weekly help of a caregiver who assists him with cleaning and laundry. Having lost the lust for novelty, he keeps to a regular routine of bridge, physical therapy, and various online aphasia groups. He reads *The New Yorker* and a wide variety of books, though he retains very little.

Marshall is still working on social skills, and on this trip he comes equipped with a list of questions from his speech therapist to help him converse with Janet and me. I have my own list of questions for him. His long-term memory is sharp, and one reason for this visit is that I've begun this memoir. When I ask him about our past, he always gives honest, detailed answers.

Each time we're together, Marshall insists that I play the piano for him. I find the task awkward and embarrassing. I think back to our days in a trailer, when he would shake his head in exasperation as I fumbled my way through a piece that he could sight-read effortlessly.

This time Janet has a new suggestion. "Marshall, your left hand works fine. Why don't you play the bass clef while Philip plays the treble with his right hand?" And so we do. As we work to synchronize two hands controlled by different brains, Janet records it on her iPhone.

When I watch the video later, something occurs to me. As brothers, we used to compete in everything: chess, debating, tennis, golf. Now Marshall's disability forces us to work together. Every week or so he calls me about a problem at his apartment he can't solve or a balky computer program or a financial matter. Once known for his eccentric autonomy, now my brother has become contentedly dependent.

I WOULD LOVE to end our family story with a scene of reconciliation, of two brothers gathered around the matriarch in a hospital room receiving a final blessing. As a son and brother, I find my heart crying out for such a scene of resolution and healing. I have seen thawing in my family, especially from my mother, but nothing so sanguine as that scenario. Life rarely follows a fairy-tale script.

As I write, our mother has passed her ninety-sixth birthday. A few years ago, when Marshall wrecked his motorized wheelchair, she dipped into her savings and sent me $2,000 to buy him a new one. He rides it almost every day, a visible token that at some level she still cares.

"You've had my prayers and best wishes through your life, even if you can't think of me as your Mother," she wrote in their final communication, which I read aloud to Marshall. That last phrase haunts her even now, and perhaps she clings to life in hopes of reversing it.

"Could you do one thing for me?" she asked me recently. "Please ask Marshall if he still thinks of me as his mother." Of course I agreed.

I've asked him several times, and each time he tells me he's still working on the right answer. "I don't know what to say" is all he can get out.

Presume not that I am the thing I was,
For God doth know, so shall the world perceive,
That I have turn'd away my former self . . .

—Shakespeare, *Henry IV, Part 2*

CHAPTER 25

AFTERMATH

A painful memory resurrects one day when I receive a letter from Hal, the political zealot whom I crushed in high school with my sham Student Rights Party. Early in my journalism career I wrote about that episode in a magazine article, painting an unflattering picture of both myself and Hal and making the foolish mistake of using his actual first name. Now, years later, I break into a sweat as I finger the unopened letter, fearing what I will find inside: legal action, perhaps, or at least a well-deserved rebuke.

In the first paragraph Hal reveals that he has indeed come across that old article. He assures me, though, that he takes no offense at what I wrote. My blood pressure returns to normal, and I sit down to continue reading.

On six pages of lined paper, Hal recounts his life after high school. As expected, he plunged into political activism, truly believing he could change the world. Instead, he became disillusioned with politics. After a stint in the air force during the Vietnam War, he returned to a broken marriage. Fighting depression, he decided to read the Gospels, something he had never done.

"Jesus came alive for me—it was then I met him personally, for the first time," the letter says. I stop and let that sentence sink in. The Hal I knew had no interest in religious faith.

The letter goes on to describe a major turnabout. Abandoning his political ambitions, Hal enrolled in seminary and earned a PhD from the Candler School of Theology. He settled on John Wesley as a model Christian leader who worked for social justice. I can hardly believe it—my high school nemesis is now a Wesley scholar.

I weep as I read Hal's letter. In a loving, humble way, he has offered forgiveness for my cruel high school prank. I follow up his invitation to visit in person, and we become fast friends.

That experience puts to rest a burden of guilt I have carried for decades. Even as I'm savoring his act of grace, however, other conscience-nagging incidents flood into my mind. Some I've alluded to in my writings, but never have I directly confronted the individuals from my past whom I may have hurt or offended. I decide it's time to honestly face the dark side of my past.

I BEGIN BY traveling to Georgia and revisiting the high school where Hal and I sparred. The school now bears the name of Ronald McNair, an African American astronaut killed in the *Challenger* disaster. Before my graduation, no minority student had dared to integrate this school named for a Confederate general. Now, roaming the hallways, I see no white faces. The school's transformation is complete.

Next I turn to the churches of my childhood. I find that my mother's spiritual home, Maranatha Tabernacle in Philadelphia, has closed, selling its buildings to a mixed-race congregation. Surrendering to such a church must have been a bitter pill to swallow for George H. Mundell, now dead, who had taught the racist Curse of Ham theory. In another shocking twist, I learn that Mundell's son, who carried the torch of his father's Victorious Christian Life message, was arrested for taking photos of nude boys in the shower of a boys' home that he operated.

I reach out to Paul Van Gorder, the former pastor of Colonial Hills Baptist Church in Georgia, who attracted a national following on radio and television. In a sharply worded letter, he once let me know that some of my words had hurt him deeply. I apologize for the pain I've caused and reassure him that I have many positive memories of Colonial Hills.

A transplant from the North, Van Gorder did not have the native racism of Southern churchmen of that era. ("He can't be a racist," my mother insisted, "he's from Pennsylvania!") Nonetheless, the church under his leadership took a go-slow approach to integration, for a time banning Blacks from attending its church and school. Colonial Hills was also where I first heard the Curse of Ham theory. I discover that the white congregation has moved out to the suburbs, with the old building now occupied by an African American group called The Wings of Faith.

A natural-born racist myself, I have much to atone for. At a conference I meet with Priscilla Evans Shirer, the daughter of megachurch pastor Tony Evans. He was the Carver Bible Institute student refused membership at Colonial Hills—before Priscilla's birth. I tell her about a service of repentance held at the church before the building sold, and we swap stories of how much Atlanta has progressed. Priscilla survived with her faith intact and is flourishing as a Christian author and motivational speaker.

Later, I go on a book tour with her brother Anthony Evans— a scout for the TV show *The Voice*—providing the music. He smiles as I remind him of those days. "Yeah, I remember, but it's a distant memory," he says. "I guess some things have changed for the better."

I schedule a lunch meeting with Dr. John McNeal Jr., whose daughter was barred from the kindergarten at Colonial Hills. Over several hours Dr. McNeal, a graying, soft-spoken man, recalls stories of growing up in the South before civil rights. During World War II he volunteered for the air force and left his hometown in rural Georgia to report for duty. At the bus station, a cashier sold him a ticket, looked him over, and said, "Well, it's against the rules, but since you're serving my country, I reckon you can use the front door rather than the Colored door in the back."

After his military service, McNeal applied to twenty evangelical seminaries. All but one rejected him on account of his race. He became the first African American professor at the historically black Carver Bible Institute—the school where my father taught—and went on to serve as its dean. Even so, when he tried to enroll his four-year-old daughter in the kindergarten at Colonial Hills Baptist, our church rejected her.

Dr. McNeal reminisces with a gentle spirit. "I harbor no bitterness," he says. "My mother taught me that God is no respecter of persons, so I didn't grow up feeling inferior. I knew things were going to change someday, and I just kept plugging away."

Listening to him, I feel remorse and shame, remembering the racist jokes I told as a child. I *was* a respecter of persons—but only white persons. The words get caught in my throat as I try to apologize. Dr. McNeal comforts me, rather than the other way around.

I leave the restaurant newly aware of my complicity in injustice. After his term at Carver, Dr. McNeal founded a church in Atlanta, which he pastored for more than fifty years. I marvel that any African Americans would adopt the religion of the enslavers who once "owned" them and the white descendants who oppressed them. Yet who ended up showing more of the spirit of Jesus?

As PART OF my amends tour, I also attend the final service of Faith Baptist, the defiantly fundamentalist church where I spent my high school years living in a trailer on the grounds. When the racial makeup of the neighborhood diversified, the church moved farther out from the city—not far enough, evidently, for Faith found itself once again surrounded by minorities.

In a sweet irony, I discover that this church, too, is selling its building to an African American congregation.

I slip into Faith's concluding service, a reunion open to anyone who ever attended. Of the two hundred or so in the crowd, I recognize only a few. I've entered a time warp in which I find my teenage friends now paunchy, balding, and middle-aged.

The pastor Howard Pyle, who has led the congregation for forty years, reiterates the church motto, "Contending for the Faith." "I have fought the fight," he says. "I have finished the course." His posture stooped from age, he seems smaller than I remember, and his flaming red hair has turned white.

During the lengthy service, people testify how they met God through this church. As I listen, I envision a procession of those not present, people such as my brother who turned *away* from God in part because of Faith Baptist. I want to stand and speak on their behalf, but opt against adding more negativity to a church's closure.

Later, I schedule a private meeting with Brother Pyle at a Starbucks. He has recently turned seventy-eight and the years have mellowed him. He has buried one wife, married another, and lost a granddaughter in a tragic accident. After we exchange pleasantries I ask, "I'm curious—how have you changed over the years?"

"My basic beliefs haven't really changed," he replies, "but I'm sure I made some mistakes. I know you remember some of the church splits we went through."

I have arranged this meeting to apologize for some of my own behavior—especially at summer camp—and to learn whether I've wounded him in my writing. Instead, he ends up thanking me for a book I wrote, *What's So Amazing About Grace?* "I wish I'd known more about the grace side of God," he says, wistfully. "My mind goes back to your teen days with your brother and mother across the driveway in that trailer. I was a young preacher with so much need for growing in God's grace. I'm afraid I showed the Ungrace that you now write about."

REFLECTING ON MY visits, I begin to view church, like family, as a dysfunctional cluster of needy people. Life is difficult, and we seek ways to cope. I think about the members at Faith Baptist who faithfully showed up each Sunday to hear our pastor threaten them with hellfire, punishment for sins, and an imminent Armageddon. They came in part from fear, but also because, like a family, they needed each other in order to withstand the assaults of life. Working-class people, they didn't sit at home evenings fretting over the fine points of theology; they worried about how to pay bills and feed the kids. When a family's house burned down or a drunken husband locked out his wife or a widow couldn't afford her groceries, where else could they turn but church?

I think, too, of my own mother. Dozens of times over the years I've run into individuals who were deeply affected by her Bible teaching. In addition, several times she provided shelter for young women fleeing troubled families. Her public reputation stayed intact; only Marshall and I witnessed a different side.

A nephew once sent me a quote that gives me perspective on the church: "An idea cannot be responsible for those who claim to believe in it." I have spent my adult life sorting through the gospel message that I heard from those who claim to believe in it, searching for the "idea," the life-giving Essence itself.

On the same trip in which I attend the final service of Faith Baptist Church, I join a reunion of my Bible-college class. The campus is as spotless as ever, thanks to the students who diligently scrub floors and mow the lawn and pick up litter. Saplings from my college days have grown into mature shade trees, a visible token of passing time. I feel disoriented, stepping back on a campus where the dean interrogated me and the faculty debated expelling me. Now, thirty years later, I am treated as an honored guest.

Before dawn I rise to jog on a familiar dirt trail along the river. The early sky is clear as water, barely tinged with gold, and I shiver in the morning cool. I tune my portable radio to the college radio station and find that, like many things at the school, music has undergone a drastic change. Albums that Bob Larson would have incited us to incinerate now play on the school's station. I listen to a few samples of contemporary Christian music until a lovely solo voice comes on, singing a cappella an old song written by George Beverly Shea:

> I'd rather have Jesus than silver or gold;
> I'd rather be His than have riches untold . . .
> I'd rather have Jesus than men's applause;
> I'd rather be faithful to His dear cause;
> I'd rather have Jesus than world-wide fame,
> I'd rather be true to His holy name.

A sense of calm descends on me as I run the trail. It strikes me that, although I often felt like a misfit on this campus, on this point we agree. I, too, would rather have Jesus. Everything else I experienced at the school pales in significance beside the fact that God met me there.

At the reunion later that day, my classmates speak in phrases we learned as students: "God is giving me the victory . . . I can do all things through Christ . . . All things work together for good . . . I'm walking in triumph." Yet they speak a different vocabulary when relating their lives after college. Several are suffering from chronic fatigue syndrome, and others from clinical depression. One couple has recently committed their teenage daughter to a mental institution. I wince at the disconnect between these raw personal stories and the spiritual overlay applied to them.

While on campus, I also visit with some of the professors and administrative staff. "Why do you defame us?" asks the former president. "Why concentrate on the negative? We give you the Alumnus of the Year award, and you turn around and lambaste us in your writing every chance you get."

Blindsided, I don't reply right away. Finally, I say, "I don't intend to demean anyone. I guess I'm still trying to sort through the mixed messages I got here."

He doesn't back off. "I know all sorts of juicy stories about people in Christian ministry," he says. "But I would never write about them because of the pain it would cause. I go by the Golden Rule: Do unto others as I would have them do to me."

Later, as his comment sinks in, I realize that is the very reason I probe my past, even though it may cause others pain. My brother's question plagues me still: *What is real, and what is fake?* I know of no more real or honest book than the Bible, which hides none of its characters' flaws. If I've distorted reality or misrepresented myself, I would hope someone would call me out.

The Bible-college visit contrasts sharply with another meeting I arrange, with five of my brother's old hippie friends in Atlanta. As they look back on their commune days, it's clear that the 1960s remain the high-water mark of their lives. They talk with more enthusiasm about that era of sex, drugs, and rock 'n' roll than about marriages, children, career, or anything else.

"Where's Jack?" I ask, referring to a friend who followed Marshall around like a puppy.

"Sad story," comes the reply. "Jack can't be here. He sits with his head down on a table, rocking back and forth, virtually brain-dead. He's worthless without speed. He still works as a phlebotomist, drawing blood at the hospital, and has to drug up before he goes to work. Jack and his wife both mainline through IVs they get at the hospital."

They tell me other, similar stories. Linda, the naïve nurse whom Marshall invited into his commune, fought against the downward slide. After becoming addicted to marijuana and Xanax, she sought treatment and has been sober for two decades. As I listen to my brother's friends, my Bible-college classmates do not seem so unhealthy after all.

AFTER I'VE WRITTEN these words and closed the cover of my laptop, my aged mother calls. "Thank you for sending the recent picture of your brother," she says. "I notice his arm is bandaged. Is he hurt?" I explain that he badly scraped his arm in a fall and had to go to a hospital emergency room for treatment. Long pause. Then she asks, "Listen, if I write him a note and send it to you, would you forward it?"

"Of course," I say, conscious of the indignity of a mother having to ask one of her two sons if he would forward a message to the other. Then follows her plaintive question, "Do you think he would read it?"

The amends tour has not yet ended with my family. After her call, I sit awhile in silence. What happened to tear apart our small family?

I have read accounts on Fundamentalists Anonymous websites that tell of church upbringings much stricter than ours. I've read memoirs in which alcoholic fathers chase their children with baseball bats, not mere tennis rackets. Mothers lock them for days in a closet without food. Parents disown or banish their children because they determine to become artists rather than doctors or rabbis.

"I did the best I could," Mother claims, and the more I learn about her past, the more I believe her. Surely, though, something else lay at the heart of all that followed.

Like every mother, she must have held us naked against herself, counting our fingers and toes, awed by what her own body had produced nine months after an act of love. She must have smiled with joy as we took our first wobbly steps and pronounced our first words.

In our teenage years, our steps and our words propelled us away from her, in ways she could not comprehend and furiously sought to prevent. The sons who had shown such promise in childhood now slouched in and out of her life, barely speaking. How terrifying it must be for a mother to release her children to the unknown. How distressing to experience the wonder of bringing new persons into the world, only to rue what they become.

As teenagers we preferred *MAD* magazine to *Israel My Glory*. We longed to see the movies and hear the music our classmates talked about. We wanted a real education, not simply more Bible. But she knew how Satan worked—as the angel of light as well as the roaring lion seeking whom he may devour. Satan tempts by degrees: a cigarette before heroin, Elvis Presley before the Beatles, *Othello* before pornographic movies. She had constructed a monument of faith made of cards perilously stacked atop one another, and her sons, *her own sons,* were tugging at the bottom cards.

Corruptio optimi pessima goes an old Latin saying: "The corruption of the best is the worst." What begins as love may, in fact, corrode into something akin to its opposite. An Afghan mother, out of devotion to her religion and country, straps a suicide vest onto her ten-year-old daughter. Or a young widow in Atlanta assumes the role of God: deciding, first, what's best for a man in an iron lung and, then, for his two sons left behind.

The mystery of my mother circles back to the scene she described to us as children: her prayer of consecration as she lay stretched across the damp soil of our father's grave. Burdened by grief and betrayal, Mother staked her future and even her faith on Marshall and me. She made an offering as solemn as Hannah's of Samuel—or, better, as Abraham's of Isaac. As our lives took their own courses, her sacred offering vanished like smoke.

I turn again to my least favorite of biblical stories, Hannah relinquishing her son Samuel to the priest Eli. Late at night, while lying down in the house of the Lord, three times the boy Samuel hears his name called out, "Samuel!" Each time he runs to Eli, who says, "I did not call; go back and lie down." Finally, the wise old priest realizes it is the Lord who is calling the boy.

In a flash I see that scene in an entirely new light. Neither Eli nor Samuel's mother commissions the boy; *God* issues the call. All our lives Marshall and I have lived under the weight of a mother's vow, one that was beyond her prerogative to invoke.

Marshall made his own choices, many of which proved self-destructive. Was he a tormented genius? Was he really schizophrenic? I do not know, and since his stroke in 2009 those questions have become moot. To this day he fights against a mother with whom he has no contact and against a God whose existence he denies. He attends what he calls an "atheist church," a Sunday assembly of humanists who expend much energy opposing a God they don't believe in. On my last visit, he had a copy of *The God Delusion* on his coffee table, along with a ticket to attend a lecture by its author, Richard Dawkins.

The wounds of faith embed like permanent tattoos. "Do you think he will ever change?" friends ask me, and I have to answer no. It is never too late for grace and forgiveness—unless a person determines it is.

WE LIVE DAY by day, scene by scene, as if working on a thousand-piece jigsaw puzzle with no picture on the box to guide us. Only over time does a meaningful pattern emerge. In this memoir I have written a sort of prequel to my other books. In retrospect, it seems clear to me that my two life themes, which surface in all my books, are suffering and grace.

I explore the topic of pain in my writing because many who suffer receive more confusion than comfort, especially from the church. Early on I learned that what we believe has lasting, sometimes fatal, consequences. The people who prayed for my father, and became convinced that he would be healed, did so with stalwart faith and the best of intentions—and were tragically wrong.

My brother, Marshall, dealt with suffering by way of amputation: dropping out of college, abandoning his musical ambitions, forsaking our family, divorcing two women and severing relations with others. In part because of his example, I have sought instead to stitch together all the strands, good and bad, healthy and unhealthy.

The New Testament presents suffering as a bad thing—Jesus, after all, devoted himself to acts of healing—yet one that can be redeemed. We have hope that on this broken planet pain can be somehow useful, even redemptive.

I've even learned to find gratitude for those years under extreme fundamentalism. I emerged with a deep sense that the choices we make profoundly matter, that life need not be just one thing after another but rather can become a kind of destiny. I gained a love for music and language, especially the language of the Bible. I learned self-discipline and avoided most reckless behavior. Nothing, in the end, was wasted.

Grace is my second theme, for I know the power of its opposite. Ungrace fuels the dark energy between my brother and mother: a wounded, vengeful spirit on the one side arrayed against a righteous judgment on the other. What power has kept them from speaking for half a century? The same force of stubborn pride that so often divides families, neighbors, politicians, races, and nations.

In the churches of my youth, we sang about God's grace, and yet I seldom felt it. I saw God as a stern taskmaster, eager to condemn and punish. I have come to know instead a God of love and beauty who longs for our wholeness. I assumed that surrender to God would involve a kind of shrinking—avoiding temptation, grimly focusing on the "spiritual" things while I prepared for the afterlife. On the contrary, God's good world presented itself as a gift to enjoy with grace-healed eyes.

My faith was put to a test in 2007 when the Ford Explorer I was driving slid off an icy Colorado road and tumbled over and over, five times in all, down a hillside. I staggered around in the snow in shock, until a passing car called 911.

An ambulance carried me to a small-town hospital, where the doctor tried to discern from CT scans whether one of the bone fragments in my broken neck had nicked a major artery. "We have a jet standing by if needed to airlift you to Denver," he said. "But, truthfully, if the carotid artery has been pierced, you won't make it to Denver. You should call the people you love and tell them goodbye, just in case."

For seven hours I lay strapped to a bodyboard staring at harsh fluorescent lights—the same view, it suddenly occurs to me, that my father had from an iron lung and that Marshall had for months after his stroke. I used those hours to review my life, and on that day I made a firm commitment, should I survive, to write a memoir.

I had always expected that, in the face of death, old fears would come surging back. An upbringing under a wrathful God does not easily fade away. Instead, as I lay there facing death several hundred miles from home, I experienced an unexpected serenity. I had an overwhelming sense of trust, for I now knew a God of compassion and mercy.

Lying helpless and strapped down, I would have felt utterly and inconsolably alone—except for the strong, sure sense that I had not made the long, winding journey unaccompanied. I walked out of the hospital late that February evening, wearing a neck brace and grateful to God for another chance at life.

As a boy wandering in the woods, a teenager constructing a psychic survival shell, a lovesick college student running from the Hound of Heaven—in all those places I felt what T. S. Eliot called "a tremour of bliss, a wink of heaven, a whisper." I came to love God out of gratitude, not fear.

Above all else, grace is a gift, one I cannot stop writing about until my story ends.

AUTHOR'S NOTE

My writing career began fifty years ago, and I have been contemplating this book ever since. I had read fine memoirs about growing up Orthodox Jewish, or Jehovah's Witness, or Irish Catholic, but none that fully captured the peculiar subculture of my own Southern fundamentalist upbringing. Yet I hesitated to delve into my past, knowing that doing so would open old wounds and inevitably cause others pain.

I have lived through KKK cross burnings, the civil rights movement, the Billy Graham era, the Jesus People movement, Jimmy Carter's "Year of the Evangelical," a lurch into politics led by Jerry Falwell, and the more recent anomaly of evangelicals' support for Donald Trump. Throughout, I've noticed that the general media—magazines, newspapers, movies—seem tone-deaf in their portrayal of religion, often presenting more caricature than reality.

Immersed in an extreme form of faith in my youth, I had the sense of being in on something that outsiders could not possibly comprehend. Over the years I have encountered some of the worst that the church has to offer and some of the best. Looking back, I wanted to understand myself, as well as the environment that helped form me. The time had come to attempt to make sense of the confusion of life in the only way I know how—by writing.

A memoir is a kind of verbal selfie, with one figure in the foreground, reflecting that person's singular point of view. I have relied on letters, diaries, and interviews with relatives and others from my past, but this interpretation of events is mine alone—the point of memoir, after all. "Memory is a complicated thing," says Barbara Kingsolver, "a relative to truth, but not its twin."

Versions of some of these anecdotes appear in the two dozen other books I have written, often in a disguised form. In this book I have sought to give an unvarnished account of what actually happened, although for privacy's sake I have changed names and details in a few instances.

I began by writing down everything I could remember about my early life. In order to trim that sprawling volume, I relied heavily on other readers for advice. I have unending gratitude for my literary agent, Kathryn Helmers, and my superb editor at Convergent Books, Derek Reed, who painstakingly guided me through multiple drafts as the book took shape. Other colleagues and friends—John Sloan, Carolyn Briggs, Tim Stafford, Elisa Stanford, Laura Canby, David Graham, Ellyn Lanz, and David Bannon—plowed through the 240,000 words of an early draft before I winnowed it down to 100,000. Harold Fickett, David Kopp, Lee Phillips, Mickey Maudlin, Charles Moore, Jon Abercrombie, Evan and Elisa Morgan, Pam Montgomery, and Scott Bolinder contributed further editorial insight for the slimmed-down version. I am blessed to have such talented and generous readers—as well as an outstanding publishing team at Penguin Random House.

Two assistants, Melissa Nicholson and Joannie Degnan Barth, spent hundreds of hours helping me bring some order to stacks of notes, books, and database entries, as well as adding their own editorial expertise. And my wife, Janet, supported me sacrificially yet cheerfully throughout the long process. She plays a starring role in this memoir as well as in my life; fittingly, I ended the project the year we celebrated fifty years of marriage.

Thank you, one and all.

ALSO BY PHILIP YANCEY

PHILIP YANCEY wrestles in print with God, with the church, and with fellow believers. In the process he has authored more than two dozen books, including the bestsellers *The Jesus I Never Knew, What's So Amazing About Grace?,* and *Soul Survivor: How Thirteen Unlikely Mentors Helped My Faith Survive the Church.* Yancey's books have garnered thirteen Gold Medallion Book Awards from Christian publishers and booksellers. He currently has more than seventeen million books in print and has been published in over fifty languages worldwide. Yancey worked as a journalist and freelance author in Chicago for some twenty years, editing the youth magazine *Campus Life* while also writing for a wide variety of publications, including *Reader's Digest, The Atlantic, National Wildlife,* and *Christianity Today.* In 1992, he and his wife, Janet, moved to the foothills of Colorado, where they live now.

ABOUT THE TYPE

This book was set in Garamond, a typeface originally designed by the Parisian type cutter Claude Garamond (c. 1500–61). This version of Garamond was modeled on a 1592 specimen sheet from the Egenolff-Berner foundry, which was produced from types assumed to have been brought to Frankfurt by the punch cutter Jacques Sabon (c. 1520–80).

Claude Garamond's distinguished romans and italics first appeared in *Opera Ciceronis* in 1543–44. The Garamond types are clear, open, and elegant.